W9-CNI-591

TREACHERY

ALSO BY BILL GERTZ

BREAKDOWN: How America's Intelligence Failures Led to September 11

THE CHINA THREAT: How the People's Republic Targets America

BETRAYAL: How the Clinton Administration Undermined American Security

TREACHERY

HOW AMERICA'S FRIENDS AND FOES ARE SECRETLY ARMING OUR ENEMIES

BILL GERTZ

CROWN FORUM
NEW YORK

TO MY CHILDREN

Published by Crown Forum, New York, New York.
Member of the Crown Publishing Group, a division of Random House, Inc.
www.crownpublishing.com

CROWN FORUM and the Crown Forum colophon are trademarks of Random House, Inc.

Printed in the United States of America

DESIGN BY BARBARA STURMAN

Library of Congress Cataloging-in-Publication Data
Gertz, Bill.
Treachery : how America's friends and foes are secretly arming our enemies / Bill Gertz.—1st ed.
p. cm.
Includes index.
1. National security—United States. 2. Illegal arms transfers.—History—21st century. 3. World politics—1995–2005. 4. War on Terrorism, 2001– I. Title.
UA23.G56 2004
355'.033073—dc22 2004012387

ISBN 1-4000-5315-3

10 9 8 7 6 5 4 3 2 1

First Edition

CONTENTS

Introduction TREACHERY 1

Chapter 1 THE FRENCH CONNECTION 11

2 GERMANY: TYRANTS, TERRORISTS, AND OTHER VALUED CUSTOMERS 37

3 RUSSIA: SLEEPING WITH THE ENEMY 55

4 THE NORTH KOREAN NUCLEAR THREAT 71

5 IRAN GOES NUCLEAR 89

6 CHINA: LIES AND DECEPTION 113

7 LIBYA AND SYRIA: THE NEW "AXIS OF EVIL" 137

8 THE UNITED STATES: PROLIFERATION NEGLIGENCE 169

9 THE UNITED NATIONS' FAILURES 185

10 THE ULTIMATE PROLIFERATION NIGHTMARE 203

Conclusion THE WAY AHEAD 217

Appendix TREACHERY EXPOSED 233

Acknowledgments 274

Index 275

Whatever enables us to go to war secures our peace.

—Thomas Jefferson, 1790

INTRODUCTION

TREACHERY

Air Force Major Jim Ewald climbed into the cockpit of his A-10 Thunderbolt jet in the midday Iraqi heat. The jet was called a Warthog because of its ugly appearance, but the U.S. troops on the ground loved it. As they fought their way into Baghdad, the only sound sweeter than the whine of the Warthog's turbofan jet engines was the staccato sound of its 30-millimeter machine gun, a seven-barrel Gatling that chewed up Saddam's troops.

Ewald, a thirty-seven-year-old Air National Guard pilot from St. Charles, Illinois, was part of the 110th Fighter Squadron. Although the war in Iraq had begun just three weeks earlier, Ewald had already flown several missions as part of the U.S. military's lightning advance on Baghdad. He was also a veteran of combat and training missions in Kosovo, Kuwait, and South Korea. But this mission, on April 8, 2003, would be unlike any he had ever flown.

Ewald took off from Tallil air base, some two hundred miles southeast of Iraq's capital city. In less than thirty minutes, the A-10 had reached western Baghdad and the target of the day: Iraqi troops who were firing on the U.S. Army's 3rd Infantry Division, which had begun its assault on one of Saddam's twenty-three known palaces.

The American pilot made three passes, firing the jet's guns on the Saddam loyalists, but then he got into trouble. A surface-to-air missile

streaked from the southwest and slammed into the back of his jet. Ewald never saw it coming.

The A-10 shuddered as if hit by "the hand of God," Ewald later recalled. "I could see a reddish glow on my cockpit instruments from the fire behind me."

Ewald struggled to keep the aircraft in the air, knowing he was over enemy territory. "My next thought was 'I don't want to bail out right over Baghdad or I'm going to be in it deep,'" he recalled. His objective was to make it to Baghdad International Airport, which was under the control of U.S. forces.

"It was physically hard [to fly the plane]," Ewald said. "I was manipulating everything with all the muscles in my body. I had flight control problems, I had engine problems, I had fuel-flow problems, I had hydraulic problems . . . not to mention that I had an airplane that was disintegrating. I looked back once and I could see little parts falling off the engine and I thought, 'I really don't know what that is, but I think I need it.'"

Finally one of his two engines went out, before he had reached the airport. He had to bail out.

Ewald pulled the ejection seat handle and parachuted to the ground, landing not far from where his A-10 crashed. Suddenly bullets were flying in every direction, and he dove into a drainage ditch, thinking that he was under fire from fedayeen Saddam guerrillas—Saddam's black-clad terrorist fighters.

Fortunately, just a short time later he was rescued by members of the U.S. Army's 54th Engineer Battalion who had seen him parachute to earth. As it turned out, Ewald wasn't under attack from Iraqi forces: The flames from his jet's wreckage had cooked off scores of 30-millimeter rounds from the Gatling gun.

Major Ewald was one of the first American pilots to be shot down in the Iraqi conflict. He had nearly been killed, and of course his $13 million aircraft was destroyed.

Was this just part of the normal costs of waging war against an enemy? Hardly. As the Army quickly discovered, the reason that an American pilot had been put in the line of fire and his aircraft destroyed was that a supposed ally of the United States was in bed with the enemy.

"It was a Roland missile," one U.S. military officer told me. That is to say, it was a French missile. Traditionally an ally of the United States, France had armed an American enemy—illegally. And according to Army intelligence, the French had sold the missile to the Iraqis *within the past year.* The French government claimed that Roland missiles had been sold to Iraq before the United Nations imposed sanctions in 1991, but a report produced for the Defense Department in February 2004 disputed that claim. The report concluded that "while Iraq had Roland missiles before Operation Desert Storm [the 1991 war], the serial number on the missile indicates that transfers occurred after 1991."

The fact that a French missile had nearly killed an American pilot was a stark reminder that illegal-arms shipments to rogue states come with a price—and that such illegal-arms deals, which began decades ago, continue even today, putting Americans and our allies at great risk.

Indeed, the missile that shot down Ewald's A-10 was just one of many French weapons the Iraqis used against U.S. forces during—and after—the Iraq war. Only a week after Ewald's crash, a U.S. Army team searching Iraqi weapons depots at Baghdad International Airport discovered caches of French-made missiles. In one cache the team found fifty-one Roland-2 antiaircraft missiles, which had been produced through a partnership of French and German arms manufacturers. One missile bore the label "05-11 knd 2002," indicating that the batch had been produced just months earlier.

There was even more. Nearby, Army Lieutenant Greg Holmes, a tactical intelligence officer with the 3rd Infantry Division, found the burned-out metal of what was a Roland-3 missile launcher, a more advanced version of the antiaircraft systems.

Nor were missiles the only French-made war-fighting equipment the Americans discovered in the early weeks of the war. Captured Iraqi military trucks had French radios, and surrendering Iraqi officers were driving French-made pickup trucks. Americans captured numerous RPGs—rocket-propelled grenades—that had French-made night sights; many of these were dated 2002.

In fact, for many months after the United States declared the end of major combat operations in Iraq, Saddam loyalists were using these French-supported RPGs to launch daily attacks on American and coalition troops trying to pacify Iraq. The grenade launchers, which are lethal against Humvees, had killed scores of soldiers by 2004.

The discovery of French weapons and equipment disgusted many American soldiers and leaders. France's behavior in the months leading up to the war—particularly when, at the United Nations, it blocked the United States from forcing Saddam to disarm peacefully, as required by sanctions dating to the end of the 1991 Persian Gulf War—led many to question whether America's NATO ally had become Saddam Hussein's friend in the West. Now, with graphic evidence that the French had illegally shipped arms to Iraq even in the last months before the war broke out, it became clear that France had abandoned its supposed ally the United States.

The Iraq war of 2003 exposed the danger to the United States of allowing rogue states to acquire weapons and military supplies that threaten and kill American troops. But shockingly, France is not the only nation that has placed greed over principle in arming tyrants like Saddam Hussein. Other supposed allies and friends, like Germany, Russia, and China, have been involved in illegal-weapons deals. The Germans have worked on their own and in tandem with the French and other arms merchants. Russia and China have been among the worst offenders in arming deadly regimes for the sake of a profit. More European countries have gotten into the illegal-arms game as well, including Ukraine and Belarus. Even the United States itself has helped rogue regimes build up their militaries.

A Pentagon report on weapons found in Iraq after the Iraq war revealed a staggering amount of armaments, almost all of the weapons foreign-made. The report reached this stark conclusion: "Foreign munitions were used against coalition forces during the war and continue to be a potential source of explosives for improvised explosive devices still being used to kill U.S. soldiers."

According to the report, twenty-four nations had supplied armaments to Saddam Hussein. The total amount was between 650,000 tons and 1 million tons. By contrast, the entire U.S. military arsenal is between 1.6 million and 1.8 million tons. The big three arms suppliers were Russia (and the Soviet Union), China, and France: Russia had supplied 122 different types of arms and a total of nearly 13 million items; China had provided 19 different types of arms and almost 380,000 items; France had supplied 12 different armaments and more than 115,000 items. The other source countries listed were Austria, Belgium, Brazil, Bulgaria, Canada, Chile, Czechoslovakia, Egypt, Germany, Iran, Italy, North Korea, Pakistan, Romania, Singapore, South Africa, Spain, Sweden, the United States, the United Kingdom, and Yugoslavia. The report (part of which can be found in this book's appendix) made clear that deadly arms merchants operate in every corner of the globe.

And Saddam Hussein was not the only tyrant allowed to illegally procure some of the most deadly weapons available. America's ostensible allies and other scofflaws are arming rogue states like North Korea, Iran, Libya, and Syria—all of which pose a growing threat to the United States and our allies around the world, including the threat of attack by nuclear, chemical, and biological weapons.

North Korea, one of the last Communist totalitarian regimes and one of the most repressive in history, is a real danger. Pyongyang's rulers admitted in the fall of 2002 that they had been clandestinely building a nuclear arsenal for years. The news came as no surprise to U.S. intelligence, which had been closely tracking North Korea's efforts to become a nuclear power. The North Koreans have received substantial help from Germany and France, as well as from China and Pakistan. With the deadly weapons and missiles it is developing, North Korea has said it will turn its enemies into "seas of fire." And, of course, the North Koreans are not always the receiving end of illegal-weapons deals; they have helped other dangerous regimes enhance their weapons programs.

Iran, too, has been developing a nuclear weapons program, which is a particularly frightening prospect given the radical Islamic regime's calculated and widespread anti-American strategy. And with their Shahab-3 missiles—which North Korea helped them develop—the Iranians can target U.S. forces and American friends and allies throughout the Middle East and Southwest Asia. North Korea's aid to Iran shows the danger of

cooperation among the "Axis of Evil," but Iran has had others support its arms buildup, including China, Russia, and even Ukraine.

Libya and Syria—both designated as state sponsors of international terrorism—have been secretly developing deadly nuclear, biological, and chemical weapons. Like other rogue states, they could not have made the progress they have without illegal aid from unscrupulous arms dealers around the world. Libya appears to be taking steps to change. But it remains ruled by a dictator with deep past involvement in terrorism.

The world has grown only more dangerous, not safer, since the Cold War ended more than a decade ago. Even as the United States prosecutes the war on terrorism, we must keep in mind that the transfer of dangerous weapons and related technology is the most significant threat to U.S. national security.

THE MOUNTING THREAT

By 2004, many Americans were focusing on Iraq and the question of how far along Saddam Hussein's regime actually had been in its quest for nuclear, chemical, and biological weapons and missiles to deliver them. The issue became heated in late January, when the CIA's former chief arms inspector, David Kay, told Congress that he had concluded that Iraq probably never had "large stockpiles of deployed, militarized chemical and biological weapons." Kay did not address the issue of whether Saddam's regime might have moved the weapons out of Iraq prior to the war, perhaps to Syria and Lebanon, or whether some weapons might have been buried in the desert. (Many did not consider this latter possibility, when in fact a U.S. search team in August 2003 found more than thirty Russian-made MiG-25 jets buried in the sand at an airfield west of Baghdad.)

But Kay did put the issue in a larger context: "In a world where we know others are seeking [weapons of mass destruction], the likelihood at some point in the future of a seller and a buyer meeting up would have made that a far more dangerous country than even we anticipated." The former weapons inspector was right. By focusing narrowly on what Iraq's capabilities might have been at the time of the U.S. military action, we overlook the more important issue of how weapons proliferation is an ongoing problem that can make our enemies even more dangerous.

The issue of the spread of arms and weapons technology is an "enormous subject," says Defense Secretary Donald H. Rumsfeld.

"I would also say it's a critically important subject," Rumsfeld told me during an interview inside the executive cabin of a U.S. Air Force C-32A jetliner, a militarized Boeing 757. "Over the coming decade, depending on how the world community conducts itself, there could be another five nuclear powers. There could be several more countries with chemical and biological programs, and there could be additional countries with the ability to deliver those capabilities long distances. The effect of that to the extent that those countries are not democracies, but rather countries on the terrorist list—the inevitable effect of that is to make the world a more dangerous place." Worse still, enemy nations are no longer the only customers for dangerous weapons; what Rumsfeld calls "nonstate entities"—organized terrorist groups—are actively working to procure weapons.

The problem is only getting worse. Part of the problem is that as soon as a country develops new weapons capabilities, it can market and transfer those capabilities to others; that nation itself becomes a dangerous proliferator. Rumsfeld recalled how one nuclear engineer from the former Soviet Union told him that the Soviets provided nuclear training to North Koreans, Iranians, and others from around the world. Similarly, Pakistan obtained nuclear weapons design information from China and Western Europe and has shared that with North Korea, Iran, Libya, and possibly others.

In addition, more and more technologies are becoming "dual-use" in nature—that is, they can be used for military as well as commercial purposes. Thus equipment and technology designed for making medicine and agricultural products also is used for biological and chemical weapons. Rogue states have also learned that U.S. intelligence can photograph practically any location on earth from the air or from space—with images clear enough to read license plates—so arms proliferators have moved to underground facilities. North Korea, Iran, and Libya have extensive underground facilities where hidden programs are (or were) carried out.

As Rumsfeld makes clear, our enemies have many reasons to arm themselves with weapons of mass destruction and advanced conventional arms. "In some cases it's a legitimate feeling that you are potentially threatened and therefore you need a deterrent," he says. "In some cases it's a country that wants to intimidate and threaten its neighbors or others." Still other nations have sought arms as "aggrandizement," the idea being that "you're not somebody unless you have this type of a capability, an aircraft carrier or a nuclear weapon or whatever."

But why would our purported allies be willing to help tyrants and terrorists become more lethal? Money, for starters. "There is no question but that a lot of countries do it for money," Rumsfeld says. In the case of a country like Russia, the defense secretary observes, "they're making nuclear weapons and they have people who know how to do that. And they have people who are unemployed." Also, as we will see, anti-Americanism has become a powerful force even in nations that we have considered allies.

For example, a contentious Belgian law allowed an attorney who was also a left-wing parliamentary candidate to charge the commander of Operation Iraqi Freedom, Army General Tommy Franks, with "war crimes." The 1993 Belgian law allowed Belgian courts to try war-crimes and genocide cases no matter where the offenses allegedly occurred or what the nationalities of the parties involved were. Thus the prosecuting attorney was representing a group of seventeen Iraqis and two Jordanians. That the Belgian government would permit a hero of the Iraq war to be subjected to the suit shows how low the European allies had sunk when it came to dealing with the United States. Only when the U.S. government threatened to pull NATO headquarters out of Brussels did the Belgian government make changes to the embarrassing law; the Belgian High Court ultimately threw out the case against Franks.

This book is the inside story of how America's supposed allies, as well as some of its foes, are secretly arming our enemies, and how in many cases the illicit-weapons deals have been going on for decades. While many Americans have condemned nations like France and Germany for opposing the United States at the United Nations before the war in Iraq, the truth is that those actions do not even hint at their treachery.

The danger of weapons proliferation is growing, and the world needs to take note of how the most deadly weapons are available to regimes run by bloody dictators and to terrorist groups. Donald Rumsfeld aptly summarizes the increasing risks we face when he points out that, thanks to improved technology, rogue states and terrorist organizations can now, with a single strike, "kill not simply thousands of people but tens of thousands of people."

And as the story of Air Force Major Jim Ewald makes clear, as long as we allow illegal-arms deals to continue, we will be putting Americans directly in the line of fire.

THE FRENCH CONNECTION

CHAPTER 1

THE U.S. MILITARY INTELLIGENCE TEAM WAS IN IRAQ to find weapons. Not ones Saddam Hussein may have hidden. The 75th Intelligence Exploitation Group, a unit set up by the U.S. Central Command, was out to find the chemical and biological weapons that Saddam had indicated he would use on advancing U.S. troops.

The rapid fall of Baghdad to U.S. and allied military forces in April 2003 created a different kind of problem for the Army spooks: looting. Hundreds of Iraqis, freed from Saddam Hussein's tyranny, began pillaging bombed-out ministries and burning government buildings. But the Army intelligence team was still able to get information about Saddam's regime. And in May, members of the team made an unusual discovery: Stashed away in an Iraqi ministry were a dozen blank French passports.

For the soldiers, the passports confirmed suspicions about the French that had been growing since Paris sought to block U.S. efforts to oust Saddam before the war: They were clear evidence that the French were aiding the enemy.

Earlier in 2003, U.S. intelligence officials had discovered that the French government had secretly helped officials from Saddam's dying regime flee from Iraq. French officials in Syria provided the passports to the Iraqis, intelligence revealed, and the travel documents gave Saddam's henchmen an easy exit. France is a member of the European Union, and the so-called Schengen Agreement provides that an EU passport holder can travel freely—that is, without any careful scrutiny by immigration authorities—through all but three EU countries (Britain, Denmark, and Ireland).

The news that the French had enabled key Saddam aides to flee Iraq was a closely guarded secret even within the U.S. intelligence community. U.S. operatives used sensitive intelligence-gathering methods to uncover the truth about the passports, and the intelligence was distributed to a very small group of senior government officials. But those who did learn what the French had done—including officials in the Pentagon, the State Department, and the military—were angry. The French had helped the Iraqi officials escape from justice. Coalition troops were uncovering more and more mass graves in Iraq, but the French had made it much harder to find out who was responsible and to put them on trial for war crimes. Even after Saddam Hussein was captured in a hole in Iraq in December 2003, many senior Saddam loyalists remained at large, and it was clear that large numbers had fled the country.

"It made it very difficult to track these people," a senior Bush administration official said. Another official said, "It's like Raoul Wallenberg in reverse," referring to the Swedish diplomat who supplied travel documents to help Jews escape Nazi Germany in World War II. "Now you have the French helping the bad guys escape from us."

After the *Washington Times* broke the story in early May 2003, some officials publicly commented on the relationship between France and Iraq. Secretary of Defense Donald Rumsfeld said simply, "France has historically had a very close relationship with Iraq. My understanding is that it continued right up until the outbreak of the war. What took place thereafter, we'll find out."

Rumsfeld had developed a reputation for poking his finger in the eye of news reporters whenever he had the chance; if he found one fact wrong, he never hesitated to embarrass a reporter in public or private over the error. But when asked specifically whether France had helped Iraqis escape, he said, "I've read those reports, but I don't have anything I can add to them." In a meeting before that press conference, Rumsfeld had been more direct; when aides told him that he would be asked about the French assistance, he replied, "Gertz had that story already." The secretary knew from the intelligence that had passed his desk that the report was true. Privately, the defense chief's aides say that he was livid that the French had aided Saddam's regime.

But France's government bristled at the suggestion that it would betray the United States by helping the Iraqis. A French Embassy spokeswoman, Nathalie Loiseau, stated, "France formally denies this type of allegation, which is not only contrary to reality but is intended to discredit our nation. It is certainly time for rumors of this type—totally unfounded and a dishonor to those who spread them—to stop."

Of course, those official comments came weeks *before* it became known that the 75th Intelligence Exploitation Group had discovered a dozen blank French passports in the Iraqi ministry. When, on May 24, the *Washington Times* broke the news that the U.S. team had found those passports, the French spin machine went into full action. Spokesmen again denounced the American press for heaping scorn on France.

But to anyone who had closely followed France's illicit relationship with the Iraqis—which went back decades—the French government's denials rang hollow. On the passports specifically, the French denials seemed implausible in large part because it was difficult to believe alternative explanations for why an Iraqi ministry would have blank French passports. A Defense Intelligence Agency official who confirmed the existence of the dozen French passports suggested that they could have been looted from the French Embassy, since embassies often keep blank passports on hand to assist visiting nationals whose passports are lost or stolen. "And if embassies are looted, blank passports would be a great commodity in the right hands," the official said. "The French had a lot of business interests in Iraq through the [UN] oil-for-food program."

But that explanation proved false. The French Embassy had not been looted, even after coalition forces took Baghdad on April 9. The reason was simple. In the days after the fall of Baghdad, France had protected the embassy with armed guards and barbed wire. Looters had sacked a French cultural center in Baghdad, but the center would not have had passports.

Another explanation for the passports was that the Iraqis had forged them. "The Iraqis are adept at forging passports," the defense official said. Even Secretary of Defense Rumsfeld, in an apparent effort to play down America's rift with France, later told me that he did not view the passports as a smoking gun in the case against the French. "We all know that there are forged and stolen passports from a variety of countries," he said, noting that trading and selling passports was a widespread problem in the Middle East.

But analysis by intelligence teams determined that the passports found in the Iraqi ministry were in fact genuine French travel documents.

According to a senior Defense Department official, a large group of Saddam's henchmen had managed to get out of Iraq and ended up crossing the porous Syrian border. The Iraqis managed to make it to a hotel in Damascus and were there without their characteristic Saddam-style mustaches. "They stayed one night and were out of there the next day with French passports and on Air France to who knows where," the senior official told me.

The unmistakable conclusion was that the French were actively helping America's enemy, an enemy that has killed hundreds of Americans and millions of Iraqis.

And France's aid to the Iraqi regime went far beyond passports. The evidence that France had sold out its allies to aid a rogue state led by a bloody tyrant was simply staggering. After all, by the time the U.S. military intelligence team discovered the French passports, U.S. forces had already found caches of French-made missiles and other weapons in Baghdad, and the Iraqis had already shot down an American pilot using a French missile. Even those discoveries, however, revealed just a small part of what the French had done to cozy up to a dictator.

"RANK HYPOCRISY AND BLATANT DISLOYALTY"

Americans had reacted angrily to France's support for Iraq in the lead-up to the war, well before the public—and even most U.S. government officials—knew the depth of France's treachery. Some people had taken to the streets to pour bottles of Beaujolais Nouveau wine into the streets. In New Jersey, California, and Illinois, people had thrown out imported French Evian bottled water, Dijon mustard, and Brie cheese. In a symbolic gesture, on March 11 Congress had banned the terms "french fries" and "french toast" from the House cafeteria; thereafter the House would be eating "freedom fries" and "freedom toast." Although French president Jacques Chirac would claim that France did not suffer any economic penalties from the American backlash, economic statistics showed that the country lost some $500 million in business from Americans who canceled vacations in France. The state of Montana showed its displeasure by divesting itself of $15 million in French stocks.

Those angry at the French could not understand why a longtime ally of the United States would stand against the United States and defend a tyrant like Saddam Hussein. As the noted French anticommunist intellectual Jean François Revel observes in his 2003 book *Anti-Americanism,* French leaders and intellectuals harbor a deep disdain for the United States, and these anti-Americans condemn the United States for prosecuting a war on terrorism. "Obsessed by their hatred and floundering in illogicality," writes Revel, "these dupes forget that the United States, acting in her own self-interest, is also acting in the interest of us Europeans and in the interest of many other countries threatened, or already subverted and ruined, by terrorism." Even before the war on terror, former French foreign minister Hubert Védrine had condemned what he called America's "hyperpower," and for months before the 2003 war in Iraq, France was trying to rein in American power.

Along with Germany, another supposed U.S. ally, France refused to support any U.S. effort to remove Saddam Hussein. French leaders also argued that there could be no justification for war against Iraq unless the United Nations Security Council approved that strategy. In March 2003, Congressman Curt Weldon, Pennsylvania Republican and vice chairman of the House Armed Services Committee, pointed out France's "rank hypocrisy and blatant disloyalty." Weldon recalled that just four years earlier, France had not sought UN support for its effort to remove Serbian dictator Slobodan Milosevic from power because French officials knew that Russia, a traditional friend of the Serbs, would have blocked the measure. Instead the French asked the United States for help. "For the first time and only time in NATO's history," said Weldon, "along with our president, at that time Bill Clinton, they used a NATO military force to invade a non-NATO sovereign nation to remove the head of state." In a letter to Chirac, the congressman stated that "your sudden reverence for the inviolability of the United Nations is laughable." Noting that Saddam Hussein was a far worse dictator than Milosevic ("The atrocities perpetrated under Hussein's regime are well documented by organizations such as Human Rights Watch, the International Federation for Human Rights, Amnesty International, the Coalition for International Justice, and even the United Nations"), Weldon concluded, "Convenience, not principle, seems to be France's guiding compass."

As Weldon observed, in using all their power to block Saddam's removal from power, the French were blatantly disregarding not only the long record of Saddam's crimes but also Iraq's constant flouting of United Nations resolutions since the end of the 1991 Persian Gulf War. Interestingly, France's repeated efforts to block the United States at the United Nations might have actually made military action necessary. In the fall of 2002, France had watered down the language in UN Security Council Resolution 1441 that required Iraq to disarm all its chemical, biological, and nuclear weapons programs. Privately, Deputy Defense Secretary Paul Wolfowitz said that France's diplomatic subversion had made it more difficult to resolve the problem of Iraq peacefully. (Later, when he learned that the French had helped Iraqi officials escape, Wolfowitz would begin to think of France not as an unfaithful ally but as a new enemy, albeit an enemy not in the same category as Syria, Iran, and North Korea, or even Russia and China.)

In early March 2003, shortly before the war began, French foreign minister Dominique de Villepin told reporters in Paris that France "will not allow a resolution to pass that authorizes resorting to force." He declared that "Russia and France, as permanent members of the Security Council, will assume their full responsibilities on this point."

According to Jacques Chirac, however, France was not opposing the United States or "appeasing this dictator," Saddam. Chirac testily told a television interviewer, "Why would France want to restrain American power? And even if France wanted to do so, how could we? It's an absurd line of reasoning. It is absolutely not reasonable [or] realistic. I am trying to be more serious and more honest of our assessment of things and world affairs today. It is ridiculous, really." Meanwhile, in denying that he was trying to appease Saddam, Chirac revealed how lenient he would be with the Iraqi tyrant. "I think the more we threaten him, the more he will react as a wounded animal," he said. "Again, every day there [is] one more step toward cooperation done by Iraq."

But if France's actions seemed illogical or hypocritical, it was only because Americans did not understand that the French had long ago sold out to the Iraqis.

GETTING IN BED WITH A TYRANT

The American soldiers who found caches of French missiles in Baghdad in 2003 may have been startled that a U.S. ally would secretly arm Saddam Hussein, but the problem was not new. French aid to Iraq goes back decades, and it has included transfers of all types of advanced conventional arms and even components for weapons of mass destruction.

The central figure in France's weapons ties to Iraq was none other than Jacques Chirac. Chirac's relationship with Saddam Hussein went as far back as 1975, when the French politician first hosted Saddam Hussein in Paris. Investigative reporter Kenneth Timmerman, a specialist on arms proliferation, outlined the Chirac-Saddam ties in his 1991 book *The Death Lobby.* As a Paris-based journalist, Timmerman closely followed France's addiction to selling deadly arms to Iraq.

As Timmerman documented, in September 1975 Chirac, then the French premier, rolled out the red carpet for Saddam when the Iraqi strongman visited Paris. "I welcome you as my personal friend," Chirac said to Saddam, who was then vice president of Iraq. "I assure you of my esteem, my consideration, and my affection." The French put Saddam up at the Hotel Marigny, an annex to the l'Élysée presidental palace, and gave him all the trappings of a head of state, including formal state receptions. The French wanted Iraqi oil, and by establishing this friendship with Saddam Hussein, Chirac would help France replace the Soviet Union as Iraq's leading supplier of weapons and military goods.

In fact, Chirac helped sell Saddam the two nuclear reactors that started Baghdad on the path to nuclear weapons. So involved was Jacques Chirac in the deal for the Iraqis' first nuclear reactor, the

Osirak, that those who opposed the sale referred to the reactor as the "O-Chirac." In June 1981, however, Israeli jets launched a daring bombing raid against the reactor, reducing the facility to rubble before it could be put on line and begin producing material that could be used for a nuclear bomb. The raid stopped Iraq from getting a nuclear bomb.

The Israeli bombing raid proved to be a key international lesson in counterproliferation, one that stands today as an example to the world. David Ivry, the major general in charge of the operation, said that in the early 1990s the U.S. secretary of defense, Dick Cheney, presented him with a large satellite photograph of the bombed-out Osirak facility. Cheney signed the photo, noting that the operation showed that the Israelis knew how to deal with threats from weapons of mass destruction. Ivry would go on to be the Israeli ambassador to the United States. In 2000, he showed me a drawing hanging in his embassy office of one of the U.S.-made F-16 fighters that took part in the 680-mile raid known as Operation Opera. Each of the Israeli Defense Forces pilots who took part in the raid had signed the drawing. One of the pilots had written, in Hebrew, "To the conductor of the opera, from the orchestra."

John Shaw, the deputy undersecretary of defense for international technology security, who for a time lived in Paris, told me that it is well known in France that Chirac "has been kind of in a godfather relationship with Saddam" dating to the time when France jump-started Iraq's nuclear program. Shaw said it was "an accepted fact in France" that Chirac was getting financial help for his various political campaigns from Baghdad. He also observed that Army and Defense Department investigators had discovered that France was one of the largest weapons sellers to Iraq and that tons of the armaments were still in bunkers spread out in the Iraqi desert.

During the 1980s, when Paris backed Iraq in its war against Iran, France sold Mirage F-1 fighters, Super Entendard aircraft, and Exocet antiship missiles to Baghdad. By the 1990s the ties between France and Iraq apparently were so strong that on the eve of the first Persian Gulf War the French government tried to conclude a secret deal with Baghdad to protect Saddam Hussein's regime from coalition forces. In January 1991, the CIA revealed in a classified report that French officials had contacted Iraqi government officials and promised to help prevent a U.S.-led military operation if Iraq would agree to withdraw half its troops from Kuwait. According to the report, the French said they would also try to address the problem of Palestinians in Israel if the Iraqis agreed to withdraw troops, but the Iraqis rejected the deal. U.S. government officials who learned of the secret negotiation felt that the French were undermining the coalition against Iraq by "freelancing" their own settlement plan.

After the Persian Gulf War, the United Nations imposed a strict arms embargo against Iraq, but numerous intelligence reports revealed that the French continued to back Iraq throughout the 1990s. For example, a CIA report from late 1996 showed that the French sent Iraq weapons to boost the power of Saddam's French-made Mirage fighters. A squadron of Iraqi Mirage F-1 fighters began receiving pairs of the advanced French Magic 2 air-to-air missiles in July 1996, according to the CIA. The Magic 2 missiles gave the Iraqis significantly improved air-combat capabilities and made patrolling the UN-mandated no-fly zone over Iraq much more dangerous for American and British pilots. "Something like that makes the hair [of fighter pilots] stand up on the back of your neck," said Robert Gaskin, a former Air Force fighter pilot. A major French arms maker, Matra, produced the missiles, and U.S. intelligence officials believed that the Iraqis could not have obtained the improved missiles without the covert support of some members of the French government, which tightly controls arms exports from France and any other defense deals.

The signs of France's corrupt dealings with Iraq were everywhere. In fact, according to a senior member of Congress who declined to be identified by name, by 2000 France was Iraq's largest supplier of military and dual-use equipment.

To get around the UN arms embargo, Saddam Hussein also developed illegal-parts networks that enabled an Iraqi military buildup in the years before U.S. forces launched a second assault on Iraq. One spare-parts pipeline flowed from a French company to the Al Tamoor Trading Company in the United Arab Emirates, which then sent the parts through a third country, Turkey, and into Iraq by truck. Through this pipeline the Iraqis obtained spare parts for their Mirage F-1 jets and Gazelle attack helicopters. U.S. intelligence would not discover the pipeline until 2003, on the eve of war; sensitive intelligence indicated that parts had been smuggled to Iraq as recently as January.

Two CIA reports provided further evidence that these transfers were occurring. In a report to Congress made public in January 2003, the CIA revealed, "A thriving gray-arms market and porous borders have allowed Baghdad to acquire smaller arms and components for larger arms, such as spare parts for aircraft, air defense systems, and armored vehicles." Another report, from October 2002, stated, "Iraq imports goods using planes, trains, trucks, and ships without any type of international inspections—in violation of U.N. Security Council resolutions."

U.S. intelligence agencies later came under fire over questions about prewar estimates of Iraq's stockpiles of weapons of mass destruction. But intelligence on Iraq's hidden procurement networks was indeed confirmed. An initial accounting by the Pentagon in the months after the fall of Baghdad revealed that Saddam had acquired between 650,000 and 1 million tons of foreign conventional weapons covertly. The main suppliers were found to be Russia, China, and France. By contrast, the U.S. arsenal is between 1.6 and 1.8 million tons.

By 2003, Iraq owed France an estimated $4 billion for arms sales and infrastructure construction projects, according to French government estimates. U.S. officials believed that this massive debt was one reason France opposed a military operation to oust Saddam Hussein. Of course, the French must not have been concerned only with unpaid bills for past arms transfers; the fact that the illegal deals were continuing even as war loomed indicated that France viewed Saddam's regime as a future source of income.

THE WEAPONS DEALS CONTINUE

As the United States prepared for military action against Iraq in the late winter of 2003, the new intelligence revealing that the French continued to aid Saddam Hussein's regime infuriated many U.S. officials, but it also helped explain why France had refused to deal harshly with Iraq. When the parts sales were discovered in early 2003, one intelligence official remarked, "No wonder the French are opposing us." That official was careful to stipulate that the intelligence reports did not indicate whether the French government had sanctioned or known about the parts transfers; the French company at the beginning of the pipeline remained unidentified in intelligence reports. Again, however, France's government tightly controls its aerospace and defense firms, so it would be difficult to believe that the transfers took place without the knowledge of at least some government officials. Iraq's Mirage F-1 was made by France's Dassault Aviation. Gazelle attack helicopters were made by Aerospatiale, which later became part of a consortium of European defense companies.

A senior administration official declined to discuss Iraq's purchase of French warplane and helicopter parts. "It is well known that the Iraqis use front companies to try to obtain a number of prohibited items," the official said. The State Department, meanwhile, confirmed that intelligence had indicated the French had given support to Iraq's military. Spokeswoman Jo-Anne Prokopowicz said, "UN sanctions prohibit the transfer to Iraq of arms and matériel of all types, including military aircraft and spare parts. We take illicit transfers to Iraq very seriously and work closely with our allies to prevent Iraq from acquiring sensitive equipment."

Other members of the U.S. government expressed their outrage. For example, Senator Ted Stevens, Alaska Republican and chairman of the powerful Senate Appropriations Committee, declared that France's selling military equipment to Iraq was "international treason." After pointing out that such deals violated a UN resolution, Stevens said, "As a pilot and a former war pilot, this disturbs me greatly that the French would allow in any way parts for the Mirage to be exported so the Iraqis could continue to use those planes." For his part, Congressman Weldon declared, "The French, unfortunately, are becoming less trustworthy than the Russians. It's outrageous they would allow technology to support the jets of Saddam Hussein to be transferred."

The U.S. military was about to go to war with Iraq, and thanks to the French, the Iraqi air force had become more dangerous. In his February 5, 2003, presentation to the United Nations, in which he summarized the intelligence about Iraq's ongoing weapons procurement, Secretary of State Colin Powell revealed another reason why Iraq's French-made Mirage fighters posed a threat. During the presentation,

Powell showed a videotape of an Iraqi F-1 Mirage that had been modified to spray anthrax spores, which gave the Iraqis a means "to disperse lethal biological agents widely, indiscriminately into the water supply, into the air," the secretary said.

Just days before the U.S. and coalition forces launched the military campaign against Iraq, yet more evidence of French treachery emerged. In fact, this was one of the most egregious cases: In mid-March 2003, U.S. intelligence and defense officials confirmed that exporters in France had conspired with China to provide Iraq with chemicals used in making solid fuel for long-range missiles. The sanctions-busting operation occurred in August 2002, as the U.S. National Security Agency discovered through electronic intercepts.

According to intelligence reports, the chemical transferred to Iraq was a transparent liquid rubber called hydroxy terminated polybutadiene, or HTPB. U.S. intelligence traced the sale to China's Qilu Chemicals, which "is the largest manufacturer of HTPB in China," according to a U.S. intelligence official. A French company known as CIS Paris helped broker the sale of twenty tons of HTPB, which was shipped from China to the Syrian port of Tartus. The chemicals were then sent by truck from Syria into Iraq to a missile-manufacturing plant. The Iraqi company that purchased the chemical shipment was in charge of making solid missile fuel for long-range missiles.

Technically HTPB is a dual-use chemical, since it can also be used for commercial purposes, such as for space launches. Of course, Iraq often disguised military purchases as commercial sales, when in reality it was all for the military, as documents found in Iraq would later confirm. Indeed, the chemical HTPB was listed as a controlled export on a list of missile-related goods that the Chinese government made public in August 2002—about the same time that the HTPB transfer to Iraq occurred.

In the same report to Congress that revealed that a "thriving gray-arms market and porous borders" had enabled Baghdad to acquire arms and spare parts, the CIA stated that Iraq had constructed two new "mixing" buildings for solid-propellant fuels at a plant known as al-Mamoun. The facility was originally built to produce the Badr-2000—also known as the Condor—solid-propellant missile. The new buildings "appear especially suited to house large, U.N.-prohibited mixers of the type acquired for the Badr-2000 program," the CIA report stated. "In fact, we can find no logical explanation for the size and configuration of these mixing buildings other than an Iraqi intention to develop longer-range, prohibited missiles (that is, to mix solid propellant exclusively geared for such missiles)." The second plant at al-Mamoun had casting pits that "were specifically designed to produce now-proscribed missile motors," the report said. Despite controversy over its Iraq pre-war intelligence the CIA said its estimates of Iraqi missiles were on target.

Representatives of the French and Chinese governments went on the attack when the *Washington Times* asked them about the chemical sale. Chinese Embassy spokesman Xie Feng did not address the specific charges but said that "irresponsible accusations" about China's exports had been made in the past. French Foreign Ministry spokesman François Rivasseau declared, "These accusations are devoid of all foundation. They are a part of a polemic that we do not want to get involved in. In line with the rules currently in force, France has neither delivered, nor authorized, the delivery of such materials, either directly or indirectly." But by that point, many in the U.S. government were fed up with French denials. After the chemical shipment was disclosed in March, Deputy Defense Secretary Paul Wolfowitz called in the French ambassador to the United States, Jean-David Levitte, to complain about France's covert and overt support for Saddam Hussein's regime. Levitte went to the Pentagon to lobby Wolfowitz against U.S. military action, but instead received an earful of harsh complaints. "Twelve years of waiting was too costly in terms of the growing threat from Baghdad," Wolfowitz told the ambassador, according to a U.S. official present at the meeting.

AMERICANS IN THE LINE OF FIRE

The U.S. military action in Iraq began on March 19, and although the main assault was swift and effective—Baghdad fell less than three weeks later—the war provided disturbing evidence that France's treacherous dealings come at a steep cost to the United States.

Early on, of course, came the downing of Major Jim Ewald's A-10 fighter and the discovery that it was a French-made Roland missile that had taken down an American pilot in the war and had destroyed a multimillion-dollar U.S. aircraft. Soon thereafter the military intelligence team found the stack of blank French passports that only confirmed what U.S. intelligence had already determined: that the French had helped Iraqi war criminals escape from coalition forces and therefore escape justice. Then, too, there were the deadly grenade launchers known as RPGs that had French-made night sights and that Saddam loyalists were using to kill American soldiers long after the toppling of Saddam's regime.

But that was not all. The intelligence team that was sent to find Iraqi weapons also found documents outlining covert Iraqi weapons procurement leading up to the war. The CIA, however, refused to make public the documents on assistance provided by France or by other so-called allies of the United States.

The clandestine arms procurement network was disclosed by the *Los Angeles Times* in late 2003. Documents showed that a Syrian trading company, SES International Corporation, was the conduit for millions of dollars' worth of weapons purchased internationally, including from France. The documents revealed that the Al Bashair Trading Company, in Baghdad, was the major front used by Saddam to buy arms abroad.

A Defense Department–sponsored report produced in February 2004 identified France as one of the top three suppliers of Iraq's conventional arms, after Russia and China. The report revealed that France supplied twelve different types of armaments and a total of 115,005 pieces.

A major reason Iraqi militants posed a threat to U.S. forces for so many months after the main military campaign ended was that they had access to the weapons that Saddam had stockpiled in violation of UN resolutions, and many of those weapons had been provided by the French.

One of the most frightening examples of how the Iraqis could put French weapons to use against the Americans came on October 26, 2003. That morning, at about 6 o'clock, Iraqis bombarded a Baghdad hotel with French missiles. Staying in the Rashid Hotel that morning was Deputy Defense Secretary Paul Wolfowitz.

The French rockets nearly killed Wolfowitz, whom Donald Rumsfeld has called "the brains" of the Pentagon. The deputy defense secretary had just gotten dressed in his hotel room that Sunday morning when a car stopped several hundred yards from the hotel. As the car stopped, it dropped off what appeared to be one of the blue electrical generators that were common to the power-starved Iraqi capital. The driver stayed just long enough to open a panel on the end of the metal box that was pointing upward toward the hotel.

The car sped off, but minutes later a pod of forty artillery rockets began firing at the hotel, their trails leaving sparks as they flew. The rockets hit just one floor below where Wolfowitz and about a dozen aides and news reporters were staying.

A remote-control signal had set off the missiles. One rocket slammed into the room of Army Lieutenant Colonel Charles H. Buehring, who was working with public affairs in Baghdad. The explosion hit him in the head. A reporter discovered him and tried to help him, but Buehring, forty, of Fayetteville, North Carolina, died a short time later.

In all, between eight and ten missiles hit the hotel. The casualties could have been higher, and might have included Wolfowitz, if the improvised rocket launcher had fired all its missiles, but because of a malfunction, eleven rockets had failed to go off.

Half the missiles were French-made Matra SNEB 68-millimeter rockets, which have a range of two to three miles, while the others were Russian in origin. The French missiles were in "pristine" condition, according to U.S. Navy SEAL commandos. "They were either new or kept in very good condition," said one SEAL who had inspected the rocket tubes. The rockets were believed to have been taken from Iraq's French-made Alouette or Gazelle attack helicopters.

The fact that brand-new French missiles were showing up in the hands of Saddam loyalists months *after* the fall of Baghdad made Wolfowitz and his close aides livid. Still, others in the U.S. government worked hard to defend the French from charges of supporting Saddam's forces. In particular, officials from the State Department and the CIA shielded Paris, offering the implausible and all-too-familiar explanation that French companies had often made deals without the government's knowledge or support. The CIA, for its part, played down the French role in helping Saddam, to avoid upsetting its ties with French intelligence. The agency had a weak human intelligence–gathering capability, and France, because of its history of ties to Iraq, was much better at penetrating Saddam's regime.

The State Department's response was not surprising. After all, Secretary of State Powell had shown himself eager to forgive the French. As early as May, when the blank French passports were discovered in Iraq, Powell had revealed that he would not take a hard-line position with the French. Asked about French support for Iraq while on a fence-mending mission to Paris, the secretary had said, "We're not going to paper over it and pretend it didn't occur. It did occur. But we're going to work through that." Powell, the retired four-star general and former chairman of the Joint Chiefs of Staff, was playing a new role as America's top diplomat, and unfortunately he was too inexperienced in the ways of diplomacy. As a result, he had largely turned over control of State Department policymaking to the Foreign Service, the corps of diplomats sent abroad. The problem with the Foreign Service is its culture. It trains its diplomats to "get along" with the foreign governments they work for. Not insignificantly, Paris is among the most coveted postings in the world for members of the Foreign Service.

The impulse to accommodate the French spread beyond the State Department. Although hard-liners in the Pentagon like Rumsfeld and Wolfowitz had carried the day early in the war, the accommodationists within the upper councils of the Bush administration took control as the conflict went on. Among those who took a softer position on France was National Security Adviser Condoleezza Rice, the former Stanford provost who had surrounded herself with State Department officials and Foreign Service officers.

Thus, while Rumsfeld had been openly critical of the French before the war, he had toned down his rhetoric by late 2003. The defense secretary drew a great deal of attention—and created a backlash within the State Department—in January 2003 when he let fly a verbal salvo against France and Germany. During a meeting with foreign reporters in Washington on January 22, when asked about why France and Germany appeared to be siding with Saddam Hussein over George W.

Bush, Rumsfeld declared, "Now, you're thinking of Europe as Germany and France. I don't. I think that's old Europe. If you look at the entire NATO, Europe today, the center of gravity is shifting to the east. And there are a lot of new members. And if you just take the list of all the members of NATO and all of those who have been invited in recently—what is it? twenty-six, something like that?—you're right. Germany has been a problem, and France has been a problem. But you look at vast numbers of other countries in Europe. They're not with France and Germany on this, they're with the United States." He also criticized French and German political leaders for making policy based not on "their honest conviction as to what their country ought to do" but on opinion polls that reflected ever-shifting public sentiments.

As the accommodationists in the Bush administration gained the upper hand, Rumsfeld and other administration officials were ordered to tone down the anti-Europe rhetoric. By late 2003, the defense secretary's critics within the Foreign Service were crowing that Rumsfeld had been "tamed." Rumsfeld did defend his now-famous "old Europe" comment during a press conference in late September 2003, explaining, "I was getting a little tired of people casting their questions with the premise being that France, Belgium, and Germany constituted all of Europe." But he also noted that he had stopped using the phrase out of deference to the Europeans. Just a day after the Iraqi attack on Paul Wolfowitz's hotel in Baghdad, in an interview with the *Washington Times,* Rumsfeld took an even softer approach toward the French. "I think back over my adult life and the relationship between de Gaulle and General Eisenhower," he said, "[and] I don't think there's been a five-year period my entire life where there hasn't been highly visible issues in one way or another that for a period spike up and then recede. People tend to look at what's taking place today and opine that it is something distinctive. I don't find it distinctive. I find it an old record that gets replayed about every five or seven years."

The public soft-policy line was, in many ways, a great victory for France. Even as new evidence poured in that the French had betrayed the United States and cost the lives of many American servicemen and -women, the U.S. government was publicly backing down from a confrontation with its erstwhile ally.

"BLOOD FOR OIL," THE FRENCH WAY

With the war came yet another indication that the French had worked closely with Saddam Hussein's regime right up to the outbreak of war. And in this case, the evidence pointed directly at the French government.

On April 24, 2003, Saddam's deputy prime minister, Tariq Aziz, gave himself up to U.S. authorities. According to a senior U.S. intelligence official, Aziz told interrogators that Saddam had misjudged the United States, believing that the Americans would not launch a military campaign. The reason: French and Russian government officials had assured Saddam in late 2002 and early 2003 that the United States would not attack. And if the Americans did try to attack, they said, Paris and Moscow would take steps within the United Nations Security Council to block the war.

A senior U.S. official related that, according to Aziz, Saddam's discussions with French and Russian officials had led the Iraqi leader to conclude that any conflict would be preceded by a long aerial bombing campaign, as had occurred in 1991. Saddam, said Aziz, planned to ride out the bombing campaign and count on France and Russia to reach a cease-fire on his behalf. As a result, Saddam refused to order a military response to the massing of U.S. and British ground forces on Iraq's border with Kuwait. The Iraqi leader refused to order military attacks even after receiving reports that American ground forces had begun pouring through the sand berms along the Iraqi border, according to Aziz.

At the time of Aziz's capture, some officials cautioned that U.S. intelligence questioned Aziz's credibility. For example, Aziz insisted that Iraq did not have weapons of mass destruction before the war. The United States is trying to figure out what happened to the weapons or whether intelligence estimates of the arms were wrong. Moreover, Aziz claimed that the U.S. pilot who remained missing from the 1991 Persian Gulf War, Navy Captain Michael Scott Speicher, was dead. The United States, meanwhile, had evidence that Speicher might still be alive: U.S. forces had just found the initials "MSS" carved into the wall of a cell in a Baghdad prison. Months later, when Saddam Hussein was captured, the Iraqi despot claimed that he didn't know what happened to

Speicher. In February 2004, Vice Admiral Lowell Jacoby, director of the Defense Intelligence Agency, testified to the Senate that despite a massive investigation in post-Saddam Iraq, the agency still considered Speicher missing. "Our assumption is that we will continue to look for Captain Speicher as if he is alive until such time as we find out otherwise," Admiral Jacoby said.

Despite the doubts raised about Aziz's testimony, U.S. intelligence had independently corroborated that the French had had close contact with Saddam in the months before the war. An early March 2003 defense intelligence report showed that French and Russian oil companies were working to conclude deals with Saddam's regime, hoping that the oil contracts "would be honored later," in a post-Saddam Iraq, as one official reported. Although the French company tried to use the Russian firm to mask its involvement, U.S. intelligence agencies detected the French effort and reported it to senior Bush administration officials the week before military operations began. According to intelligence officials, during these oil negotiations, Paris and Moscow might also have been working to help Saddam stay in power.

John Shaw, the deputy undersecretary of defense for international technology security, told me another story of how the French helped Saddam. According to Shaw, the French government had helped arrange for Saddam Hussein to flee Iraq three or four years before the war of 2003. The plan called for the French to keep an Airbus 300 jetliner stationed at the Baghdad airport and for Saddam to flee to Mauritania, a former French colony in northwest Africa. "If it was true, it got rid of Saddam without any bloodshed," Shaw said. "But what could be nicer than having Chirac have to deal with him as his keeper for the rest of his life." The problem of Saddam would have gone away and Chirac would have continued getting some of the money he was getting from Saddam. "They deserved each other, but nothing ever came of it," Shaw said. Officially, the French government denied the plans for sending Saddam to Mauritania, but privately French officials acknowledged the plan.

Shaw dismissed French government claims that its arms sales to Iraq took place before Saddam's invasion of Kuwait in 1990. The weapons flow continued through 2003. "There was no break in the flow of stuff going in there," he said, adding that documents recovered from Iraq were expected to produce additional details on how France armed Saddam Hussein.

ARMING THE "AXIS OF EVIL"

The war against Iraq has provided the most graphic evidence of French treachery. After all, many Americans have lost their lives because French arms dealers unscrupulously provided missiles and other weapons to Saddam Hussein's regime. But France's support for rogue states has not been limited to Iraq.

The French have also helped Iran, which President Bush named as part of the "Axis of Evil." The dual-use equipment that the French have given Iran is, U.S. government officials believe, helping Iran's nuclear program.

In 2003, U.S. export control officials investigated a French company for supplying Iran with four specialty pumps made in the United States. Treasury and Commerce Department officials suspected that the dual-use pumps, described as cryogenic-fluid transfer pumps, were sold illegally and could be used as part of the cooling system for Iran's nuclear reactors, which can be used to produce weapons-grade material. "That's the immediate concern," a Commerce Department official told me.

The investigation centered on the French firm Technip-Coflexip. According to investigators, in January 2003 the firm diverted the pumps it had purchased for an oil-related project to Iran's nuclear program. The electric pumps are submersible and used to transfer extremely cold fluids.

Technip contacted at least two U.S. transfer pump manufacturers, including the U.S. subsidiary of the Japanese-owned company Ebara International Corp. The French company was trying to get two ethylene and two ethane transfer pumps for its petrochemical complex in Asaluyeh, Iran, the Ninth Olefins Complex. In March 2003, an informant close to Ebara provided the Treasury Department's Office of Foreign Assets Control (OFAC), which monitors adherence to export controls on Iran, with documents that outlined this diversion effort.

Ebara "has knowingly engineered, manufactured, tested, and shipped the above-referenced pumps to Technip of France for delivery to

Iran," the informant stated in a document sent to Treasury's chief of enforcement, Hal Harmon. According to the informant, Ebara's corporate lawyer in 1998 warned the company "not to engage in the sale of goods or engineering services to countries that are on the restricted list per OFAC regulations." The informant also stated that an inspector working on behalf of Technip refused to authorize the shipment of the pumps because of concerns that the pumps would be sent to Iran. The pumps were exported without nameplates, the informant added.

When questioned by investigators, Richard Mitchell, the Ebara corporate counsel, denied that the company had sent pumps to Technip and also asserted that Ebara scrupulously abides by laws and regulations related to sales to Iran. "I have asked everyone in the organization in a position to know and they have manifestly and devoutly stated that nothing was done" in violation of export rules, Mitchell stated.

U.S. investigators, however, remain convinced that the diversion took place.

Technip concluded a deal in 2001 with the National Petrochemical Company of Iran to build the Ninth Olefins Complex, and in September 2002 it agreed to build a second facility at Assaluyeh, the Tenth Olefins plant. The second plant would produce 1.3 million tons of ethylene a year. The French construction deals were estimated to be worth about $1.2 billion.

The deals showed that France's major oil company had no qualms about doing business with a country governed by a radical Islamist regime that is a major backer of international terrorism.

Another dangerous regime to which France has provided weapons is China. Thus, not only have the French conspired with Chinese firms to make another rogue state more deadly, but they also have helped the Chinese government build up its military in its effort to dominate the Pacific. According to intelligence reports, France helped arm China's Luhu-class destroyers, supplying advanced Crotale surface-to-air missiles, Sea Tiger naval surveillance radar, Dauphin-2 helicopters, and the TAVITAC combat data system, which is used to integrate the various combat systems on the destroyers. The French also sold China the Super Frelon helicopters, which are used for antisubmarine warfare.

These deals should be particularly troubling to Americans, because the arms could be used against U.S. military forces. For years tensions between China and Taiwan have been mounting (as I documented in my book *The China Threat*), and U.S. policy currently commits the United States to support Taiwan in any conflict. Although the war on terrorism is the preoccupation of American policymakers, let there be no doubt that the U.S. government is closely monitoring the simmering tensions in the Taiwan Strait. If those tensions were ever to boil over into a conflict and the United States were to get involved militarily, once again American servicemen and -women would be directly threatened by French weapons. For years ahead we may be paying the price for France's deadly dealings with the enemy.

FRENCH ESPIONAGE

When Donald Rumsfeld told the *Washington Times* that the 2003 Iraq war didn't mark the first time when there were "visible issues" between the United States and France, he was not merely being conciliatory, he had a point. Years before the Iraq war, the U.S. government had encountered problems with the French that were unrelated to France's continuing proliferation of weapons to rogue regimes.

In the early 1990s, for example, U.S. intelligence agencies became wary of French intelligence, because the French spy service was conducting aggressive operations against visiting U.S. officials and businessmen. French intelligence electronically intercepted telephone calls, planted electronic listening devices in hotel rooms, broke into visitors' hotel rooms, and searched luggage and portable computers. "The French have completely wired most hotels," one official said at the time. Additionally, in May 1994, the CIA ordered all U.S. intelligence-sharing with Canada cut off because of concerns that the French intelligence service had planted agents within the Canadian government; at the time the French-speaking Quebec province was considering seceding from Canada. "France's [intelligence] service is no longer considered a friendly intelligence service," an official said.

Relations between the CIA and the French civilian intelligence service, the Direction Générale de la Sécurité Extérieure (DGSE), hit

rock bottom in 1995. That's when Paris expelled five CIA officers who were caught in a sting operation as they attempted to recruit a French government official as a spy. But in fact Paris was engaged in aggressive technology spying at the time. In 1993, a French intelligence document was made public showing that the DGSE had targeted about fifty U.S. firms for economic spying activities. The intelligence plan, produced in 1991 by the DGSE's Department of Economics, Science, and Technology, listed the companies, products, and information the DGSE sought from U.S., British, and Swiss firms and government agencies. Among the intelligence the French tried to collect was "technical-industrial" information on "computers, electronics, telecommunications, aeronautics, armaments, nuclear, chemical, space, consumer goods, capital goods, raw materials, and major civilian contracts." The U.S. firms the French targeted included Allied Signal, Bell, Boeing, Ford Aerospace, General Dynamics, Grumman Aerospace, GTE, Honeywell, Hughes Aircraft, Lockheed, Los Alamos and Lawrence Livermore national laboratories, McDonnell Douglas, NASA space centers, Northrop, Pratt and Whitney, Texas Instruments, TRW, United Technologies, and Westinghouse.

Indeed, French intelligence had become a kind of economic KGB, trying to steal proprietary information from U.S. companies. In early 1994, U.S. intelligence agencies disclosed a worldwide French intelligence operation to help a French company corner the market in high-technology abrasives. Abrasives technology is important for ceramics, a material being developed for automobile engines and missile nose cones, and microabrasives are used to make computer microchips. According to FBI sources, France's government was developing abrasives technology as part of a national industrial program, and the French targeted a leading American abrasives manufacturer, 3M.

According to a document that 3M obtained outlining France's intelligence effort, the French had some twenty corporate agents worldwide working to collect information on 3M's abrasives technology. Many French agents called 3M facilities seeking specific information on 3M's exclusive manufacturing technology; some callers even disguised themselves as researchers conducting "safety surveys." In one case, intelligence agents posing as fire inspectors tried to enter a 3M facility in Canada.

The French government denied this operation as it has denied so many others. But former 3M executive William E. DeGenaro, a one-time Pentagon counterintelligence official, and journalist Michael J. Stedman uncovered the economic spy operation. According to DeGenaro and Stedman, the French began their operation in the summer of 1990, shortly after the French company Saint-Gobain bought a major 3M competitor, the Norton Company of Massachusetts. DeGenaro reported that the French ramped up their operation the next year, using three different corporate intelligence firms, including one based in Paris. DeGenaro found no hard evidence linking Saint-Gobain and French intelligence to the espionage attacks, but the former counterintelligence official remarked, "Let's just say there was overwhelming circumstantial evidence." At the very least it seemed Saint-Gobain had a major economic incentive to keep on top of its rival 3M: It paid $1.9 billion for Norton.

"I'M NOT MAD"

In 2003, after the war in Iraq had begun, President George W. Bush was often asked to assess America's relationship with France. In late April he indicated that tensions remained when he remarked of French president Jacques Chirac, "I doubt he'll be coming to the ranch anytime soon"; Bush had invited other world leaders to join him at his ranch in Crawford, Texas, the following week. He also acknowledged, "There are some strains in the relationship, obviously, because it appeared to some in our administration and our country that the French position was anti-American."

Like others in his administration, President Bush softened his tone over time. At the end of May, in an interview with French television, he said that he had forgiven France and that there would be "no sanctions—I'm not mad." He went on, "I mean, I'm disappointed, and the American people are disappointed. But now is the time to move forward. And there's a lot of issues that we can work together on." Bush's comments summed up the U.S. government's position on France. Relations between Washington and Paris were chillier, to be sure, but the rift was informal. This remained the status quo for many months after the fall of Baghdad.

For most reporters who asked President Bush about U.S. relations with France, the only real issue was France's diplomatic opposition to the Iraq war. As we have seen, however, France's repeated efforts to block attempts to hold Saddam Hussein accountable were just one small part of that nation's treachery. The American government may in its public statements pretend that the French did not have a decades-long relationship with the tyrant Saddam Hussein, but mountains of intelligence and other evidence tell a much different story. Worse, the record reveals that France's deadly dealings continue, and that the French have made some of the worst rogue states even more dangerous.

"There are consequences to what these people did to us, to our soldiers, and our Marines," said Edward Timperlake, the Pentagon's director of technology assessment, who helped catalogue Iraq's weapons. "A lot of people cheated, a lot of people made a lot of money, a lot of people left a mess in the desert, a lot of people profited, and a lot of Americans paid the price because of their greed."

By long tradition France is a friend and ally of the United States, but we would be well served to cast a cold eye on an "ally" that continues to put Americans in the line of fire.

GERMANY: TYRANTS, TERRORISTS, AND OTHER VALUED CUSTOMERS

CHAPTER 2

SHORTLY AFTER 8:45 A.M., THE TWO U.S. ARMY CH-47 Chinook helicopters lifted off from a base at Habbaniya, about thirty miles west of Baghdad. The helicopters were ferrying a group of soldiers to Baghdad International Airport so they could catch a return flight to the United States for much-needed rest and relaxation.

It was November 2, 2003, but even now, nearly seven months after the toppling of Saddam Hussein's regime, many Iraqis in this area remained loyal to Saddam. One of those Iraqis lay in wait on the ground below, hiding in a dense patch of palm trees. He was carrying a shoulder-fired missile. As the noise of the twin-engine helicopters got louder, the Iraqi took aim. The first missile hit the critical tail rotor of one chopper, sending it crashing into a field. Thanks to the Chinook's ALG-156 anti-missile system, a second missile missed the other American helicopter, barely.

Describing the attack, one of the soldiers aboard the first helicopter later recalled, "I heard a loud boom. I closed my eyes and I prayed. After that I don't know." Sergeant Christopher Nelson, twenty-seven, of Orange, Texas, was knocked out when the helicopter hit the ground. He suffered a broken hip and ankle and had a large bruise over his left eye. But he was lucky. In all, fifteen Army soldiers were killed in the attack. It was the single largest number killed in action since the end of major combat operations in April.

Iraqi fighters had a huge arsenal of shoulder-fired missiles—at least five thousand, U.S. intelligence agencies estimated, most of which remained unaccounted for by the fall of 2003. Attacks like the one on the Chinook helicopters were not unusual. In fact, not long before the Chinook crash, the State Department had put out a notice warning that "coalition forces have reported possible missile attacks directed at aircraft over the past few weeks." And just five days after the crash, an Iraqi missile brought down a Black Hawk helicopter near Saddam's hometown of Tikrit, killing six American soldiers.

In the fall of 2003, U.S. forces were still discovering stockpiles of Iraqi weapons throughout the country. Some suspected that Saddam's forces, which had disbanded as U.S. troops entered Baghdad, had deliberately hidden weapons and ammunition around the country in preparation for the insurgency that followed. Army Lieutenant General Ricardo Sanchez, the commander of coalition ground forces in Iraq, said in October that he had "literally thousands and thousands of soldiers" tracking down just ammunition. "Every single day we find ammunition," the three-star general said. "We find caches, huge caches, where we're operating."

Particularly troubling were the shoulder-fired missiles, which were being used to such effect against American forces. But where did the Iraqis get the missiles? U.S. officials knew that the type of missile the Iraqis were using in the helicopter attacks was what the military calls a manpad, or man-portable air defense missile. The Iraqis had two kinds of manpads. The first was the Russian SA-7 missile, also known as the Strela. This low-altitude missile with a passive infrared homing device carried a filter design to reduce the effectiveness of flares, which U.S. helicopters like the Chinook used as part of their antimissile systems. The missile had a range of a little over two miles from the firing point and could hit targets at a range of between 45 feet and 4,500 feet. The SA-7 was a "tail-chaser," locking on to a heat source on low-flying jets or helicopters.

But U.S. intelligence officials believe it even more likely that the shoulder-fired missile used in the attacks against U.S. helicopters was the other kind of Iraqi manpad: a hybrid weapon built from components that Germany had illegally supplied to Iraq. In fact, the surface-to-air missiles might well have been copies of the U.S. Stinger, America's premier short-range antiaircraft missile. Like the Russian SA-7, the Stinger has passive infrared homing guidance and can defeat antimissile defense things like flares and chaff. Intelligence officials report that the Germans were helping Iraq with a Stinger copy months before coalition forces began their push toward Baghdad.

The Stinger deal was by no means an isolated incident. In late 2002, in a last-ditch effort to avert a war with Iraq, the United Nations pressed Baghdad into making a declaration of its arms, and the dossier the Iraqis provided showed that German companies were key suppliers of Iraq's weapons equipment and technology. The leftist Berlin newspaper *Die Tageszeitung* obtained a portion of a UN arms report stating that more than *half* of the eighty companies that had supplied Iraq with weapons materials were German. Still, the newspaper listed only three German companies, indicating that German government officials intent on minimizing the political fallout had leaked the document. The German companies included in the report were automaker Daimler-Benz, which merged with the American company Chrysler in 1998; MAN Nutzfahrzeuge AG, a major manufacturer of space technology, satellite navigation equipment, and aircraft technology; and Siemens, a conglomerate specializing in electronics. Siemens continued to supply Saddam Hussein well into the 1990s. From December 1998 to June 1999, the company sold Iraq special medical interrupters designed to split kidney stones. But like many other technologies the Iraqis acquired, the interrupters were a dual-use technology: They could potentially be used as electrical fuses for nuclear bombs.

Like their French counterparts, German companies have taken advantage of lax export controls to sell weapons to rogue states like Iraq. They have also capitalized on government indifference. Even on the rare occasions when the German government has caught arms dealers, the proliferators have usually received no more than a slap on the wrist—a fine, in most cases. The message is clear: The German government does not view selling arms to states that support terrorism as a major crime.

THE STINGER DEAL

Among the most startling German deals was the effort to help Iraq develop a copy of the Stinger antiaircraft missile. The effort became public in early 2003, when a German businessman was caught selling missile goods to Iraq. Details remain closely held, but U.S. officials have said that the case was one of several indicators that Germany was a key location for Iraq's weapons-procurement efforts.

Two Germans, identified only as Klaus H. and Khidir R. in German court records, were the central figures in the Stinger deal. Klaus, sixty-three, was a businessman from Steinfurt, in western Germany, who ran a company called Military and Security Projects. In reality, he was an electronics specialist looking to make some money selling illegal-weapons goods to Iraq. He was typical of the shady arms merchants and exporters often found in Germany who would sell out their mothers to the likes of Saddam Hussein, Iran's ayatollahs, and North Korea's totalitarians. Khidir, meanwhile, was a native Iraqi who worked as a street vendor in Steinfurt.

Klaus's business was hurting. Looking for opportunities, he asked Khidir to arrange some contacts in his native Iraq. Khidir traveled to Baghdad in the spring of 2002 to take part in a conference for Iraqis living abroad. Iraq's intelligence services used the conference to recruit expatriate Iraqis, urging them to do everything possible to work for Iraq's interests. Khidir filled out a questionnaire in which he told the Iraqis about his friend the military electronics specialist who was looking for quick deals.

Six months later, Iraqi officials showed up in Steinfurt with invitations to the Baghdad International Exhibition in November 2002. The Iraqis also provided the Germans with two airline tickets from Frankfurt to Amman, Jordan.

At the fair, Klaus met three Iraqi generals involved in arms procurement. Not interested in Klaus's offer of night-vision equipment for helicopters, the Iraqis asked him to provide them with large numbers of missile parts. The Iraqis mailed the two Germans samples of parts they wanted reproduced by a manufacturer in Germany, including bearings and electronic components for missiles.

The scheme came unraveled only when Klaus called on a friend to help him clean out a virus from his computer. While working on the computer, the friend noticed drawings that appeared to be military or weapons technology. The friend told police about what he saw, and the investigation was launched that led to the arrests of Klaus and Khidir in January 2003. Investigators discovered that the two German men had made a list of fifteen to twenty militarily useful parts that were to be sold to the Iraqi military. The prosecutor in the case, Eckhard Baade, said, "We don't know what type of missile the components were intended for but the Stinger missile was mentioned." Indeed, the parts looked similar to the components used in the Stinger. At Klaus's firm investigators also found a diagram of a missile guidance system; Klaus claimed the diagram was for a street-sweeping machine. All told, it was quite clear that the missile parts were designed for control-and-stabilization systems. The case provided yet more evidence that the Iraqis were upgrading their missile program. A U.S. Defense Department official said that it was possible the Iraqis were building copies of the Stinger but that it was more likely they were seeking the Stinger know-how to upgrade the targeting mechanisms of their existing missles.

In fact, the trade fair that Klaus and Khidir attended made clear that Iraq was aggressively pursuing arms. Saddam's government gloated over its ability to entice foreign nations, and Germany in particular, to cut deals with Iraq. At the time of the fair, an article in the government-run newspaper *Iraq Daily* stated, "Iraqi-German relations have witnessed a notable improvement after the firm positive stand of Germany in rejecting the launching of a military attack against Iraq by the U.S. Accordingly, President Saddam Hussein has ordered to give priority to German companies to enter the Iraqi market." At the opening of the trade fair, Iraq's vice president, Taha Yassin Ramadan, made a point of tying the fair participants' political support to Iraq's defiant stand against the United States and Britain. Ramadan said, "The friendly countries will not permit the U.S. and Britain to get the U.N. consent to launch the war against Iraq."

Of course, Germany was not the only nation to have a presence at the Baghdad fair. More than 1,200 companies from forty-nine nations, including France, Russia, Turkey, China, Spain, Italy, Sweden, Denmark, Iran, and Saudi Arabia, took part in the trade fair. Iraq signed some $500 million in contracts with companies from Saudi Arabia, the United Arab Emirates, Iran, France, and Germany. (No American firms were present.) France alone had eighty-one companies represented in Baghdad. A representative of the French satellite telephone company E-Sat put it bluntly, telling one reporter, "We are not here for politics but for pure business."

THE SUPERGUN

According to U.S. officials, several other cases of illegal-arms-related exports from Germany were under way at the time of the Stinger deal. German authorities uncovered these cases, usually with the help of the CIA, and U.S. officials say that these are but a small sampling of the deals that were occurring.

In one case, two German businessmen were caught illegally shipping special drilling equipment to Iraq. Weapons specialists say that Saddam's military purchased the 33-foot-long drills to make tubes for long-range cannon as part of a program to build delivery systems for chemical and biological shells. In the 1980s, Canadian artillery specialist Gerald Bull had sold Saddam Hussein on the idea of a "supergun" that could launch missiles and projectiles hundreds of miles. The Iraqi company that was building the cannon, Al Fao, was reportedly trying to build a truck-mounted gun that could fire a 100-kilogram projectile some thirty-five miles—far enough, according to U.S. intelligence officials, that the Iraqis could fire chemical or biological warheads at advancing U.S. troops.

The main architect of the drill deal, fifty-nine-year-old engineer Bernd Schompeter, purchased the drills from two German companies and then shipped them to Jordan. From there, they were trucked into Iraq.

Schompeter was convicted, as was fifty-three-year-old Willi Heinz Ribbeck, who worked at the machine company that produced the drills. According to investigators, these men had also tried unsuccessfully to sell howitzer gun barrels to Iraq through a Swiss company in 1999 and had brokered deals through Ukraine to allow the Iraqis to purchase bulletproof vests and braking parachutes for MiG jets in 1997 and 1998.

THE NUCLEAR BUILDUP

The Germans' role in Iraq goes back decades. Germany even provided Iraq with materials and goods for nuclear weapons.

Although United Nations inspectors had discovered evidence of Iraq's clandestine nuclear program after the 1991 Persian Gulf War, the West did not know how far Saddam Hussein had gone to fulfill his nuclear ambitions until the director of Saddam's nuclear program, Khidhir Hamza, defected from Iraq in 1994. According to Hamza, Iraq purchased nuclear technology from abroad, claiming it was for peaceful research. As seen in the last chapter, France provided the nuclear reactor, but the Iraqis also sought help from places like Poland and Germany. "Everything we asked for was approved," Hamza said. "Actually, there was no discussion except for prices. There's no limitation on what one can get [from other countries]."

Hamza said he met representatives from the German chemical company Degussa AG at the Iraqi embassy in Bonn. The Iraqis were seeking a high-temperature foundry to forge uranium metal that could be used as the core of a nuclear weapon. The Iraqi representatives told the German company that the foundry would be used for working with tungsten, which only prompted laughter from the Germans. According to Hamza, the Germans clearly suspected that Iraqis wanted the foundry for a nuclear bomb program, but they did not object to that.

The Iraqis never purchased the foundry, but they used its technical specifications to build their own foundry. And the Germans came through in other ways, reported Hamza. The Iraqis relied on foreign expertise, and among those who provided help were German engineers who disclosed top-secret information on high-technology methods of acquiring highly enriched uranium.

Hamza faulted Western intelligence, including the CIA, for failing to pursue Iraq's nuclear bomb program. He believed the spy agencies looked closely at goods and technology but did almost nothing to locate, recruit, or gather information from the people involved in the program. "For example, we had 400 people in France and Italy training," Hamza said. "Nobody contacted them. Why nobody was interested? We had a main figure in the program defected to the U.S. in the '80s.

OK. Actually, we were worried for a while . . . that he might try to reveal something. Apparently neither he talked nor was he asked."

An even more important Iraqi defector who disclosed details of German support to Iraq was General Hussein Kamal, a brother-in-law of Saddam and director of Iraq's Military Industrialization Corporation, which ran the Iraqi weapons program. On the night of August 7, 1995, he and his brother, Colonel Saddam Kamal, fled by car across the Iraqi border into Jordan. Saddam coaxed the brothers back to Iraq in February 1996 and summarily shot them, but not before they had revealed new details of Iraq's secret program to develop a nuclear bomb. The defections had also forced Saddam's hand; the two defectors had brought with them documents that were turned over to the United Nations, prompting Baghdad to disclose new details of its secret program to develop nuclear bombs, biological weapons, and ballistic missiles.

The information that Hussein Kamal provided to UN arms inspectors proved vital. He revealed, for instance, that before the first Gulf War, the Iraqis had been manufacturing their own centrifuges, the high-speed spinning machines that are critical to producing nuclear weapons because they create highly enriched uranium as weapons fuel. Kamal said the Iraqis disguised the centrifuge program by placing it under the nominal control of the Iraqi agriculture ministry and by lying about where the centrifuges were being built.

The defector also identified who had been building the centrifuges: a German nuclear energy company known as Interatom GmbH, a subsidiary of Siemens. These were part of the Al Furat facility, where Saddam hoped to complete a "cascade" of one hundred centrifuges by 1993. (A "cascade" is a series of centrifuges that is designed to turn uranium hexafluoride gas into highly enriched uranium.) Although Kamal said that U.S. and allied bombing raids during the 1991 Gulf War had destroyed Iraq's nuclear program, he revealed that the centrifuge method continued. He did not think Iraq was carrying out nuclear arms work at the time of his 1994 defection, but he noted that "blueprints are still there on microfiches."

Another German company figured prominently in Iraq's centrifuge program. In 1989, the Iraqi procurement agency known as the Industrial Projects Company (IPC) took charge of Iraq's program to build gas centrifuges in Iraq and commissioned the German firm Strabag AG to help build steel and aluminum pipe and to provide technology, training, and machinery, including helium leak detectors and vacuum pumps. In 1990 Strabag sent a twenty-truck convoy of equipment to the central plant; six of the trucks were blocked because of a United Nations embargo imposed after the invasion of Kuwait. The company also concluded an agreement with IPC to train twenty-two Iraqi engineers in Germany with the help of the German companies Lurgi GmbH and Zertz und Scheid Ingenieurgesellschaft (ZSI). The specialists involved in the training were experts in uranium-enrichment plants. In late July 1990, just days before Iraqi forces crossed the border into Kuwait, German customs officials blocked the exporting of a specialized laboratory for the Iraqi centrifuge project.

Leybold, a subsidiary of German firm Degussa, also took part in the Iraqi nuclear program. From 1984 to 1989, the company built and delivered two electron beam welders to the Iraqi Atomic Energy Commission. The welders were used to make centrifuge rotors and thus were key to building nuclear weapons. The German company also trained Iraqi technicians. In 1989, Leybold sold the welders to Iraq's State Establishment for Heavy Engineering Equipment, which set up the Al Furat factory and produced magnets, vacuum chambers, ion sources, and collector components for calutrons—huge machines that the United States used to develop the first nuclear weapons. Leybold tried to disguise the transfers by using front companies in Switzerland and Liechtenstein, but German officials caught some of the deals.

OIL FOR ARMS

In the 1990s the United Nations instituted the "oil-for-food program," which greatly loosened exports to Iraq, ostensibly for humanitarian goods. But it hardly served its purpose. In fact, Army General Tommy Franks, the commander of the operation that ousted Saddam Hussein, called the oil-for-food program the "oil-for-palace program" because Saddam used the oil revenue to buy goods for his own personal aggrandizement and build numerous palaces throughout the country.

The program served another purpose as well: It provided a cover for Iraq to get what it needed for military and military-related projects. As the CIA observed in a January 2003 report to Congress, Iraq acquired "dual-use and production items that have applications in the [advanced conventional weapons] arena through the oil-for-food program." In some cases Iraq was foiled in its attempt to procure weapons-related material by pretending the goods were for commercial purposes. In fact, in June 2003 the United Nations released a list of goods that Iraq had been blocked from purchasing because they would have contributed to Iraq's military power. The list clearly indicated that German companies were major military suppliers for the Iraqis. According to the UN data, German companies had tried to supply Iraq with truck parts, liquid natural-gas pumps, machine tools, mobile air compressors, laboratory equipment, steel reinforcing bars, pharmaceuticals, a spectrophotometer, turbines, and other goods that could have enhanced Iraq's arms programs. All together, fifty-four German contracts with the Iraqis had been turned down.

But proliferation experts point out that many other German-Iraqi arms deal went through. Gary Milhollin, director of the Wisconsin Project on Nuclear Arms Control, has been tracking German and French weapons sales to Iraq for nearly twenty years. He reveals that most of Iraq's weapons goods came from those two allies. In March 2003, as U.S. forces began the military assault on Iraq, Milhollin said, "It is a sad if not outrageous fact that we must wage war once again to counter an arsenal that Western companies helped create."

Germany, in particular, was instrumental to Saddam's efforts to build up the Iraqi war machine. Milhollin found that fully half of Saddam's arms-related transfers came from Germany. Without this material, much of the other foreign-made equipment that the Iraqis obtained was of little use.

As Milhollin learned, a German firm was one of two major companies behind Iraq's poison gas efforts in the 1980s. The German company Karl Kolb, along with the French firm Protec, sold Saddam millions of dollars' worth of sensitive equipment; it went to six separate Iraqi plants that were used for making mustard gas and nerve agents. According to intelligence estimates, these plants could produce hundreds of tons of nerve agent per year.

"These companies had to know what the specialized glass-lined vessels they peddled were to be used for," Milhollin said. "It is insufferable that, like Pontius Pilate, Germany and France now wash their hands of the whole affair, and even chastise others for cleaning up the mess their companies helped create."

Germany also made a major contribution to Iraq's missile development, according to Milhollin. The German firm ThyssenKrupp sold Iraq thirty-five turbopumps to boost the capability of Iraqi rocket engines. German companies like Deutsche BP, Carl Zeiss, Degussa, and Tesa supplied specialists and training in wind tunnels and missile electronics. Siemens provided the switches and electrical systems that control the production of missile fuel.

Milhollin believes that the Iraq experience provides a lesson about future threats. "If Western powers sell the means to make horrific weapons, war is going to be the price we pay," he said. "Without a change in our export behavior, we will have to send our soldiers somewhere else to disarm another tyrant. Wouldn't it be cheaper—and more humane—not to create the problem in the first place?"

Addressing the endemic problem of weapons proliferation is, indeed, the first step in formulating an effective foreign policy. Until America and its allies—its *real* allies—address this problem, our enemies will only grow more powerful, and bolder.

SADDAM'S WEB

In August 2003, U.S. intelligence agencies set up what became known as the Iraq Survey Group. The aim was to search for Iraq's hidden stocks of nuclear, chemical, and biological weapons. Although the hundreds of intelligence analysts failed to turn up stockpiles of weapons of mass destruction, they did turn up valuable information on the networks Saddam Hussein used to procure arms.

The Survey Group talked to two key Iraqi scientists involved in the nuclear arms program who confirmed that in November 2002, when UN inspectors returned to Iraq after Saddam had barred them for four years, the Iraqis hid materials and documents relating to their nuclear weapons program.

The Iraqis also made use of the supergun that United Nations arms inspectors had dismantled in the mid-1990s, according to the Survey Group. Iraqi missile developers were taking portions of the barrel and using them to make missile motors. "They had reestablished a large-scale casting facility and were moving ahead for a 1,000-kilometer solid-fuel missile," said David Kay, the CIA's representative to the Survey Group. Kay's group discovered that sometime in 1999 and 2000, Iraq switched gears and began developing a whole new family of missiles. The group theorized that Saddam Hussein, deciding to wait until sanctions were lifted to restart his nuclear, chemical, and biological weapons programs, chose to focus on the delivery systems for the weapons. The United Nations, after all, had allowed Iraq to build short-range missiles; if Iraq could work on short-range missiles, making their range longer was only slightly more challenging technically.

The Survey Group also uncovered thousands of documents that exposed the tentacle-like web of Iraqi procurement connections. "This is an ongoing operation," said Kay. "It is important not only in Iraq. It's important because of the fear that these same countries, companies, and individuals are likely to have been involved with proliferant activities and other states, so it's an ongoing operation that would put people's lives in jeopardy if I told you much more." Kay revealed that the Iraqis had received a lot of foreign assistance for their missile programs. "We have a series of companies, not North Korea, that were involved in dual-use and other precursor sales of chemicals to the Iraqis after 1998, and that also is a subject of continuing investigation to see exactly what it means," he said. He added that some European companies were involved in the missile program in Iraq, but he declined to name them.

Kay offered a different picture several months after his first interim report. In a move that surprised the CIA, he announced that with 85 percent of the Iraq Survey Group's work finished, he believed that Iraq did not have large stockpiles of chemical and biological weapons, as U.S. intelligence agencies had asserted before the war. He criticized U.S. intelligence analysts for failing to properly assess Saddam's weapons of mass destruction. CIA Director George Tenet countered in a speech that the agency's analysts did the best they could and that arms inspectors were not done searching. "We are nowhere near the end of our work in Iraq; we need more time," he said in a speech at Georgetown University in February, a few months before he resigned. The new Iraq

Survey Group chief, Charles Duelfer, believes Iraq once had weapons of mass destruction and he will try to find out what happened to them.

TERRORISTS AND DICTATORS

The evidence is so voluminous as to be undeniable: German companies were arming Saddam Hussein's regime even after the United Nations imposed sanctions against Iraq and right up to the time U.S. and coalition forces launched their assault on Iraq in 2003. But why would these companies be so willing to send arms and related equipment to Iraq?

The answer is that they took the lead from their government.

Under Chancellor Gerhard Schroeder, the left-center German government continually displayed its indifference to the Iraqi threat and also its aversion to the United States. In fact, in September 2002, as the world community fiercely debated how to deal with Saddam Hussein, Schroeder's government rode a wave of anti-American sentiment to reelection, and that set the stage for a major political rift between the United States and its longtime ally. The split was not serious enough for the United States to pull out the tens of thousands of troops stationed in Germany, but the differences were nevertheless sharp, the rhetoric harsh. At one point in the reelection campaign, Schroeder lashed out at the United States and said, "Under my leadership, this country will not be available for adventures."

"Germany did not hesitate to offer solidarity in the fight against international terrorism," Schroeder said. "I say: yes to pressure on Saddam Hussein. . . . But I can only warn against playing games with war and military intervention."

Germany's defense minister, Peter Struck, challenged the United States on Iraq's support for terrorism and its hidden arms program. "Iraq is no threat to us," he said.

Germany's anti-Americanism stemmed from the left-wing radicals who had moved gradually into positions of power in Schroeder's government. Although Schroeder was the leader of the German government, he was not the most virulent of Germany's anti-American leaders. Just a week before the 2002 election, Schroeder's justice minister, the Social Democrat Herta Däubler-Gmelin, criticized U.S. war preparations, telling the regional newspaper *Schwäbisches Tagblatt,*

"Bush wants to divert attention from his domestic problems. It's a classic tactic. It's one that Hitler also used." Later, when questioned about the statement, Däubler-Gmelin only made things worse, saying, "I didn't compare the persons Bush and Hitler, but their methods."

White House spokesman Ari Fleischer condemned the statement by saying it was "outrageous, and it is inexplicable." He noted that President Bush "continues to view this as a troubling event."

Schroeder tried to make up for the Hitler remarks with a letter to Bush. The chancellor stated in the letter that Däubler-Gmelin "has assured me that she never made the remarks attributed to her. She has said this publicly as well. I would like to assure you that no one has a place at my Cabinet table who makes a connection between the American president and a criminal."

But the White House was not buying the German spin. "It really didn't read like an apology," Fleischer said. "It read more as an attempt at an explanation."

Still, Schroeder did not fire Däubler-Gmelin. Only after he had won the election did he allow her to resign.

Richard Perle, a Pentagon adviser, believed Schroeder himself should have resigned because of the damage caused to ties between the United States and Germany. "Never in my life have I seen relations with a close ally damaged so fast and so deeply as during Chancellor Schroeder's election campaign," he said.

As troubling as those developments were, however, they did not indicate just how radical some of Germany's leaders were. The most vigorous opposition to U.S. efforts to stop Saddam Hussein emanated from Germany's leftist foreign minister, Joschka Fischer. Fischer, of the left-wing Green Party, claimed that a U.S.-led ouster of Saddam would disrupt the Middle East. "It would lead to a new order in the Middle East," Fischer said, "and there is a big question mark as to whether this consequence has been thought through and discussed in the United States. . . . That is why we have made our position clear, that we reject mistaken steps and will not take part in them." Fischer used the opposition to U.S. military action in Iraq to boost the standing of the Green Party, which won 8.5 percent of the vote in September 2002, the party's largest showing ever.

Though a member of the pro-environmental Green Party, Fischer was by no means a pacifist environmentalist. He was a hard-core Marxist-Leninist who took to the streets in the 1960s and 1970s, as a series of photos published in 2001 revealed. The photographs, taken during an April 1973 demonstration in Frankfurt, showed Fischer among a group of toughs kicking an unarmed police officer who had fallen down during a street battle. The photos demonstrated that Fischer started the fight with the police officer. Wearing a crash helmet for protection, he punched the officer, then, after the policeman had fallen to the ground, Fischer joined other leftists in kicking him. The publication of the photographs forced Fischer to apologize publicly for his past activities as a left-wing militant.

Critics of the foreign minister say he also was involved in firebombing a police car in 1976 and nearly causing a policeman to burn to death. Fischer denied involvement in that attack.

But it is Fischer's friendship with another German radical that exposes his true past. Fischer testified at the trial of Hans-Joachim Klein, who had been charged with three counts of murder and three counts of attempted murder for his role in a terrorist attack in Vienna in 1975. Klein had been on the run for more than twenty years before his capture in 2000, but Fischer nevertheless agreed to testify on his behalf. It's little wonder, then, that prosecutors described Klein as Fischer's old friend. The description also seemed appropriate because Klein was with Fischer when he was photographed stomping the police officer in Frankfurt.

The 1975 terrorist attack in which Klein was involved, which targeted a meeting of ministers for the Organization of Petroleum Exporting Countries (OPEC), was organized and led by Ilich Ramírez Sánchez, better known as Carlos the Jackal. And that was not the only terrorist attack Klein was linked to. In that second attack, Klein used Fischer's car to ferry the weapons used in the attack, although Fischer said he knew nothing about it. Klein was convicted of murder in 2001 and sentenced to nine years in prison. He was pardoned after serving two years.

When asked why he would testify on behalf of an alleged terrorist, Fischer said, "I do not regard it as awkward. Without my biography, I would be a different person today and I would not like that at all." Fischer also made clear that he was no pacifist. Violence, he said, should not be ruled out as an option. "I have never been a pacifist and will never become one, because I never exclude the reason to fight for your freedom and for your life."

Fischer might have been even more closely linked to Klein's terrorist activities than he let on. Former high-ranking Romanian intelligence officer Ion Mihai Pacepa, who now lives in the United States, revealed that in preparation for the 1975 terrorist attack on OPEC, Libyan dictator Moammar Qadhafi asked Romanian leader Nicolae Ceausescu for the blueprints to OPEC's Vienna headquarters, which Ceausescu directed his intelligence services to supply. Carlos the Jackal, who carried out the attack, was arrested by the French in 1997, and he disclosed to France's DST counterintelligence service that his deputy for the OPEC attack was Hans-Joachim Klein, who operated under the code name "Angie." Carlos also told the French that the weapons used in the OPEC attack in Vienna were stored in the Frankfurt apartment used by Klein and two others: Daniel Cohn-Bendit, who would become a member of the European Parliament, and Joschka Fischer.

Fischer vehemently denied being linked to the arms in the Frankfurt apartment or to Communist-backed revolutionary cells in West Germany. But Pacepa questioned those denials. He pointed out that Qadhafi had sent Ceausescu a thank-you message in January 1976 in which the Libyan leader said that the operation could not have been carried out without the help of the Romanian DIE intelligence service and the "West German revolutionary group in Frankfurt/Main." Pacepa said that Fischer was a product of the old anti-American intelligence community of which the Romanian himself was a part. The violent demonstrations that Fischer took part in in the 1970s were "not spontaneous demonstrations," Pacepa said. "They were all financed by the Soviet bloc foreign-intelligence community, including my own DIE [intelligence service] when I was at its helm."

Pacepa went on: "It may never be possible to prove beyond the shadow of a doubt Joschka Fischer's connection with the Soviet KGB, but I do know that the KGB—and my DIE—was financing West Germany's anti-American terrorist movements in the 1970s, while I was still in Romania. Fischer's evidently ingrained anti-Americanism is now spreading throughout the German government, and beyond. This is a monumental display of ingratitude to the 405,399 American soldiers who gave their lives to defeat Berlin's old Axis, as well as to the millions of American taxpayers who spent trillions of dollars to rebuild Germany's war-torn economy and to protect West Germany from falling into Communist clutches."

The German government's strident anti-American rhetoric, and its repeated efforts to block U.S. attempts to bring Saddam Hussein to justice, showed that Pacepa was right about Joschka Fischer's "ingrained anti-Americanism" spreading through Germany's leadership. That anti-American attitude, combined with lax attitudes toward Saddam's Iraq, left German companies free to violate United Nations sanctions and arm a brutal dictator. For unscrupulous arms dealers, it didn't matter that Germany had been part of the coalition that went to war against Iraq in 1991, or that they were making a tyrant even more dangerous.

No, the Germans showed no concern for the consequences of their illicit-arms deals. And their illegal-weapons proliferation was not confined to Saddam Hussein's Iraq. German companies were willing to trade with anyone who could pay the right price. More evidence of this emerged in February 2004, when German investigators found that a company in Marburg, Germany, had been involved in shipping nuclear weapons–related equipment to Pakistan, which is itself one of the worst weapons proliferators, as we will see in more detail later in the book. The German company sent alpha-gamma spectrometric systems to Pakistan in late 2002 as part of the covert nuclear supplier network headed by Pakistani scientist Abdul Qadeer Khan. The Khan network unraveled after a shipment of nuclear weapons goods was uncovered in Libya. The components were supposed to be shipped to a medical facility, but in reality the recipient was a front for Pakistan's nuclear arms program. German prosecutor Hans-Joachim Woelk told reporters that equipment was used illegally in Pakistan's nuclear arms program.

Another state that, like Germany, has a totalitarian past is Russia, one of the most aggressive nations involved in arming America's foes.

RUSSIA: SLEEPING WITH THE ENEMY

CHAPTER 3

THE U.S. GENERALS HAD BEEN MUZZLED. POLITICALLY correct government officials, not wanting to offend, had made sure that American spokesmen scrupulously avoided mentioning the uncomfortable truth: that one of our so-called friends was helping the enemy.

But as much as certain U.S. officials wanted to ignore the truth, they could not get around the fact that Russia had supplied the Iraqi military with systems meant to defeat one of America's marquee weapons systems—a bomb guided to its target by satellite navigation.

It was late March 2003, and the war to oust Saddam Hussein's regime had been under way for just a few days. To defend themselves against the U.S. military's highly advanced precision-guided bombs, the Iraqis had purchased six electronic jammers from the Russian company AviaConversia. Saddam's military had spread the small boxes in a circle around Baghdad, believing that the jammers—which emit electronic noise to disrupt navigation signals sent from Global Positioning System (GPS) satellites, the heart of several of the U.S. military's key advanced weapons—could prevent U.S. bombs from hitting their targets.

The jamming didn't work, because the Pentagon had learned, from several years of testing, that it could negate the jammers by altering the GPS signals. Still, U.S. electronic-warfare aircraft had trouble locating the jammers, which put out only between four and eight watts of power, making them difficult to detect. In the early days of the war, the U.S. Air Force had to conduct multiple bombing raids to find and eliminate the Iraqis' GPS jammers.

A day after the final raid, Air Force Major General Gene Renuart said he was "happy to report that we have destroyed all six of those jammers." But as part of the U.S. government's effort to pretend that the Russians were not aiding the enemy, General Renuart did not specify who had supplied Iraq with the GPS jamming system, saying only that "they have procured [the jammers] from another nation." At the Pentagon, Army Major General Stanley McChrystal took the same approach when asked about the GPS jammers. He noted that the Iraqis had deployed jammers but did not address the question of where Saddam had gotten the system.

Privately, however, the U.S. government called Moscow on its aid to the enemy. A day before the bombing raid that knocked out the last Russian-made GPS jammer in Iraq, a U.S. embassy official in Moscow delivered a formal protest note, or démarche, to the Russian Foreign Ministry. The note criticized Russian companies and military technicians for selling key military equipment to Iraq in violation of United Nations sanctions, and it urged the Russians to halt all assistance to Iraq immediately. The note carried an implicit warning to Moscow that any Russian personnel helping the Iraqis with jamming gear would probably be blown up in the U.S. air strikes. Nevertheless, the note was typical of what former Pentagon official Richard Perle calls a "démarche-mellow"—a protest note that has virtually no impact.

On March 24, the day after the last GPS jammer had been bombed, President George W. Bush showed that the United States was serious. He called the Russian president, former KGB spy Vladimir Putin, to express his anger that Moscow had done nothing to stop Russian companies from helping an enemy that was now at war with the United States and many other allies. According to White House officials familiar with the phone call, Bush let fly a verbal fusil-lade at Putin. The Russian leader politely said he would look into the problem.

That afternoon, White House spokesman Ari Fleischer took the Bush administration's complaint public. He also indicated that the Russians' assistance to Iraq went far beyond a onetime sale of military equipment. "We are very concerned that there are reports of ongoing cooperation and support to Iraqi military forces being provided by a Russian company that produces GPS-jamming equipment," Fleischer said, noting that such trade violated United Nations sanctions against Iraq. "This is what was discussed in the phone call. There are other causes of concern, as well, involving night-vision goggles and antitank guided missiles." According to Fleischer, "Senior U.S. government officials have repeatedly raised these concerns with their Russian counterparts over the past year." The goal, he said, was to get the Russians to "move aggressively to cut the cooperation."

Unfortunately, the Russians did not halt their cooperation with the Iraqis. As happens so often with weapons proliferators, Moscow simply denied the charges. But as reams of intelligence reports make evident, Russia's denials were disingenuous. In January 2004, U.S. officials disclosed that they had found the illegally exported night-vision goggles and jamming equipment in Iraq. This intelligence confirmed that Russian companies had sold Saddam Hussein military equipment that threatened U.S. forces during Operation Iraqi Freedom.

Russia never provided honest explanations for its arming of America's enemy. The Russians had supplied Saddam with all kinds of military equipment and technical support, and had shared intelligence with Iraq. Worse still, Saddam's Iraq, though a favorite client, is just one of several dangerous regimes the Russians have armed. Russia remains one of the world's most dangerous sellers of weapons, weapons technology, and dual-use equipment.

CLOSE TIES WITH A DICTATOR

Long before the Russian-Iraqi GPS jammer deal came to light, President Bush had argued that United Nations sanctions did little to prevent Iraq from getting military equipment and weapons. In February 2001, Bush noted, "Our sanctions are like Swiss cheese; that means they are not very effective." By 2003 the problem had gotten to the point that Russian military equipment was directly threatening U.S. troops.

John Bolton, the Bush administration's undersecretary of state for arms control and international security, highlighted this problem when he said, "The critical point here is that some of this equipment can be used against American forces." He added, "That's why we've been especially concerned about it, really going back months and months now." Bolton, who had taken part in numerous meetings with the Russians when their record of selling dangerous arms and equipment was discussed, said that Russia had always flatly denied the charges. When confronted with the intelligence about the GPS jammer transfers, the Russians claimed the company AviaConversia did not even exist. After the U.S. government identified it to the Russians, someone apparently tipped the company off and it quietly went out of business—or, it is more likely, began business under a different name.

But the Russians actively helped Iraq right up to and even after the outbreak of war, according to U.S. officials. The arms deals have put American soldiers at risk. A report prepared for the office of the Defense Department revealed that Russia had violated United Nations sanctions on Iraq by selling Saddam Kornet-E antitank guided weapons. The report said that in March 2003, Kornet missiles, first developed in 1994, were fired at two U.S. Army M1A1 tanks near Najaf, disabling them. The report also stated that Syria purchased five hundred to a thousand Kornets from Ukraine "on behalf of Iraq"; the transfers took place in early 2003, the report said. The Ukrainians had bought the missiles from Russian manufacturers. The report concluded, "Possession of the Kornet-E violates U.N. Security Council Resolution 687," which barred arms sales to Iraq.

John Shaw, the deputy undersecretary of defense for international technology security, said that the Russians had been "working overtime" in early 2003 to help Iraq's military with both weapons deliveries and technical expertise, specifically on Iraqi air defenses. The Russian help continued during the early stages of the war, he said: "One source of irritation was that we would take out some of their [air-defense] equipment and they had it up and running the next day because there were some of their own people there." After President Bush addressed the matter with Vladimir Putin, "it stopped," Shaw said.

Russia's last mission in Iraq before U.S. forces entered the country was to provide Saddam's forces with "the highest level of capability they could get," according to Shaw. Russia viewed Iraq as a major arms market and some of the weapons manufacturers were operating semi-autonomously. "There was no adult supervision in a political sense," Shaw remarked. The Russian military also needed the hard currency that arms sales to Iraq could bring. As Shaw said, "The Russian armed services needed to support some of their activities."

"It seemed that the provision of whatever important weapons system the Iraqis needed was made available," Shaw revealed. "You had everybody getting into the game." In addition to Russia, France was eager to supply the Iraqi military with arms and equipment, and China got involved as well. "If the price got too high," Shaw said, "the Chinese would say [to the Iraqis], 'Oh, you don't need to go with Pierre on this. We can provide it for you for X percent less.'" Saddam was probably directing the arms trades himself, according to Shaw, "not for efficiency, but to ensure that cash flows that went out to the individuals were not known to anybody else."

It was not simply a matter of hardware either. Russia had worked diplomatically on behalf of Saddam's Iraq and had supplied critical intelligence to the regime. Documents uncovered by reporter David Harrison of the London *Sunday Telegraph* in April 2003 revealed an extensive conspiracy between Russian intelligence and Iraq's spy agencies. The documents were recovered from the ruins of the Iraqi intelligence service's Baghdad headquarters. They showed that in the months before the war began, officials from the Russian Federal Security Service had informed Saddam that the U.S. government hoped the Iraqis would block United Nations weapons inspectors so it could justify going to war in Iraq. In one report, dated November 13, 2002, the Russians told the Iraqis that the United States under President Bush had launched a two-month "propaganda" offensive "to secure a United States military operation against Iraq." The Russians told the Iraqis, "In Washington, they think that during this period they will manage to provoke a conflict between the UN inspectors and Iraqi authorities and render the [UN inspectors'] work 'impossible'; accuse Iraq of breaking agreements, and open the way to a military operation against Baghdad."

Attached to the Russian report was this note from an Iraqi intelligence officer: "We will pass this to M4 [chief of the Iraqi intelligence service] and take it to the President."

Other documents that the *Telegraph* exposed showed how Russia and Iraq had signed agreements to share intelligence and to help each other acquire visas for intelligence agents. Moscow was willing to share all kinds of information with Saddam Hussein, including a list of assassins and details of Osama bin Laden's plans to fund terrorist training camps to support operations in the Russian enclave of Chechnya. The documents also revealed Russia's arms deals with Middle East nations. For example, one report, dated January 27, 2000, said that in 1999 Russia had sold Syria rockets for $138 million. Other Middle Eastern clients for Russian arms included Egypt and Kuwait.

The ties between the spy agencies were so strong that the head of the Iraqi spy service exchanged Christmas cards with his counterpart in Russia; copies of the cards were found among the documents recovered from Iraq's spy headquarters.

U.S. intelligence officials confirmed the Russia-Iraq intelligence sharing, saying that they had learned of the arrangement from other means, such as electronic intercepts, before the discovery of the documents in Baghdad.

The cooperation between Russia and Iraq continued up to the end of the Saddam Hussein regime. "There were literally hundreds of Russian specialists that were going through there trying to shred all evidence [of their involvement] in the days before the war started," said John Shaw. "It's sort of like the days of the Third Reich. When you have a totalitarian government, everything has to be done in multiple copies. But there is never enough shredding capability to get them all. At least that's my hope."

"ON THE TAKE"

U.S. officials familiar with reports of the Russia-Iraq intelligence ties said that the connections were left over from the Soviet period, when Yevgeni Primakov was the Kremlin's top Middle East specialist and later head of the KGB. Primakov harbors hard-line anti-American views, and in a Russian government dominated by former KGB intelligence officers as well as current intelligence officials, his power continues to grow. Primakov backed Iraq in the early 1990s and unsuccessfully attempted to avert the 1991 Persian Gulf War through last-ditch negotiations in the Middle East. Russian intelligence remained opposed to the use of force in Iraq in 2002 and 2003. Sergei Lebedev, the head of Russia's foreign intelligence service, SVR, told reporters in Moscow in December 2002 that any use of military force against Baghdad "could significantly complicate the situation in the region and in the world." Lebedev said that Moscow wanted to use "political and diplomatic methods" to prevent "a military catastrophe."

Many senior U.S. policymakers viewed Primakov with distrust—and for good reason. He rose within the Soviet system as a hard-line Communist who favored close relations with radical Middle East governments that directly supported international terrorism. A personal friend of Saddam since 1969, when he was a Baghdad correspondent for the Communist Party newspaper *Pravda,* Primakov had strengthened his ties to Iraq during his tenure as head of the KGB.

A highly classified U.S. intelligence report disclosed that in November 1997, Primakov, as Russia's foreign minister, arranged for his deputy to secretly inform the Iraqis that the United States would not launch air strikes if Saddam Hussein opened up sites to United Nations weapons inspectors. The top-secret report indicated that Russian deputy foreign minister Viktor Posuvalyuk made the secret offer to Iraqi foreign minister Tariq Aziz, using information that Primakov himself had learned from a U.S. official. The intelligence report did not identify that U.S. official, but some American officials suspected that it was Deputy Secretary of State Strobe Talbott, who was the Clinton administration's point man on Russian affairs. White House officials denied that the Clinton administration had used the Russians to send a message to the Iraqis, however. White House press secretary Michael McCurry suggested that the Russians had engaged in diplomatic "freelancing" with Baghdad. "We cannot account for what the Russians may have told Iraq," McCurry told me.

Whatever the Clinton administration's intention, Baghdad interpreted the Russian overture to Iraq as an official U.S. appeal and a way out of a crisis that only days earlier had appeared headed toward an inevitable military exchange, according to the top-secret report. A day after the Russians made the appeal, Iraq announced that it would permit UN inspections on a conditional basis. The United States put off air strikes against Iraq. But a year later, when Iraq refused to allow U.S.

members of the United Nations weapons inspection team to take part in efforts to destroy all nuclear, chemical, and biological weapons facilities, as required by UN resolutions, Russia could not protect the Iraqis. The United States launched strikes in December 1998.

In 1999, Primakov blocked UN efforts to search Iraq's presidential palaces, where intelligence officials believed that Saddam had hidden weapons. Richard Butler, the head of UN weapons inspections, later recounted how Primakov said "that these presidential sites were deeply important to the dignity of the regime and thus should be kept out of UNSCOM's [U.N. Special Commission] reach." In his book *The Greatest Threat,* Butler described his reaction: "I could not believe it. This was, of course, in violation of the very resolution that Russia had helped the Security Council adopt." Primakov was so solicitous of the Iraqis, according to Butler, that he argued for lifting the sanctions against Iraq so that the Iraqis could sell oil for profit. "Why should Russia care about Iraq's economic fortunes? Primakov volunteered the answer: Iraq owed Moscow some $7 billion (for Russian tanks, helicopters, and other weapons dating back to the Iran-Iraq War), and Russia wanted the money." Butler went further and stated that intelligence reports "from an outstanding source" revealed that "the Russian foreign minister had been getting personal payments from Iraq."

"For God's sake, I thought, here we are trying to disarm a rogue regime, and a person who should be a prime mover in this grand enterprise was on the take," Butler wrote. "Since then, Russian officials have publicly denied these reports. But in intelligence circles, the reports' credibility has deepened over time." The reports showed that Primakov had received some $800,000 in payoffs from Saddam.

And when war loomed in Iraq, Primakov made sure the Russians got to Baghdad. According to U.S. officials, in February 2003, just weeks before Operation Iraqi Freedom began, Moscow dispatched two senior Russian military representatives to Baghdad to meet with the head of Iraqi intelligence. They wanted Iraq to protect sensitive intelligence files, some of which eventually ended up in newspapers (including the *Sunday Telegraph*) and in the hands of U.S. intelligence officials. Primakov himself arrived in Baghdad on February 22 to negotiate with the Iraqis for the files and for Saddam and his two sons, Uday and

Qusay, to flee the country. Moscow claimed that Primakov was in Iraq to explain the Russian government position that Iraq should cooperate with United Nations inspections. But it was widely reported in the news media that he was there to cover up the support Russia had given to Saddam's brutal dictatorship.

Indeed, according to at least one knowledgeable source, Primakov and the two Russian generals were in Baghdad to help the Iraqis hide their weapons from the soon-to-be-advancing U.S. military forces. Ion Mihai Pacepa, the former head of the Romanian foreign intelligence service who defected to the United States, said, as "someone who used to take orders from the Soviet KGB," he knew that Russia was behind Baghdad's efforts to hide weapons in post-Saddam Iraq. In the late 1990s, Primakov had made sure that the Russians sent Iraq plenty of goods—many with military applications—through the UN's oil-for-food program. In fact, Primakov's close friend Grigori Rapota was in charge of the state-owned arms-exporting company Rosvooruzheniye. But according to Pacepa, the Soviet bloc had been arming Saddam Hussein for years before that.

And the Soviets were adept at hiding weapons, the Romanian reported: "The Soviet Union and all its bloc states always had a standard operating procedure for deep-sixing weapons of mass destruction—in Romanian it was code-named Sarindar, meaning emergency exit." Pacepa knew from experience, for he had been in charge of hiding all traces of chemical weapons in Libya if Western nations ever came close to them. The chemical arms would be burned or buried at sea, he said, but technical documentation would always be preserved on microfiche or buried in waterproof containers for future reconstruction. Thus he was convinced that the Russians not only sold the Iraqis weapons of mass destruction but also "showed them how to make them disappear."

Like Primakov, the two supposedly retired generals who were in Baghdad in February 2003 represented the dark Soviet past. They had been involved in the 1993 coup attempt against Boris Yeltsin. Each had significant military experience, one in special forces and the other in air defenses. If they weren't there to help with hiding weapons, as Pacepa believed, a logical conclusion would be that at the very least they were helping Iraq prepare their defenses against U.S. troops. Certainly the

Iraqis showed their appreciation for the Russians' help: The Iraqi defense minister presented the Russian generals with medals, as photographs posted on a Russian Internet site revealed. When asked why he was in Baghdad getting the award, one general, Vladislav Achalov, refused to answer directly but noted, "If they're awarding you a decoration, it must be for something."

David Kay, the former head of the Iraq Survey Group, the intelligence team that searched for Iraq's hidden arms, told me he was familiar with Pacepa's theory. The Iraqis "certainly destroyed things and it looks systematic, and it looks thought-out in advance and continues," he said. "But I can't tie it directly to [Pacepa's] report."

This would not have been the first time Russia helped Iraq hide its weapons program from inspectors. When Hussein Kamal defected from Iraq in 1995, he pointed UN inspectors to more than a hundred metal trunks of documentation on the weapons program that he had overseen. Moreover, Kamal's tips led to the discovery of Russian-made missile-guidance components that had been hidden in containers submerged in the Tigris River.

On January 28, 2004, Kay, who days before had stepped down as head of the Iraq Survey Group, spoke of the difficulty of determining what weapons a rogue regime like Iraq might have. "Certainly proliferation is a hard thing to track," he told a Senate committee, "particularly in countries that deny easy and free access and don't have free and open societies." And after Saddam expelled all inspectors in 1998, he had ample time to hide everything he could. Earlier Kay had acknowledged that he and his inspectors were considering the possibility that Saddam had hidden weapons, saying, "It's one of five to six . . . major hypotheses." Another theory, for example, was that prior to the war, the Iraqis had moved weapons and weapons material to countries like Syria.

ALMIGHTY OIL

Yevgeni Primakov's eleventh-hour trip to Baghdad was just one sign that Russia was cooperating with Saddam Hussein's regime right up until the very end.

Moscow attempted to block the United States at every turn as the Americans tried to put pressure on Saddam. In late 2002 and early

2003, Russia's government blocked new resolutions aimed at pressuring Saddam to go along with UN inspections. Vladimir Putin expressed Russia's anti-U.S. sentiments when he said, "We oppose the drawing up of black lists"—a reference to the president's identifying Iraq, Iran, and North Korea as part of the "Axis of Evil." But Moscow's leaders must have been aware that U.S. military action would expose the hidden hand of the Kremlin in supporting and arming Iraq.

The Russians had good reason to stand by Saddam against the United States. As noted in Chapter 1, classified intelligence reports based on sensitive information revealed that Russia, along with France, secretly attempted to conclude lucrative oil deals with the Iraqi government in the days before U.S. military operations began. "They believed they could get the contracts and then hope they would be honored later," one official told me. The Russian oil deal (with the French company working behind the scenes) was to be done through the UN oil-for-food program. But U.S. intelligence agencies picked up on the arrangement and reported it to senior Bush administration officials just a week before the launch of Operation Iraqi Freedom.

Russian oil contracts were a key element in Moscow's pro-Saddam policies. U.S. officials identified the Russian firms involved in the last-minute negotiations with Iraq as Zarubezhneft and Lukoil. Zarubezhneft (in Russian, "Outside the Frontiers Oil") was set up as a special government entity by the Russian Foreign Economic Affairs Ministry to conduct foreign oil development. It is considered the top overseas oil company in Russia. Lukoil, meanwhile, is Russia's largest private oil company and is the most active Russian company abroad. Saddam had granted the companies contracts for Iraq's two largest fields, West Qurna and Bin Umar. Lukoil's stake in the West Qurna field was worth a whopping $20 billion. It is little wonder, then, that the Russians would want to shore up those arrangements on the eve of war. Lukoil officials had been more confident the previous September, bragging publicly that the Russian government had assured the company that its stake in Iraq would not be lost if Saddam was ousted.

Ultimately, however, the Russian oil firms would lose out. After the fall of Saddam's government, the Bush administration denied Russia, France, Germany, China, and others who had opposed the U.S. liberation of Iraq access to some $18 billion in oil-related contracts.

It seems the Russians took advantage of almost every opportunity to do business with Saddam. In January 2004, a new Baghdad newspaper, *Al Mada,* published a list of hundreds of foreign companies reportedly involved in an illegal kickback scheme that funneled money into Saddam's coffers from the United Nations' oil-for-food program. The list, which the paper had obtained from a division of the Iraqi Oil Ministry, included forty-six Russian companies and individuals. According to the list, Russians did quite well on the deals, as Iraq apparently gave them vouchers to purchase some 1.36 billion barrels of oil, which would have been worth millions of dollars. (If a voucher authorized the purchase of a million barrels of Iraqi oil, the voucher could bring in about $200,000 after it was sold to oil traders.) The Russian-Iraqi contacts appear so extensive that it is possible that the Russian government itself was involved in the deals. Indeed, one item on the list stands out: "Chief of the Russian presidential office: 5 million [barrels of oil]."

A LONG TRAIN OF ABUSES

The record of Russian proliferation—to Iraq and other dangerous countries—is long. Classified intelligence reports show that for more than a decade Moscow used its arms sales to rogue states as a strategic hammer against the United States.

In late 1990, U.S. intelligence agencies reported that more than three hundred Iraqi military officers had been sent to the Soviet Union for training. At the same time, according to one intelligence report, a thousand Soviet military advisers were in Iraq, and an additional six thousand Soviets from the defense industry were there helping with Iraq's weapons systems.

On January 16, 1991, the CIA's top-secret *National Intelligence Daily* reported that the Soviet Union had sold several hundred shoulder-fired SA-16 surface-to-air antiaircraft missiles to Iraq. The shipment was photographed as it was loaded on a ship in northern Russia. For many months after the fall of Baghdad, Iraqi insurgents were using SA-16 missiles to shoot down U.S. helicopters and cargo aircraft.

The same *National Intelligence Daily* noted that some two hundred Soviet military advisers remained in Iraq, despite the UN's ban on foreign military support to Baghdad.

The CIA also reported that the Soviet Union was secretly importing thousands of barrels of Iraqi oil. More Iraqi oil was going to Cuba through a covert network, as intelligence agencies learned in December 1990. An Iraqi oil tanker passed through the channel between Mexico's Yucatán peninsula and Cuba and then stopped at port in Mexico. U.S. intelligence observed as the Iraqi ship pumped oil onto smaller boats, which then sailed for Cuba. The Iraqi ship stayed in the port for about a month. In all about four oil shipments went to Cuba during that time.

President George H. W. Bush in January 1991 wrote a letter to Soviet leader Mikhail Gorbachev urging the Kremlin to curtail its intelligence cooperation with Iraq. But, as has been seen, Moscow's intelligence ties to Baghdad only grew stronger over the years.

An intelligence report from that same month revealed that U.S. satellite photographs had identified terrorist training camps in Iraq, where the terrorists had begun "new activities." Among those in the Iraqi camps were the Palestinian terrorist group 15 May Organization and the notorious terrorist Abu Nidal. Meanwhile, Carlos the Jackal reportedly was in Baghdad and had his group at another Iraqi camp. The collapse of Communism in Eastern Europe had driven Carlos out of Romania, and the report showed that Baghdad had picked up Carlos's operation—no doubt at the behest of Moscow. (Significantly, this report reveals that Saddam's support for terrorists was long-standing.)

On January 22, 1991, six days after the start of the Persian Gulf War, a classified U.S. intelligence report revealed that the Soviet Union was covertly resupplying Saddam's army. The evidence included satellite intelligence photographs showing a convoy of some four hundred trucks carrying military and other goods from the Soviet Union, through Iran, and into Iraq. "They were loaded with ammunition and military equipment," said one intelligence official who saw the photographs. Intelligence intercepts at the time also indicated that the Soviets were offering to send Iraq thirty MiG-29 jet fighter-bombers, which were among Moscow's best warplanes. The official Soviet airline Aeroflot continued regular flights into Baghdad despite the war.

On January 28, 1991, the *National Intelligence Daily* showed that Soviet intelligence had informed Iraq's government of the times that U.S. reconnaissance satellites passed over Iraq. The information would be useful in conducting military movements without being detected by spy satellites. The next month, U.S. intelligence agencies reported that Russian voices were being heard on Iraq military communications channels, another sign that Moscow was covertly helping Saddam's forces.

On June 9, 1991, the *National Intelligence Daily* reported that U.S. military forces had captured Iraqi short-range missiles and determined that the missiles had parts or components that had originated from Russia, China, and North Korea.

In November 1991, a classified CIA report revealed that nuclear weapons technicians were attempting to smuggle plutonium out of Russia.

On December 2, 1991, just before the collapse of the Soviet Union, the CIA reported that Soviet officials were helping North Korea with nuclear weapons–related technology. U.S. officials who saw the report did not specify what this covert cooperation entailed, but it could have marked the beginning of North Korea's nuclear buildup, which, as we will see in the next chapter, led to a nuclear crisis in late 2002.

Certainly all of that weapons proliferation and aid to enemies of the United States was dangerous, but then again, it was not particularly surprising coming from our Cold War antagonist. More troubling is that Moscow's aiding of America's enemies persisted after the fall of the Soviet Union and continues to this day.

On February 9, 1994, U.S. intelligence agencies intercepted communications between Russia and China indicating that the Russians were trying to sell cruise missile technology to China, specifically the Nanjing Aircraft Company. They would eventually sign a deal to transfer the missile technology to China, though the U.S. State Department tried to block the deal.

On August 18, 1998, U.S. intelligence reported that Russia had concluded an agreement with Syria to help that terrorist-sponsoring nation develop a nuclear reactor. That same month, the CIA said in a classified report that Russia was selling missile technology to Pakistan, using front companies. Pakistan threatens America's ally India, and it has become a serial weapons proliferator in its own right.

In November 1998, U.S. intelligence made the alarming discovery that Russia was supplying China the chemicals and technology to develop a high-technology rocket fuel designed to reduce the signature of a missile plume—the key indicator that enables U.S. spy satellites to detect a missile launch. Later that year, according to the National Security Agency (NSA), the Russian equipment company Morion sold China equipment intended for mobile missile launchers.

In March 1999, U.S. intelligence agencies uncovered information indicating that Russia and China were working jointly to develop high-powered lasers that could be used in antisatellite warfare. The intelligence included imagery obtained from U.S. spy satellites.

On April 1, 1999, the NSA uncovered electronic intercepts indicating that Russia had secretly lifted all restrictions on the export of weapons and dual-use technology to China. The move was a sign that Moscow was stepping up its cooperation with China on weapons development. Another NSA report, this one from April 19, revealed that China and Russia were cooperating on a high-technology weapons program that included nuclear arms, a high-powered microwave weapon, and radio-frequency weapons.

On October 26, 1999, U.S. intelligence reported that Russia was assisting Iran with a laser complex as part of that country's nuclear weapons program.

Yet another rogue state got help from Russia in 2000. On May 23, 2000, U.S. intelligence agencies reported that the Russian atomic energy export agency, known as Atomenergoexport at the time, had resumed work halted some years earlier in Libya on a nuclear reactor.

All told, the Russians have an egregious record of weapons proliferation. Rogue regimes, totalitarian states, terrorist groups—all have made themselves more powerful, and more dangerous, with the help of Russia. On December 2, 1991, just before the collapse of the Soviet Union, the CIA reported that Soviet officials were helping North Korea with nuclear weapons–related technology. U.S. officials who saw the report did not specify what this covert cooperation entailed, but it could have marked the beginning of North Korea's nuclear buildup, which, as we will see in the next chapter, led to a nuclear crisis in late 2002.

THE NORTH KOREAN NUCLEAR THREAT

CHAPTER 4

IN EARLY 2002, YUN HO JIN OF PYONGYANG, NORTH Korea, sent a letter to Hans-Werner Truppel at the German export firm Optronic GmbH KB and Company. Yun, representing Nam Chon Gang Corporation, a North Korean import-export company, wrote to Truppel, "I want to discuss certain matters with you by mail and not by phone. That is because letters are more reliable in a certain sense." Yun said he wanted to purchase special aluminum tubes on behalf of the Shenyang Aircraft Corporation, China's largest aircraft maker. He even produced a letter with Shenyang's logo. Although Shenyang does make jet fighters for the Chinese military, Yun claimed that the Chinese company would use the aluminum to make fuel tanks for commercial aircraft.

In reality, Yun was a North Korean government agent. The well-known diplomat, who wrote letters from both Pyongyang and an apartment in Beijing, had a special assignment: to buy materials for a covert program to build nuclear weapons inside the hermit Communist nation. And he convinced the German firm to cooperate. That German firm, meanwhile, had lined up assistance from a French shipping company.

When U.S. intelligence agencies discovered the deal, it marked the beginning of a major international crisis over North Korea's nuclear weapons. The tube deal was a clear indication that North Korea was pursuing a uranium-enrichment program in violation of its 1994 agreement not to build nuclear weapons.

Yun had in fact been North Korea's representative to the International Atomic Energy Agency, the United Nations watchdog group that is supposed to prevent nonnuclear nations from getting nuclear bombs, in an ironic twist, and a fitting symbol of the North Korean regime's blatant disregard for international nonproliferation standards. Indeed, Kim Jong-il's totalitarian regime defines the term *rogue state.* In 1994 Yun told reporters, "Our country has neither the intention nor the capability to manufacture a nuclear weapon." It was a lie, of course, and lies are key to fooling naïve governments into believing what they often want to believe: Nuclear weapons proliferation is not a problem.

But even more disturbing was that some of our friends in Europe helped this ruthless regime arm itself with the world's most dangerous weapons.

NUCLEAR DEALS EXPOSED

Truppel's company had had experience with military equipment before Yun approached him in early 2002. In the past, it had repaired thermal-vision equipment for the German military and had hired actors to play civilians on battlefields during U.S. military exercises. But Yun's shopping list was unusual: special aluminum tubes. Lots of them.

The North Koreans had done their homework. They understood that the specialty aluminum they needed for their nuclear weapons program was controlled for export. Under a system called the Nuclear Suppliers Group, member states, among them Germany, require exporters to obtain licenses before selling goods that can be used for nuclear arms programs. That is why Yun used the Chinese aircraft maker as a front company. Moreover, the North Koreans had carefully chosen these particular tubes, known in the trade as 6061-T6 aluminum tubing, to convince export authorities that the metal would be used for commercial purposes. Some specialists considered the tubing too soft for use in rotor tubes for gas centrifuges, which are critical to uranium enrichment, and in fact the tubing's tensile strength was below the level that would trigger the Nuclear Suppliers Group's controls on export licensing. But the metal is highly corrosion-resistant and strong enough for

use in the vacuum housings that cover tube rotors in centrifuges. Nuclear specialists believe the North Koreans planned to cut the tubes in two sections and then use them for feeding uranium hexafluoride gas in order to obtain highly enriched uranium. After Yun contacted Truppel, the German exporter called a company known as Jacob Bek GmbH in Ulm, Germany, a subsidiary of the major conglomerate the Thyssen-Krupp Group. ThyssenKrupp then ordered the tubes from British Aluminium Tubes, a German subsidiary of the British firm Luxfer, which is considered one of the best at making specialty aluminum products. The price: $4.53 per kilogram. In all, the deal was worth $906,000. Truppel reported the deal to German customs, noting that the buyer was Nam Chong Gang in North Korea and that the end user would be China's Shenyang Aircraft. German authorities didn't buy his claim that the tubes were to be used in the fuel tanks of domestic Chinese commercial aircraft. They notified Truppel in February 2002 that because the tubes could be used in nuclear weapons development, he would have to secure an export license before the goods were shipped.

Truppel ignored the advice. He went ahead with the North Korean deal, with Yun agreeing to buy 200 metric tons of the aluminum tubes. The Hamburg company Delta Trading contracted with the French shipper CMA CGM to send the cargo to North Korea. By April 2002, the first shipment of 214 tubes, weighing 22 tons, was ready to go. Yun wanted to use this small shipment as a trial run, to see if he could sneak the material past U.S. officials and other security and intelligence services. On April 4, the French ship *Ville de Virgo* sailed from the German port of Hamburg carrying the aluminum tubes.

But the North Korean procurement effort had come to the attention of the U.S. intelligence community. The CIA contacted its counterparts at German intelligence. Although the tubes had already left Germany, the German Customs Criminal Investigation Agency, known as ZKI, tracked the shipment down. American and German authorities alerted the French government that nuclear arms–related material was on its way to North Korea, and French officials ordered the ship diverted to the Egyptian port of Damietta. The tubing cargo was seized.

Based on the size of the shipment, intelligence officials believed that North Korea was planning to make a cascade of 3,500 to 4,000 centrifuges, which would be enough for Pyongyang to produce 90 kilograms of highly enriched uranium a year. One atomic bomb, using conventional explosives surrounding a nuclear core, requires less than 25 kilograms of this weapons fuel to create a devastating blast. According to U.S. officials, the aluminum tubes the North Koreans tried to purchase matched the specifications of the specialty tubes used in the G-2-design gas centrifuge, which is the centrifuge of choice for would-be nuclear weapons states. The G-2 was designed in the mid-1970s by Urenco, a conglomerate of German, Dutch, and British companies, but Pakistani scientist Abdul Qadeer Khan, the father of Pakistan's nuclear weapons program, stole the design when he worked in the Netherlands for an organization that was part of Urenco's centrifuge project. The Dutch government convicted Khan in absentia for his role in the economic espionage. Although the conviction was later overturned on a technicality, U.S. intelligence has ample evidence of Khan's, and Pakistan's, cooperation with rogue regimes, including North Korea. In the early 1990s, in a series of meetings involving high-level military and government officials—including Pakistani Prime Minister Benazir Bhutto—Pakistan and North Korea agreed to share nuclear and missile technology. Abdul Qadeer Khan himself visited North Korea in October 1997 and April 1998. Thus American intelligence is convinced that Pakistan's AQ Khan Research Laboratories supplied North Korea with the complete centrifuge design, and also with enough materials to start building the all-important cascade of centrifuges.

That conclusion was borne out in early 2004, when the covert international network of nuclear suppliers headed by Abdul Qadeer Khan was exposed. Pakistan's government, after years of denials, was pressured into recognizing that Khan was secretly working to sell nuclear weapons material and expertise to Libya, Iran, and North Korea. "We . . . believe Pyongyang is pursuing a production-scale uranium-enrichment program based on technology provided by A. Q. Khan, which would give North Korea an alternative route to nuclear weapons," said CIA Director George Tenet in February.

German law prohibits the export of dual-use goods that have applications for nuclear energy, and Truppel was eventually arrested and tried. As of this writing the trial was ongoing. According to a German court statement, however, authorities concluded that Truppel's claim that "the use [of the tubes] in gas tanks in the Chinese aircraft industry . . . was technically implausible, and on those grounds it had to be feared that the tubes would be delivered on to North Korea and used in that country's nuclear weapons program."

China was indeed complicit in the North Korean program, either through negligence or because the Chinese government was covertly assisting the North Koreans. The German government seized on that fact in a late 2002 report on domestic security. "One can assume that [North Korean] embassy personnel are still involved in the acquisition of sensitive goods," the German Interior Ministry stated in its report. "Because the previous practice to organize the export of such goods via European third countries is hardly possible any more due to extensive checks, attempts are being made to carry out such exports via China or Singapore. Not infrequently, North Korean front companies in China are given as the recipient." The report was a clear attempt to deflect blame from Germany, when in fact Germany had become a favorite shopping place for North Korea's arms and weapons programs since Berlin and Pyongyang had set up diplomatic relations on March 1, 2001. The German government was taking its cue from the Clinton administration, which had launched a major diplomatic effort to develop closer ties to one of the most repressive regimes in modern history.

"A SEPARATE PATH"

The discovery of the aluminum tube transfer was an important signal that North Korea was trying to produce nuclear weapons. North Korea had been so adept at hiding its nuclear program that U.S. and South Korean intelligence agencies had almost no information about the covert program. Many intelligence officials believed that North Korea had constructed underground nuclear facilities, just as it had built facilities for its military into rock formations throughout the nation. (One intelligence official estimated that more than 75 percent of the North Korean military is housed underground, with most of the troops and arms deployed close to the demilitarized zone separating North and South Korea.) In May 1999, the United States had even demanded to see the underground facility at Kumchangni, which was thought to be a covert nuclear facility. But the North Koreans removed all material and equipment from the plant and showed visiting U.S. officials a hollow underground cave. Still, U.S. intelligence agencies consider the clandestine procurement of centrifuge technology for uranium enrichment to be one of the red flags that a nation or group is trying to build a bomb. The reason is that once a regime or organization has the material to produce centrifuges, it can carry out the program with a small number of workers.

And once the weapons fuel is ready, a nuclear bomb is relatively easy to make, as the late nuclear scientist Louis Alvarez pointed out. Alvarez, who took part in the Manhattan Project, America's secret nuclear program during World War II, wrote that modern weapons-grade uranium poses enormous dangers because "terrorists, if they had such material, would have a good chance of setting off a high-yield explosion simply by dropping one half of the material onto the other half. Most people seem unaware that if separate [highly enriched uranium] is at hand it's a trivial job to set off a nuclear explosion. . . . Even a high school kid could make a bomb in short order."

The North Koreans in 2002 were well on their way to producing enough highly enriched uranium for at least three nuclear bombs a year. The discovery of the tube shipment had another, more dramatic consequence: It led to a fundamental altering of U.S. policy toward North Korea. In 1992 North Korea joined the International Atomic Energy Agency to gain access to nuclear technology, ostensibly for the production of electrical power. In 1994 Pyongyang signed an agreement with the Clinton administration in which it said it would freeze its nuclear weapons program in exchange for two civilian nuclear reactors. The 2002 aluminum tube deal revealed the Agreed Framework, as the agreement with the Clinton administration was called, to be what many U.S. intelligence officials had long suspected it of being: a worthless agreement. Nothing better illustrates North Korea's duplicity than the fact that Yun himself, North Korea's representative on the International Atomic Energy Agency, was the key procurement agent for the covert nuclear arms program to enrich uranium. And the tube deal was hardly Yun's only foray into illicit-arms deals. According to officials close to the case, in Germany alone Yun had purchased pumps, gas masks, dial gauges, and generators for the North Korean military. North Korea's efforts continued even after the tube deal was discovered. In May 2003, for example, the CIA notified the German government that North Korea had purchased from Germany thirty tons of sodium cyanide, a precursor for making the deadly nerve agent tabun. Authorities stopped the shipment before it reached Singapore, which has become a key transit point for North Korean goods.

At the time of the Agreed Framework, the U.S. government and others in the international community were concerned not with North Korea's uranium enrichment but with its efforts to produce the other nuclear-bomb fuel, plutonium, at the Yongbyon nuclear reactor. Now, with the aluminum tube transfer, it became clear that North Korea had and was developing a "production scope level of uranium-enrichment capability," one U.S. official said.

"While they had the whole world focused on Yongbyon, they were out developing a separate path to nuclear weapons," the official told me privately. "And we don't know where the uranium-enrichment facilities are; we don't know how big they are; we don't know how long they've been engaged in actually doing the enrichment; we don't know how much weapons-grade uranium they have; we don't know whether they've made it into weapons; we don't know anything about it."

The U.S. official affirmed that there was no doubt as to what the North Koreans wanted the tubes for. When Saddam Hussein had purchased similar specialty tubes, the intelligence community had been divided on the question of whether the tubes were for centrifuges or missiles. The North Korean tube purchase created no such divisions, however. "This time there is no argument that [the tubes] are for rockets," the official told me. "Everybody in the intelligence and policy community believes they were for uranium centrifuges that would have gone to North Korea. So they are still procuring stuff. If they've been in production for five years, they've got a lot of enriched uranium. If they haven't really gotten their act together yet, then we're okay."

The aluminum tube deal was the most glaring example of how North Korea was covertly building a nuclear arms program, but it was only one of several examples that U.S. intelligence had noticed. The Department of Energy's intelligence section had blown the whistle on

North Korea's uranium program as far back as the spring of 1999. A top-secret report that I obtained identified a North Korean trading company that had tried to buy enrichment technology from a Japanese manufacturer. The report stated that Pyongyang's attempts to get the technology were a clear sign that North Korea was "in the early stages of a uranium-enrichment capability." The Department of Energy report estimated that North Korea was "at least six years from the production of" highly enriched uranium, but it qualified that statement: "On the other hand, with significant technical support from other countries, such as Pakistan, the time frame would be decreased by several years." The intelligence confirmed that Pakistan was in fact helping the North Koreans set up a uranium-enrichment program, using special centrifuge technology—five thousand ring magnets—that it had purchased from China in 1996. (The Clinton administration had not sanctioned China for that illegal weapons technology sale because an investigation determined that senior Chinese leaders had been unaware of the technology transfer.)

By the summer of 2002, the U.S. intelligence community had come to the unequivocal conclusion that North Korea was well along in building centrifuges for making weapons fuel. That intelligence was unwelcome news to the State Department's diplomats, who were fighting within the bureaucracy to maintain the Clinton administration's policy of appeasement toward North Korea's Communist dictatorship, trying to normalize relations with Kim Jong-il's totalitarian regime. After a series of high-level interagency meetings, the State Department was ordered to send James Kelly, the assistant secretary of state for East Asia and the department's point man for all Asian policies, to Pyongyang in October 2002.

One of Kelly's key assignments was to present the North Koreans with the recent U.S. intelligence on the covert uranium-enrichment program. The State Department had used this tactic in the past when presented with unwelcome intelligence: Showing a watered-down version of the intelligence to the government in question, the State Department could elicit the expected denial. Armed with that denial, the diplomats at State could argue within the U.S. government that the intelligence was inconclusive and best forgotten. Kelly and others expected their

North Korean host, Deputy Foreign Minister Kang Seok-ju, to follow that script. And that is exactly what Kang did—at first.

Confronted with the centrifuge intelligence in the first meeting in Pyongyang, Kang said that the Americans were wrong, that North Korea had no such uranium-enrichment program. The next day, however, Kang showed that North Korea would not keep playing along. He revealed that North Korea did indeed have nuclear weapons and that the nuclear program had been under way for several years. He even blustered that in addition to its nuclear bombs, the Communist state had more powerful weapons; presumably he was referring to chemical and biological arms, though he did not elaborate. Kang added that North Korea now considered the Agreed Framework nullified.

The revelation was a huge setback for State Department officials who thought the way to get North Korea to halt its weapons and missile programs, stop threatening its neighbors, end its support for terrorism, and stop the criminal treatment of its own people was to offer Pyongyang major concessions. After word of Kelly's meeting leaked out in Washington, the State Department was forced to admit that "we are unable to pursue this approach." In a statement to the press, the State Department declared, "North Korea's secret nuclear weapons program is a serious violation of North Korea's commitments under the Agreed Framework as well as under the Nonproliferation Treaty (NPT), its International Atomic Energy Agency safeguards agreement, and the Joint North-South Declaration on the Denuclearization of the Korean Peninsula."

Despite the dramatic disclosures, the Bush administration did not adopt a tough posture. In the fall of 2002 the administration was preparing to deal militarily with Saddam Hussein's Iraq, and it was simply not possible to begin a similar track on North Korea. Instead the administration launched what it called the "diplomatic process" of trying to negotiate with a Communist regime that has threatened to turn South Korea, Japan, and the United States into "seas of fire." Three months after the meeting in Pyongyang, the administration proposed a multiparty dialogue with North Korea with the goal of reaching yet another agreement.

Shortly after the nuclear dispute surfaced, the official Korean Central News Agency issued a threat to the U.S. imperialists. "The use of force should be countered by force," the broadcast stated. "This is the DPRK [North Korean] principle of struggling against the enemy and mode of retaliating against him. If the U.S. levels a machine gun at the DPRK, the latter will return artillery fire for its fire, and if the U.S. fires an artillery piece at the DPRK, it will use a more powerful weapon in retaliation against the fire. The U.S. warhawks had better . . . think twice."

The picture grew more bleak as U.S. intelligence made new discoveries about the North Koreans' buildup. In November 2002, the CIA told Congress the bad news about North Korea's "breakout" from the Agreed Framework, revealing that "the North has continued its nuclear weapons program" despite the 1994 agreement. By 2005, the CIA said in its statement to Congress, North Korea could be making enough plutonium (275 kilograms) for more than fifty bombs a year and could have its centrifuge cascade for uranium enrichment in full swing. "We recently learned that the North is constructing a plant that could produce enough weapons-grade uranium for two or more nuclear weapons per year when fully operational—which could be as soon as mid-decade," the agency said. "We assess that North Korea embarked on the effort to develop a centrifuge-based uranium enrichment program about two years ago."

That fall, U.S. intelligence also uncovered a nuclear deal involving China. According to intelligence sources, Pyongyang purchased from several Chinese companies twenty tons of the chemical tributyl phosphate, or TBP, which is used in a process known as plutonium-uranium extraction, or purex, which produces plutonium from spent reactor fuel. In a January 2003 report to Congress, the CIA disclosed how North Korea was using front companies in China for its arms-procurement programs. North Korea "has continued procurement of raw materials and components for its ballistic-missile programs from various foreign sources, especially through North Korean firms based in China," the CIA stated in its report. One trading company in Macao, for example, was operated by the North Korean People's Armed Forces.

THREATS AND INTIMIDATION

Army General Leon LaPorte, the commander of U.S. forces in South Korea during the nuclear crisis, said in an interview with American reporters that North Korea's Communist regime was a dangerous enemy that posed an "asymmetric threat" to U.S. and South Korean forces. "They have chemical weapons. Their doctrine is to use chemical weapons as a standard munition," he warned in the November 2003 interview. "They also have weapons of mass destruction and our concern is that they have nearly eight hundred missiles. The missiles themselves are a significant asymmetrical threat. But if that was combined with a nuclear capability, now you have a capability that not only threatens the peninsula, but threatens the entire region.

"Additionally, and I think equally important, is North Korea is a known proliferator of military technology—missile technology and others. We believe that nothing will prevent them from selling weapons-grade nuclear material to other countries, rogue nations, or terrorist organizations. And now you have a situation where a terrorist organization has a weapon of mass destruction. And that's the concern we have relative to North Korea's nuclear program." The threat of exporting nuclear material or even entire nuclear weapons is real, as a North Korean official made clear to the U.S. government. In late April 2003, U.S., North Korean, and Chinese officials gathered in Beijing for the first round of talks on the North Korean nuclear crisis. At a side meeting with James Kelly, North Korean Foreign Ministry official Li Gun warned that North Korea would export nuclear arms, add to its current nuclear arsenal, or conduct a first test of an atomic bomb. Li said that whatever option Pyongyang chose would be directly related to the actions of the United States. "This was clearly a threat," said one American official closely involved in the talks.

Li made another alarming disclosure: North Korea, he said, had nearly finished reprocessing some 8,000 spent plutonium fuel rods being held in storage at a containment facility at the Yongbyon facility. U.S. intelligence agencies were caught by surprise. Before Li's revelation, the CIA had estimated that none of the fuel rods had been reprocessed. But in August 2003, the agency submitted a revised, unclassified estimate to the Senate Select Committee on Intelligence. "We assess that North Korea has produced one or two simple fission-type nuclear weapons and has validated the designs without conducting yield-producing nuclear tests," the agency reported. In the spring of 2004, U.S. intelligence agencies would increase that estimate. A new secret intelligence estimate stated that because of renewed North Korean nuclear activity, the rogue state could have as many as eight nuclear weapons.

Although North Korea had not conducted a nuclear test of its own, U.S. intelligence concluded that Pyongyang's technology had advanced enough that such a test would be unnecessary. "North Korea has been conducting nuclear weapons-related high explosive tests since the 1980s in order to validate its weapons design(s)," the CIA said in its 2003 report. "With such tests, we assess North Korea would not require nuclear tests to validate simple fission weapons."

Nevertheless, Li's claim that North Korea might test a nuclear weapon was not an idle threat. The CIA noted that it appeared Pyongyang was escalating tensions and that conducting a nuclear test would intensify the effort. "A test would demonstrate to the world the North's status as a nuclear-capable state and signal Kim's perception that building a nuclear stockpile will strengthen his regime's international standing and security posture," the CIA said.

The threat to export nuclear arms set off alarm bells. Secretary of State Colin Powell warned in public that the United States would not allow North Korea to export nuclear arms. Yet the Bush administration had internal differences on how to deal with the North Korean nuclear problem. State Department officials within the East Asia bureau still wanted to make concessions to Pyongyang in the hopes of reaching another agreement, even though little progress had been made at the April 2003 talks in Beijing. Other officials, like Defense Secretary Donald Rumsfeld and Undersecretary of State John Bolton, were skeptical that any deal could be reached. Asked in late 2003 if North Korea could be trusted to abide by a new agreement, considering that it had violated the 1994 Agreed Framework, Rumsfeld stated, "With respect to trust, I have always kind of agreed with former President Reagan: Trust but verify."

During 2004, senior Bush administration officials refused to cave in to pressure from within the bureaucracy and from abroad to make concessions at the North Korea nuclear talks. The U.S. demand was

simple: North Korea must first agree to a "complete, verifiable, and irreversible" dismantling of its nuclear program. Only then could there be talk of normalizing ties.

Bolton testified to the House International Relations Committee in March 2004 that North Korea must give up both its plutonium-based program and the covert uranium enrichment effort. "We will not follow the mistaken path of the 1994 Agreed Framework because as Secretary Powell has said, 'We bought that horse once,'" Bolton said. "We will not provide inducements or reward the North Koreans to come back into compliance with their international obligations. Fundamentally, North Korea needs to understand that the end state is not a freeze, but the complete, verifiable, and irreversible dismantlement of all their nuclear programs, including the Yongbyon facility."

Bolton said the nuclear program was only one concern. Additionally, North Korea must address the massive conventional forces poised dangerously close to South Korea, its chemical and biological and missile proliferation activities, and its abysmal human rights record. "They must make this strategic decision themselves, or face continued isolation and other unwelcome consequences," he said.

U.S. officials have said that any deal with North Korea on the nuclear program would require intrusive inspection provisions, something the reclusive Communist regime would be unlikely to approve.

"If diplomacy fails, there are two alternatives," one official told me. "Either you allow North Korea to remain a nuclear power or you exercise the military option."

In other words, there are no good options. Allowing North Korea to retain its nuclear capabilities would signal to other rogue regimes that the United States can be kept at bay with a nuclear arsenal. But a veteran U.S. military official revealed to me that "there is no way to do a surgical strike on North Korea," meaning that a military strike against North Korea could easily lead to all-out war. The North Koreans have about 10,000 artillery tubes and rocket launchers within striking distance of downtown Seoul, a bustling city of 17 million people. They could also use their bombs against Japan, as they demonstrated in August 1998 when they test-fired a long-range Taepodong-1 missile that flew over Japanese islands. Depending on how much they have developed their long-range missile capabilities, the North Koreans could possibly target even the United States.

The lack of good options with regard to North Korea sums up why weapons proliferation is such a threat to our national security.

WEAPONS IN, WEAPONS OUT

As with so many other rogue regimes, North Korea poses a threat not just because it is arming itself but also because it is selling weapons around the world. A veteran U.S. intelligence specialist on North Korea says that Pyongyang is the source of arms and weapons technology for a host of countries, including Iran, Iraq, Syria, Libya, Pakistan, and India. "There is a fair amount of information, albeit fragmentary, to show that North Korea is and has been using other countries as subcontractors for essential research, especially on their nuclear program," the intelligence official told me. "Since our narrow-minded 'experts' called attention to places such as Yongbyon, the North Koreans have intensified their use of surrogates and subcontractors to prevent being 'caught' with a smoking gun, should the [International Atomic Energy Agency] and our national collection means discover continued nuclear testing and research going on inside North Korea."

After the war in Iraq began, in 2003, U.S. intelligence picked up new information about how North Korea arms other rogue states. Right before the start of the war, North Korea and Saddam Hussein's government had been discussing a missile deal, as revealed by Iraqi documents uncovered after the fall of Baghdad and captured Iraqi officials. In February 2003, a month before the U.S.-led invasion of Iraq, two North Korean officials met the head of Iraq's Al Bashair Trading Company to discuss Iraq's purchase of major components for ballistic missiles. The meeting was held at the Damascus offices of a private company called SES International Corporation, which is headed by a cousin of Syrian dictator Bashar Assad. One document uncovered in Iraq revealed that ten months before this meeting, on April 8, 2002, the Iraqis had made a $1.9 million down payment to the North Koreans through SES.

CIA official David Kay, who headed the survey group that was looking for weapons in Iraq, described the North Korean–Iraqi deal.

Under the terms of the deal, he said, Iraq was to receive "missile technology for the Nodong, a 1,300-kilometer missile"—even though United Nations sanctions prohibited Iraq from building missiles with a range greater than 150 kilometers—"as well as other nonmissile-related but prohibited technologies." But the Iraqis had not received anything in return for the money. "The Iraqis actually advanced the North Koreans $10 million," Kay said. "In late 2002, the North Koreans came to the Iraqis as a result of the Iraqis' inquiring, 'Where is the stuff we paid for?' and the North Koreans said, 'Sorry, there's so much U.S. attention on us that we cannot deliver it.'" Baghdad demanded that North Korea return the $10 million, but the North Koreans refused, according to Kay.

"UNCONDITIONAL, INSTANT DENUCLEARIZATION"

Although the United States has learned a great deal about North Korea's capabilities in recent years, it is clear that Pyongyang is hiding a lot. We gain some insight into how the regime's weapons programs work as more and more defectors escape North Korea. From defectors, for example, the United States picked up information about Pakistan's nuclear aid to North Korea, and also learned that a key element of the nuclear program is the North Korean National Academy of Sciences complex located in Pyongsong, about forty miles north of Pyongyang. Moreover, nuclear specialists got valuable information indicating that North Korea is heading toward—in just three to five years—a strategic nuclear weapons system to threaten Japan and South Korea, at a minimum, and perhaps the United States, Russia, and China.

Defectors have also shed light on how Communist dictator Kim Jong-il and the rest of his regime operate. Hwang Jang-yop, a high-ranking North Korean Communist Party official who was close to Kim, broke with the regime in the 1990s and escaped to South Korea.

In one of his few interviews with a Western reporter, Hwang told me that Kim is a "failure" as a politician. "No one starved to death under Kim Il-sung," Kim Jong-il's father and predecessor, says Hwang. "However, after Kim Jong-il came to power, millions of people have starved to death. The economy has been destroyed. And the whole government and the country became one big prison." Hwang is right. Kim has driven his country to destitution. A secret U.S. State Department intelligence report from the late 1990s revealed that North Korean food shortages were so bad that large numbers of North Koreans had resorted to cannibalism merely to survive; the investigation that Kim himself ordered indicated that the problem had become "a national-level concern." And a report by the U.S. Committee for Human Rights in North Korea detailed the Pyongyang government's systematic use of torture and starvation, including in its prisons and labor camps, which contain perhaps as many as 200,000 political prisoners. Thousands of prisoners are worked to death or starved to death, the report noted. Hwang also told me that Kim "is very egotistical." The North Korean leader "is watching out for his own self-interest, and his self-interest only," says the former Communist Party official. "He believes that as the leader he can decide everything; [that] he owns everything; and [that] he is the center of everything. A totally egotistical man."

Kim is interested solely in "maintaining his dictatorial regime," says Hwang. That is why North Korea developed nuclear warheads—to maintain Kim's regime in power (and possibly to use them against South Korea to achieve the long-term goal of reuniting the peninsula under Communist control).

A former U.S. military intelligence official who specialized in Korean affairs agreed with Hwang that Kim Jong-il's egotism is his defining characteristic. "Going after North Korea as a Communist country does not strike at the heart and soul of the cult around Kim Jong-il, nor will it ever do so," the Korean specialist told me. "We have to get in there and work on the levels of personal avarice and greed, mistrust and cunning, that enable Kim Jong-il to exercise total control." He also agreed that North Korea's priority is regime survival. "They see their nuclear deterrent force as a hedge against a U.S. Iraqi-style invasion," he commented. "Consequently, it is very unlikely that North Korea would ever decide to launch a nuclear weapon as a first-strike attack because they know they'd be outgunned something like 3,000 to 5." Kim probably would not initiate his own demise, especially after observing what happened to his "Axis of Evil" brother, Saddam Hussein.

The best hope for a peaceful resolution, said the former intelligence official, would be to "contain" the North Koreans. By 2004, the Bush administration had indeed made steps toward a containment policy. For example, it had launched the Proliferation Security Initiative, an international effort to stop and seize illicit-arms shipments on the seas, and ultimately on land and in the air.

Of course, containment creates problems, because by failing to deal forcibly with a regime that illegally builds up its nuclear arsenal, we invite other rogue states to go nuclear. The former intelligence official therefore indicated that the threat of force must be behind any containment policy. The United States must make clear to North Korea, he said, that any use of a nuclear weapon would result in "unconditional, instant denuclearization," which would leave "only a few vapor trails to indicate where there used to be a country called North Korea."

Yet while America's superior firepower could almost certainly overwhelm North Korea, we must always recall that the Communist regime has the weapons capabilities to back up its threat to turn the United States and its allies into "seas of fire." And it has those capabilities to put the United States and its allies at risk because German, French, Chinese, Pakistani, Iraqi, and other arms traders agreed to ignore international law and sell an aggressive Communist dictatorship dangerous weapons and weapons materials.

IRAN GOES NUCLEAR

CHAPTER 5

"THERE CLEARLY IS CONCERN IN THE REGION ABOUT Iran's, not simply their nuclear program, but . . . also their ballistic missile program," Defense Secretary Donald H. Rumsfeld said in early 2004. "They have had a fairly energetic program in both areas. The missile program has been visible, reasonably visible, to intelligence. The nuclear program obviously very recently has been discovered. Indeed I believe it's now broadly agreed that they have in fact not been forthcoming about their nuclear program. Sometimes I understate for emphasis."

The defense secretary's comment was indeed an understatement. For years the Iranian government actively deceived the international community as it built a nuclear weapons program. Although the CIA and other U.S. intelligence agencies have been tracking Iran's weapons programs for years, only now are we beginning to understand the extent of Tehran's nuclear activity, and its duplicity. The most alarming discovery came in 2003, when international inspectors caught Iran secretly building centrifuge cascade facilities to make highly enriched uranium—much like the facility that North Korea was covertly building.

Iran's government steadfastly refused to admit that the secret nuclear programs were aimed at building weapons. After all, by building material for nuclear weapons, the Iranians would be violating their agreements with the United Nations watchdog group the International Atomic Energy Agency (IAEA). Tehran maintained that the nuclear program was for generating electrical power.

But the Iranian regime's denials were unbelievable. First, with huge oil reserves, Iran has no logical reason to develop nuclear stations for electrical power. Rumsfeld noted that Iran is "probably burning off more gas and wasting it at the present time than they would get out of the Bushehr [nuclear] reactors." He put it even more bluntly to NATO ministers in late 2003: "They need nuclear power about as much as they need sand." And as at least one member of the Iranian parliament acknowledged, evidence of Tehran's weapons building is overwhelming. In late 2003, in an open session of the parliament, which is known as the Majiles, Ahmad Shirzad called out his government for covering up its nuclear program, stating, "Contrary to its claims, the regime is secretly preparing to produce weapons of mass destruction." Western intelligence agencies, he rightly pointed out, "have evidence and documents to prove their claim." According to Shirzad, the Tehran regime chose "an irrational path in nuclear technology without believing that the world will discover their activities, such as their underground 50,000 [square] meter site." Despite all the intelligence revealing the nuclear arms program, the Iranian government continued to attribute such intelligence reports to "Zionist" conspiracies.

The lengths to which the hard-line Islamic regime went to build, and to cover up, its nuclear program indicate that Iranians will, in Donald Rumsfeld's words, "be willing to do that again for a good many years." Said Rumsfeld, "One has to assume that they are purposeful, that they will, if they have the opportunity, certainly continue with their ballistic missile programs, and I would estimate, continue with their nuclear programs, probably being somewhat more clever than they were the last time."

An ongoing Iranian nuclear program poses a direct threat to the United States. Iran has said it will use weapons against the United States and its allies. Iranian supreme leader Ayatollah Ali Khamenei said in June 2003 that a U.S. attack would be "suicidal." Earlier, on December 14, 2001, Iranian leader Ali Akbar Hashemi-Rafsanjani, president from 1989 to 1997, stated that "when the Islamic world acquires atomic weapons, the strategy of the West will hit a dead end—since the use of a single atomic bomb has the power to destroy Israel completely, while it will only cause partial damage to the Islamic world."

Worse, Iran has already supported and even conducted terrorist attacks against American servicemen. Though the Tehran regime has publicly said that it would support Iraq's post-Saddam government, the regime has worked secretly to destabilize the country. In August 2003, the Iraqi police raided the Al Mashriq Money Exchange Company offices in liberated Baghdad and discovered twelve agents from the Iranian Ministry of Intelligence and Security who, interrogations would reveal, were planning bombings to target U.S. and allied troops and the pro-U.S. Iraqi government. Scores of other Iranian operatives remained at large in Iraq, however. Sure enough, several days after the Al Mashriq raid, in an attack that U.S. officials believed was the work of the Iranian intelligence service, terrorists in Najaf, a Shiite Islam center, set off a massive car bomb that killed a moderate Shiite leader.

And intelligence agencies have caught the Iranians lending support to plenty of other terrorist groups. For example, in January 2002, Israeli commandos in the Red Sea captured a ship that was carrying a large cache of Iranian weapons to the Palestinian Authority. U.S. intelligence had located the ship, the *Karine A,* for Israel, and when the Israelis captured the ship, they discovered AK-47 assault rifles, mortars, rockets, rocket-propelled grenades, plastic explosives, and more. The weapons cargo was estimated to be worth $10 million. Previously, Iranian government support to terrorists in the region had been limited to groups such as Hamas and Palestinian Islamic Jihad.

Tehran's anti-U.S. strategy and its support for terrorism make Iran the number-one danger in the Middle East today. The prospect of a nuclear Iran is particularly frightening, not simply because of the threat that Iran itself poses to the United States and our friends in the Middle East, but also because the regime could supply terrorist groups with nuclear weapons.

Unfortunately, even after the 2003 discovery of Tehran's uranium-enrichment program, the U.S. government has shown no interest in letting the American people know how Iran obtained its weapons. Starting in 2003 the American public learned bits and pieces of the story of Iran's weapons programs from occasional news reports, but the secret intelligence disclosed to me tells a much different, much more comprehensive, and much more disturbing story.

Perhaps most troubling is how much help the Iranians have gotten and continue to get. Like other regimes that threaten the United States and its allies, Iran has been able to arm itself only because it has worked closely with greedy governments and arms dealers around the world. Among the many nations that have partnered with Iran's clerical regime are Russia, China, North Korea, Ukraine, Kazakhstan, and Pakistan. Certainly it comes as no shock that the rogue regimes in China and North Korea would arm a dangerous country in the volatile Middle East, but many observers are surprised and bothered by the fact that Russia and European countries like Ukraine and Kazakhstan would so willfully disregard international antiproliferation agreements. In the case of Russia, in 1995 Moscow reached a secret agreement with the United States to halt arms sales to Iran, but it spent the next several years working around that agreement.

Many other countries have placed greed over principle, even if they haven't been arming Iran. The problem is that they have turned a blind eye to Tehran's active nuclear buildup. One U.S. intelligence official told me that the world seemed to ignore the Iranian threat despite the fact that the danger was obvious for anyone to see. As the official put it, "All you have to do is look at the fact that Iran has had a vice president for atomic energy for decades to realize where they were heading." According to John Bolton, the undersecretary of state for arms control, European nations and other governments have not taken a tough position on Iran's nuclear arms programs—or on its human rights violations, for that matter—because Iran has held out the potential for lucrative oil and gas contracts.

Only by learning the full story of Iran's weapons buildup can we ever hope to stop the proliferation and curtail the Iranian threat.

THE FULL STORY

The public version of the Iranian nuclear story acknowledges Iran's buildup but leaves out many important details. In its report to Congress about Iran, which became public in November 2003, the CIA stated that Iran was continuing to work on homemade programs for making nuclear, chemical, and biological weapons, as well as missile delivery systems and advanced conventional arms. "To this end, Iran continued to seek foreign materials, training, equipment, and know-how," the agency report said. "During the reporting period, Iran still focused particularly on entities in Russia, China, North Korea, and Europe." The CIA noted that Tehran's pursuit of a "clandestine nuclear weapons program" put it "in violation of its obligations as a party to the Nuclear Nonproliferation Treaty (NPT)." According to the report, the Iranians hid the weapons program within their domestic program to develop a nuclear fuel cycle.

True enough, as far as it goes. But there are many more details that the U.S. government did not let the public know. And there are many details that U.S. intelligence agencies were not even aware of, at least initially. In fact, U.S. intelligence was not responsible for the dramatic 2003 discovery of Iran's centrifuge cascade facilities. It took a left-wing Iranian opposition group to blow the whistle and set in motion a second nuclear crisis rivaling the North Korean threat.

On August 14, 2002, just weeks before the North Koreans shocked the world by disclosing their uranium-enrichment program, the National Council of Resistance, a political arm of the People's Mujahideen of Iran, disclosed new details of Tehran's secret nuclear weapons program. The council's credibility in the past was suspect, but this time its information was correct, as the IAEA later confirmed. Using its agents and sources inside Iran, the council had pinpointed two key secret nuclear projects, which council representative Alireza Jafarzadeh revealed at a press conference in Washington, D.C. The Iranian-born Jafarzadeh announced that the Iranian regime had a major nuclear installation at Natanz and a second facility at Arak, neither of which U.S. intelligence had noticed.

The IAEA could not gain access to the two secret facilities until February 2003, but what it found proved that the Iranians had been lying about their nuclear program for nearly two decades. The Iranians, it turns out, had been building a uranium-enrichment centrifuge system for the previous eighteen years. U.S. intelligence officials were startled to learn that the Iranians were carrying out a military nuclear weapons program under the cover of a civilian nuclear power–generating program. The discovery of the uranium-enrichment program forced U.S. intelligence to reassess Iran's capabilities; the shocking conclusion was that Iran as of 2003 was only a few years away from producing enough highly enriched uranium to make nuclear weapons.

In February 2004, during a speech defending CIA lapses on Iraq's weapons of mass destruction, CIA Director George Tenet said the agency had not been "surprised" by the Iranian opposition disclosures. Tenet said the disclosures "validate our intelligence assessments." Other U.S. intelligence and policy officials said Tenet was wrong, and that the CIA never brought the information to the attention of policymakers until after the opposition group went public.

Natanz, a facility located some two hundred miles south of Tehran, had above- and belowground buildings that covered about 120,000 square yards. The six buildings aboveground housed a cascade of about 1,000 centrifuges. When the inspectors visited the plant in February 2003, about 160 centrifuges were in operation and another 820 were being assembled. Specialists say that when the cascade is finished it will produce between 10 and 12 kilograms of weapons-grade uranium a year. That spring, IAEA inspectors found particles of highly enriched uranium on the machines, a sign that the Iranians were already producing weapons-grade material. Confronted with the evidence, the Iranians told the inspectors that the centrifuge components had those traces on them before they were imported into the country.

But the Iranians kept up their nuclear weapons program even after the IAEA made these discoveries. In June, as a test, they used a single centrifuge to create uranium hexafluoride gas, and two months later they began testing a ten-machine cascade, according to Ambassador Kenneth C. Brill, the U.S. representative to the U.S. Mission to International Organizations in Vienna. Brill said in a statement to the Board of Governors meeting in September 2003 that Iran was continuing to deceive the international organization. "After an additional two months of intensive work, the unanswered questions have only grown in both number and significance," he said.

Brill identified a pattern of activity that included Iranians "working in secret, going back into the 1980s, to develop sophisticated nuclear facilities; stalling, stonewalling, and on a number of occasions first providing the IAEA false information, and then changing its story when the original version was revealed to be inaccurate." The Iranians also sought to "cover up traces of its activities to avoid detection by the Agency," Brill said.

In October 2003, the Iranians pledged to suspend their uranium enrichment, but construction and installation work at the Natanz facility continued.

The Arak facility, the planned site of a thermal heavy-water reactor, was a bigger surprise. The IAEA weapons inspectors were puzzled because Iran does not have nuclear reactors that use heavy water. When completed, the Arak reactor will use uranium dioxide and heavy water to produce plutonium, the other important fuel for making nuclear weapons. But the Iranians told the IAEA that the reactor will be used to produce radioisotopes for medical and industrial use. The problem with that claim was that the design showed no plans for "hot cells," which are large, lead-lined containers that provide shielded work areas for people engaged in radiopharmaceutical research, production, and processing. So much for the Iranians' medical research excuse.

Later Iran offered up another excuse, telling the IAEA that the hot cells would be set up in a second building at Arak. IAEA specialists remained unconvinced, however. They concluded that the Arak reactor when completed will be capable of producing between 8 and 10 kilograms of plutonium annually, enough for one or two nuclear bombs a year.

The two facilities that the National Council of Resistance revealed led to even more discoveries about the Iranian nuclear program. Iran has built an even more elaborate uranium-enrichment facility, a large-scale commercial plant, that is scheduled to begin constructing centrifuges in 2005, according to U.S. intelligence. The three massive underground facilities when completed will hold up to 50,000 centrifuges and will be able to produce about 400 to 500 kilograms of weapons-grade uranium each year—enough for the Islamic regime to produce fifteen to twenty nuclear bombs a year.

In August 2003, after months of being blocked by Iranian officials, IAEA inspectors finally got in to check a plant run by the Kalaye Electric Company, located in Tehran. There they found traces of highly enriched uranium and low-enriched uranium. The Iranians had claimed that the facility was not used for uranium enrichment, but the IAEA tests proved that Tehran was lying—again. The Iranians were forced to admit that the facility had secretly been producing centrifuge parts and assembling centrifuges and had been used for enrichment tests in 1999 and 2002.

Other Iranian nuclear facilities include the Esfahan Conversion Facility, which is used for converting uranium yellow cake ore into uranium hexafluoride, uranium oxide, and uranium metal. The hexafluoride is sent from Esfahan to Natanz for enrichment. In addition, the Iranians use the Jabr Ibn Hayan Lab–Tehran Nuclear Research Center to turn uranium tetrafluoride into uranium metal. They also used the facility to hide from the IAEA material that they had obtained from China, including uranium hexafluoride, uranium tetrafluoride, and uranium dioxide. China was a major supplier to the Iranian nuclear program, along with Russia and Pakistan.

But there was still more. In October 2003, the Iranians admitted that they had irradiated depleted uranium dioxide to produce plutonium. They said that the Tehran Research Reactor had carried out the irradiation from 1988 to 1992, producing 3 kilograms of separated plutonium.

As the IAEA said in its report, the Iranians also acknowledged in 2003 that for the past twelve years they had been working on laser isotope separation as part of a program to enrich uranium. U.S. intelligence agencies uncovered the carefully constructed procurement network the Iranians used to support this covert program. The plan called for a company in Denmark to purchase the laser from a South African company and then sell it to an Iranian front company in Italy that posed as a merchant in Persian rugs. Iran admitted that the Lashkar Abad plant had tested a laser enrichment process from October 2002 to January 2003 using 22 kilograms of natural uranium metal that Russia had transferred to the Iranians in 1993. The Iranians insisted that they had stopped the laser enrichment and dismantled all the equipment. But in May 2003 they sent all the equipment from that supposedly shelved program to yet another covert nuclear facility, Karaj.

A reactor near Iran's Persian Gulf coast, Bushehr, had been a focus of U.S. antiproliferation efforts for years. Germany had originally launched the construction of Bushehr, but the Iranians had an $800 million deal with Russia to finish the project. In the deal, Moscow agreed to deliver the fuel for the reactor and to take back the spent fuel. Intelligence reports that I obtained confirm that Russia was Bushehr's key supplier despite American appeals to stop helping Iran build the reactor complex. Refusing to listen to the United States, Moscow played an integral role in Iran's carefully managed overt-covert nuclear program. Overt in its use of nuclear reactors to produce electrical power. Covert in the drive to build nuclear bombs.

In an interview, Donald Rumsfeld told me that the Russian role in Iran's nuclear program shows how irresponsible Moscow has been. "I can't imagine why Russia sells the things it sells to the countries they sell them to," he said.

DENY, DENY, DENY

The IAEA report was a clear indictment of Iranian duplicity, but Tehran has offered only further lies in response.

Undersecretary of State John Bolton, who has taken the lead within the Bush administration on dealing with the problem of deadly arms going to rogue states, declared in late 2003 that the findings of the IAEA and U.S. intelligence made clear that Iran's claims could not be trusted. "While Iran has consistently denied any program to develop nuclear weapons," Bolton said, "the IAEA has amassed an enormous amount of evidence to the contrary that makes this denial increasingly implausible. In what can only be an attempt to build a capacity to develop nuclear materials for nuclear weapons, Iran has enriched uranium with both centrifuges and lasers, and produced and reprocessed plutonium. It attempted to cover its tracks by repeatedly and over many years neglecting to report its activities, and in many instances providing false declarations to the IAEA." In one case, for example, the Iranians claimed that uranium enriched in centrifuges had been "lost," but nuclear technicians who investigated Iran's programs revealed that claim to be false.

"I repeat: The United States believes that the long-standing, massive, and covert Iranian effort to acquire sensitive nuclear capabilities makes sense only as part of a nuclear weapons program," Bolton said. "Iran is trying to legitimize as 'peaceful and transparent' its pursuit of nuclear fuel cycle capabilities that would give it the ability to produce fissile material for nuclear weapons. This includes uranium mining and extraction, uranium conversion and enrichment, reactor fuel fabrication, heavy-water production, a heavy-water reactor well suited for plutonium production, and the 'management' of spent fuel—a euphemism for reprocessing spent fuel to recover plutonium."

Bolton also announced that the United States "will continue its efforts to prevent the transfer of sensitive nuclear and ballistic missile technology to Iran, from whatever source, and will monitor the situation there with great care." But he was worried that the IAEA would let Iran off the hook for multiple violations over a period of years, which would give the Iranians more time to develop nuclear weapons. As Bolton put it, "The real issue now is whether the [IAEA's] Board of Governors will remain together in its insistence that Iran's pursuit of nuclear weapons is illegitimate, or whether Iranian efforts to split the Board through economic incentives and aggressive propaganda will succeed." And those economic incentives were real, since Iran could dangle major oil and gas contracts in front of other nations as a way to stave off international pressure.

Staving off international pressure is critical to the Iranians, because the UN Security Council could take real action against Iran, whether it is sanctions or even the use of force. That is why Iranian government leaders insisted that the nuclear program was for peaceful purposes, despite all the evidence pointing in the other direction. They also insisted that they would not stop enriching uranium, apparently because that could be taken as a sign of kowtowing to the IAEA. "Our decision to suspend uranium enrichment is voluntary and temporary," said the head of Iran's Supreme National Security Council, Hasan Rowhani. "Uranium enrichment is Iran's natural right and [Iran] will reserve for itself this right. . . . There has been and there will be no question of a permanent suspension or halt at all."

Former Iranian president Akbar Hashemi-Rafsanjani, who remains an influential leader in Iran, said that Europeans accept Iran's claims about its nuclear programs and that "only America and Israel still dream of chantage, propaganda, and measures to prevent Iran from realizing its right." At a Friday prayer sermon at Tehran University, Rafsanjani said, "We firmly stated that we would not abandon our nuclear industry and that we have the right to have access to peaceful application of it." Rafsanjani, vice chairman of the Assembly of Experts, Iran's council of clerics, claimed that Iran had no interest in nuclear weapons. "Any effort for production and proliferation of weapons of mass destruction is considered as inhuman and un-Islamic," he said.

Of course, while publicly claiming not to have any interest in nuclear weapons, the Iranian regime is working feverishly to build the infrastructure needed for making bombs. Rafsanjani himself boasted that Iran had become "the strongest missile power in the Middle East." Included in Iran's missile arsenal—which was built with the help of Russia, China, and North Korea—are missiles with ranges of 620 miles that have no capabilities for precision guidance. The only logical conclusion is that these missiles are designed for one thing: carrying nuclear warheads capable of causing devastating destruction.

As for Iran's reaction to U.S. threats to hold Tehran accountable for its nuclear violations, Rafsanjani had threats of his own: "America should be sure that if it intends to hatch and carry out any plots against Iran, the God of Islam, the God of the Koran, the God of the Companions of the Prophet, and the God of our revolution and our people will foil these, bravely and courageously. . . . Iran is one of those places which cannot be harmed very easily. And anyone who should want to stretch their hands toward Iran will have those hands cut off."

The Iranian radical leader made clear Tehran's anti-U.S. position when he said that Iran opposed the establishment of a democratic Iraq: "We never want the U.S. to become victorious over Iraq, because the U.S. is more dangerous [to us] than Iraq, as is a viper to a scorpion and a pit to a hole." He summed up by saying, "This is our ideological position and our political experience."

Ayatollah Ali Khamenei, Iran's Islamic dictator, said during a meeting of Iranian leaders that the nuclear program was peaceful and that Iran's enemies were using the nuclear issue to attack Iran. "The point at issue is hostility, opposition, and evil deeds," he said. "That is what the Islamic Republic is confronting." Like Rafsanjani, Khamenei was not afraid to threaten the United States and its allies. "Of course," he proclaimed, "if someone has hostile intentions or has perpetrated evil deeds, then the Islamic Republic will not take into consideration anyone's desire before dealing a blow to them. It will not have any doubts about doing so either." After he said that, a crowd began chanting, "God is great, Khamenei is our leader, death to opponents of the guardianship of the supreme jurisconsult, death to America, death to Britain, death to [Iranian opposition group] Monafeqin and Saddam, death to Israel."

Khamenei also said that foreign nations, like Russia, wanted to build power stations for Iran and supply the fuel for the stations. But, he said, "The Islamic Republic does not want this." The ayatollah said that the ability to make fuel for the Bushehr facility was "an important, complicated, very sensitive process" that "will have a great impact on the country's scientific and technology sector."

It was clear why the Iranians didn't want help constructing power plants, which would be used for civilian purposes: Official denials notwithstanding, they understood that fuel production for nuclear reactors can be used to build nuclear weapons. And they wanted to conduct their nuclear program in secret.

Confirmation of U.S. government worries about Iranian duplicity arrived in March 2004. And according to senior U.S. officials, the CIA was caught off-guard a second time. A foreign intelligence service that officials declined to identify obtained new information indicating that Tehran had established a special panel in late 2003 that had the task of deceiving the IAEA—*after* the agency discovered the covert Iranian nuclear program.

A Bush administration national security official familiar with the foreign report said that the concealment committee helped hide almost three hundred Iranian nuclear facilities around the country, including those working on the centrifuge cascade. The panel was made up of officials of the Atomic Energy Organization of Iran.

An analysis of the foreign intelligence report, first disclosed by the *Los Angeles Times* and confirmed by U.S. officials, stated that the committee was examining all uranium-conversion facilities, centrifuge component manufacturing plants, and other secret installations to identify whether they were properly concealed. The Iranians wanted to ensure that international inspectors did not discover their nuclear facilities.

The IAEA learned of the existence of the concealment committee in late 2003 but the U.S. government was not informed about it until months later, officials told me.

The disclosures strengthened the U.S. government's conviction that Iran was bent on building nuclear arms and deceiving the international watchdog agency about its programs.

Representatives of thirty-five nations on the IAEA Board of Governors condemned Iran for withholding nuclear information from inspectors. A resolution that was passed March 13, 2004, stated that Iran had failed to account fully for its nuclear equipment, including the following:

- "A more advanced centrifuge design than previously declared, including associated research, manufacturing and testing activities."
- "Two mass spectrometers used in the laser enrichment program."
- "Designs for the construction of hot cells at the Arak heavy water research reactor [that] may point to nuclear activities not so far acknowledged by Iran."

The IAEA also said that Iran had failed to fully explain the sources of highly enriched uranium and the work on the advanced centrifuge design, the planned heavy-water reactor, and experiments carried out with polonium-210, a radioactive metallic substance that can trigger a nuclear blast.

The IAEA noted that the Iranian program shared "several common elements" with Libya's nuclear program, "including technology largely obtained from the same foreign sources." We will learn more about Libya's covert nuclear program in Chapter 7.

In a confidential report disclosed to the public in June 2004, the IAEA stated that Iran had failed to report to the agency its "possession of P-2 centrifuge design drawings and to associated research, manufacturing, and mechanical testing activities." The report revealed that

Iran's government had lied in an earlier statement when it claimed not to have received special ring magnets used in centrifuge rotors: "Iran has now acknowledged that, contrary to these earlier statements, it had imported some magnets relevant to P-2 centrifuges from Asian suppliers, and that the composite rotors that had been manufactured in Iran had in fact been fabricated in another workshop situated on a DIO [Defense Industries Organization] site."

The IAEA report indicated that Iran was lying to international inspectors about other nuclear weapons activities. When asked to explain the presence of highly enriched uranium on imported equipment, the Iranians had claimed that the highly enriched uranium had leaked from bottles of stored uranium hexafluoride gas. But the IAEA deemed that explanation "not credible." The traces of highly enriched uranium were found in two Iranian facilities, and "the fact that virtually no other particles similar to this group have been identified on imported centrifuge components suggests that . . . [the highly enriched uranium] was introduced in the room and the balancing machine in some other manner," the report said.

Worse, the IAEA suggested that the Iranians continued to operate covert nuclear facilities. The problem was that the agency could inspect only "those sites that have been identified by Iran." the report said. The IAEA questioned the value of "intensive verification at these sites, given that the Agency cannot provide any assurance about the possibility of component production elsewhere in the country."

By April 2004, Iran had built 855 centrifuges and was nearly finished with another 285, the report noted. The IAEA believed that the Iranian centrifuge cascade was to have between 2,000 and 4,000 machines, based on Iran's inquiries to a European manufacturer to buy 4,000 ring magnets. Two magnets are used in each of the machines' high-speed rotors. A U.S. official, meanwhile, said the Iranians were interested in "tens of thousands" of centrifuge parts.

The IAEA report showed that the Iranians were working to make highly enriched uranium on a large scale, and that it was intended for nuclear weapons. State Department spokesman Richard Boucher declined to comment on the IAEA report, noting that "circulation of the report is restricted to [IAEA] delegations and it's not a matter of public record, so I can't discuss it in any detail." But he noted that "Tehran has repeatedly failed to declare significant and troubling aspects of its nuclear program. It has interfered with and suspended inspections. It has failed to cooperate with the International Atomic Energy Agency in resolving outstanding issues related to its nuclear program."

SERIAL PROLIFERATORS

Ayatollah Khamenei's comment that Iran did not want help building nuclear power plants didn't mean that the Iranians were averse to getting any sort of nuclear aid from other countries. Quite the contrary. As the CIA acknowledged even in the report to Congress it made public in 2003, Iran has received missile goods and other material for weapons of mass destruction from a number of countries, most notably China, Russia, and North Korea. Intelligence reports indicated that weapons transfers were occurring as late as the spring of 2003, and they began many years earlier.

Intelligence reports first noted China's collaboration with the Iranians in the early 1990s. According to intelligence officials, China delivered a shipment of about fifty short-range ballistic missiles to the Iranian port of Bandar Abbas in May 1990, then sent another shipment of missiles in December. In October 1991, U.S. intelligence discovered that the China Nuclear Energy Industry Corporation was building a nuclear reactor in western Iran in collaboration with the Iranian nuclear energy ministry. In what would become a pattern, Iran denied that it was seeking nuclear weapons after this author disclosed reports of the cooperation in the pages of the *Washington Times.*

The North Koreans were arming Iran during that same period. In January 1991, an Iranian Boeing 747 cargo jet was spotted leaving North Korea with a shipment of Scud missiles (a 747 can fit up to six Scuds). Intelligence confirmed that the missiles reached Iran. In July 1992, more Iranian 747 flights were detected leaving the airfield at Sunan, North Korea, carrying Scud missiles to Iran. According to intelligence officials, the Iranians chose the 747 route because they believed that they would run less risk of interdiction or sabotage than they would by sending the missiles by ship.

Still, the Iranians did use ships to transfer Scuds from North

Korea. In 1992, intelligence detected multiple shipments of Scud missiles from North Korea to Iran. For instance, in January, intelligence picked up on the delivery of at least twenty Scud-C missiles from North Korea to Iran, and in the summer of 1991, a North Korean freighter named the *Mupo* carried eight more Scud-Cs to Iran. A third Scud shipment occurred in September.

Kazakhstan was also lending a hand. In November 1994, the Pentagon disclosed a secret Iranian program to buy more than 1,320 pounds of highly enriched uranium from the former Soviet republic in Central Asia. A covert Defense Department project prevented Iran from purchasing the fuel, but if the deal had gone through, the Iranians could have used the uranium to make as many as twenty nuclear bombs. Two months earlier, factory officials reported that a group of Iranians had visited the Ulba Metallurgy Plant at Ust-Kamenogorsk, in Kazakhstan's northeastern corner.

Meanwhile, Russia did much to boost Iran's nuclear capability with its nuclear deal in 1995. The deal called for Moscow to build two reactors at Bushehr. William Perry, the U.S. defense secretary at the time, said of his meeting with Russian officials, "I expressed my deep concern about Russia selling nuclear reactors to Iran because I was fearful that this would fuel Iran's ambition of becoming a nuclear weapons state, and that would be a threat to all its neighbors, including Russia. The Russian government did not agree to change their decision to proceed with that sale."

Russia supplied more than weapons material. In September 1995, U.S. intelligence agencies discovered that Russia's Foreign Intelligence Service had forged new ties with the Iranian secret police. In July, Iran's intelligence minister, Ali Fallahiyan, and the head of Russia's SVR spy service, Yevgeni Primakov, had hammered out the agreement, and in August, the Russians began training Iranian agents in modern spying, according to U.S. intelligence officials.

This relationship was deeply troubling because Iran's Ministry of Intelligence and Security is one of the world's most dangerous spy agencies. The Iranian spy service has been involved in terrorist activity for decades. For instance, it has backed the terrorist group Hezbollah, which has killed hundreds of Americans over the years, going back to

the 1983 bombing of the Marine barracks in Lebanon that killed 241 Marines. Additionally, Iranian intelligence operatives specialize in acquiring embargoed technology that can be used in weapons programs. U.S. intelligence agencies also concluded that the Russians compromised sensitive U.S. intelligence as part of their partnership with Iran. The United States had provided Moscow with intelligence about Iran's nuclear weapons program to try to convince the Russians not to sell the Bushehr reactors, but according to U.S. intelligence, Moscow relayed that information to the Iranians.

Foreign governments continued to help Tehran with its nuclear program through the late 1990s. A top-secret intelligence report that I obtained in mid-April 1996 reported that that week, a Chinese delegation of technicians was set to arrive in Tehran to build a new uranium facility for nuclear weapons. "The plant will produce uranium products that Iran can use to make fissile material for nuclear weapons," the report said. The deal for the Chinese facility had been under negotiation for five years, and according to the report, "The United States has repeatedly encouraged China not to move forward with this project because of its potential contribution to Iran's weapons program."

This plant, near Esfahan, would remain secret to all but those with access to the most sensitive intelligence until Iran's National Council of Resistance disclosed the existence of Iran's nuclear projects in 2002.

The Chinese were, in fact, helping the Iranians with several facilities, according to intelligence reports. The Chinese nuclear technicians who visited Iran in April 1996 were described as an advance team that would begin the detailed design phase for several plants. In March, a team of Iranian nuclear specialists had visited China to study technical documents for the new Iranian facilities.

In the spring of 1997, intelligence agencies exposed Iran's efforts to procure surface-to-air missiles from Kazakhstan. After intelligence reports about the deal were disclosed by this author in the *Washington Times,* U.S. officials pressed the Kazakh government to stop the $90 million missile sale. But even after the United States sent two notes protesting the arms sales, a colonel in the Kazakh army, Oleg Sinkin—whom Kazakh officials had alerted to U.S. objections—continued trying to send the SA-10 missiles to Iran, according to intelligence reports.

The intelligence indicated that others involved in the deal included a former Kazakh defense minister as well as the chief of military intelligence, Zhenis Raspayev, both of whom had a direct financial interest. U.S. intelligence agencies also suspected that Kazakhstan's defense minister at the time, Mukhtar Altynbayev, was part of the missile deal but that he might have backed off because of the U.S. protests. The Chinese government refused permission for Kazakh aircraft carrying the SA-10s to fly over Chinese territory. The Chinese cited concerns that the overflight request would violate the 1944 Chicago Convention on civil air transport, but some Kazakh officials believed that Beijing blocked the shipments to protect its own missile sales to Iran. In any case, other Kazakh missile deals might have gone through.

Kazakhstan was merely picking up on a deal that Moscow arms brokers had not been able to conclude because of pricing differences with Iranian officials. That deal called for selling Iran three SA-10 batteries and thirty-six missiles from components obtained in Russia, Croatia, and Kazakhstan. U.S. officials said that the missiles would have provided Iran with dangerous new capability and would have violated the secret 1995 agreement that Vice President Al Gore struck with Russian Prime Minister Viktor Chernomyrdin to keep Moscow from selling arms to Iran. (Of course, that back-channel deal, which the *Washington Times* exposed in 2000, raised many questions, especially since Gore kept the arrangement secret from Congress.) In April 1997, around the same time that Kazakhstan was trying to finish the SA-10 deal, intelligence reports showed that Moscow was seeking to sell advanced SA-12 missiles and handheld antiaircraft rockets to Iran. It was not known whether the deal went through.

In 1999, Iranian technicians made arrangements to take classes at Moscow State Aviation Technical University. On March 10, Russia shipped 100,000 kilograms of specialty steel to Iran for use in its various weapons programs. The steel could be used in the nuclear centrifuge program or for missiles. In November of that year, U.S. intelligence reported that Russia was building a nuclear fuel-fabrication facility in Iran and that Russia had helped Iran with testing of a special laser used in nuclear fuel fabrication.

China ratcheted up its aid to Iran in 1999. In January, the Penta-

gon's Joint Staff issued a special classified report about the problem, revealing that China had provided Iran with large amounts of material for missiles and nuclear programs. That same month, U.S. intelligence caught China selling Iran zirconium tubes to be used in making nuclear fuel rods. In March, the Iranians sent ten engineers to Beijing University to be trained in missile guidance and development. In July, China shipped Iran upgraded C-801 antiship cruise missiles that were part of an $11 million deal to make Iran's missile forces more powerful. The deal included adapters for the missiles that would permit the Iranians to fire the deadly antiship missiles from helicopters and from catamaran patrol boats. In August, Beijing provided Tehran with specialty steel and components to help Iran begin producing its own missiles. In October, China provided Iranian military personnel with missile training. In November, the U.S. intelligence community discovered that the China Precision Engineering Institute was selling Iran missile guidance and telemetry equipment for testing missiles. In December, the China North Industries Corporation, known as NORINCO, provided Iran with test equipment for missiles, including a U.S.-manufactured gamma dosimeter, which is used to measure radiation. The United States has repeatedly imposed economic sanctions against NORINCO, which is known as a "serial proliferator" of weapons and know-how. Finally, that same month, China sent Iran radiation detection meters that had been made in the United States.

Meanwhile, on November 21, 1999, yet another Iranian 747 flew from North Korea to Iran. The North Korean shipment included a package of twelve rocket engines for medium-range ballistic missiles, to be used on Iran's Shahab-3 missiles—which are copies of North Korean's Nodong medium-range missiles. Despite this and other uses of Iran's 747s to obtain weapons, the Clinton administration waived sanctions on Iran so that Tehran could buy spare parts from Boeing to fix the jets.

In early December 1999, the U.S. National Security Agency (NSA), which is the world's premier electronic intelligence–gathering agency, reported in a highly classified report that technicians and engineers from China and Pakistan were working in Iran's underground nuclear laboratory near Esfahan. The site and the work would remain secret until IAEA inspectors got into the facility four years later. Moreover, in March of 2000, the NSA reported that a delegation of Chinese missile technicians had visited Iran to help with the development of Iran's missile program. On July 20, 2001, the NSA discovered that China had sent electrical components "of U.S. origin" to Iran for missile programs.

By 2001, the pattern was familiar: China, North Korea, and Russia would arm Iran whenever they got the chance. For example, in April 2001, North Korea tried to ship missile goods to Iran but held up the deal because of a dispute with Tehran over payment, according to intelligence officials. China, the same month, delivered a precursor chemical that is useful for making chemical weapons. The Russians, for their part, agreed to set up a new shipping route to Iran across the Caspian Sea, and in November, U.S. intelligence caught the Russian state arms exporter, Rosoboronexport, selling Iran advanced electronic warfare systems specifically designed to defeat U.S. airborne warning and control system aircraft (AWACS).

But a new culprit emerged at the end of 2001. In December, U.S. intelligence discovered that Ukraine was sending missile goods and material to Iran.

After that, Iran seemed to go back to its favorite trading partners. According to intelligence reports, in 2002 China shipped the Iranians naval antiship missiles for patrol boats, sent a delegation to train the Iranians in how to operate the C-14 catamarans that it had sold the Iranian navy, supplied additional nuclear weapons–related components, and sent six guided missile patrol boats, including two Hodong fast patrol boats. North Korea sent Iran some fifteen patrol boats and semisubmersibles, which sail just below the water's surface and are used by special forces commandos. U.S. intelligence tracked the shipment as it made its way aboard the Iranian merchant ship *Iran Mead* from Nampo, North Korea, all the way to Bandar Abbas, Iran.

Taken together, all of these deals painted a picture of a rogue regime that was taking whatever steps necessary to make itself more deadly, whether through nuclear, chemical, or conventional weapons. They also revealed how numerous foreign governments flout international law time and again to make a tidy profit. But none of this information made its way into the semiannual reports that the CIA makes to Congress on arms transfer. The American people remained in the dark about the North Korean threat.

A NEVER-ENDING STORY

Iran, having greatly improved its weapons capabilities by working closely with serial proliferators, is extremely dangerous. The nuclear threat, which the CIA's late-2003 report to Congress gave only passing mention to ("Commercial imagery showed that Iran was burying the enrichment facility presumably to hide it and harden it against military attack"), is most frightening. But Iran's other capabilities are troubling, as well.

The CIA noted in 2003 that Iran has become nearly self-sufficient in the production of ballistic missiles, thanks to all the missile-related cooperation it has received over the years from Russia, North Korea, China, and others. According to the CIA, Iran's ballistic missile inventory is among the largest in the Middle East and includes about a dozen Shahab-3 medium-range (826-mile) ballistic missiles and several hundred short-range ballistic missiles—including the Shahab-1 (Scud-B), Shahab-2 (Scud-C), and Tondar-69 (a derivative of the Chinese CSS-8), along with a variety of large unguided rockets.

Probably spurred on by the U.S. operation in Iraq, the Iranians announced in 2003 that they had begun deployment and production of the Shahab-3 and a new solid-fuel short-range missile known as the Fatah-110. The Iranians also announced they were planning longer-range versions of the Shahab-3. A long-range Shahab-4 missile was initially announced as Tehran's answer to an intercontinental ballistic missile. But later the Iranian government backed off and said that the missile was really a space launcher—a tactic intended to avert criticism of its missile forces. The CIA noted that it believes "Iran is also pursuing longer-range ballistic missiles" than the Shahab-3.

Iran also is building chemical weapons even though it is a signatory of the Chemical Weapons Convention, which bars offensive poison weapons. According to the CIA, "Iran likely has already stockpiled blister, blood, choking, and probably nerve agents—and the bombs and artillery shells to deliver them—which it previously had manufactured." It should come as no surprise by now that China provided critical support for Tehran's chemical weapons program.

Another ominous sign is intelligence reports that Iran is working to field deadly biological weapons—in violation of Tehran's commitments under the Biological Weapons Convention. The CIA believes that Iran has an offensive biological arms program, and its weapons buyers continue to seek dual-use biotechnical materials, equipment, and expertise. The goods can be used for medical and pharmaceutical development but also will feed Iran's military biological arms program. "It is likely that Iran has capabilities to produce small quantities of [biological warfare] agents, but has a limited ability to weaponize them," the CIA said in its 2003 report to Congress.

Iran's drive for advanced conventional arms also continues. Its main suppliers remain Russia, China, and North Korea.

Given that Iran's radical Islamic regime is continually ramping up its capabilities, we can only hope that efforts to bring a democratic system to Iran prevail. One bright spot is Hossein Khomeini, the grandson of Iran's Islamic Republic founder, Ayatollah Ruholla Khomeini. Hossein moved to Iraq after becoming disillusioned with the regime, which had sent assassins from the Ministry of Intelligence and Security to murder his uncle. Hossein Khomeini has turned on Tehran, telling one Arabic newspaper that he advocates a "democratic system that does not use religion as a tool to repress the people and suffocate society." He argues that the rulers in Iran are exploiting his grandfather's name as well as the name of Islam to "continue their unjust rule" and perpetuate "the worst dictatorship in the world." Hossein believes the popular opposition to the clerics' rule in Iran will lead to a revolution in the near future, saying in August 2003, "We will witness the great event soon."

But until that "great event" comes, Iran will continue to hoard the world's most dangerous weapons, making it an ever more potent threat to the United States and our friends around the world.

CHINA: LIES AND DECEPTION

CHAPTER 6

IN THE FALL OF 2001, AS THE AMERICAN PEOPLE WERE reeling from the deadly al Qaeda terrorist attacks of September 11, U.S. intelligence discovered that the People's Republic of China was aiding the Islamist militia that was harboring terrorists from Osama bin Laden's network. The National Security Agency (NSA), the secret electronic spying agency whose specialty is picking sensitive communications literally out of thin air, revealed in September that two Chinese telecommunications companies were helping Afghanistan's ruling Taliban build a major telephone system in Kabul, the Afghan capital.

In short, Communist China was supporting a radical regime that had carried out a reign of terror against Afghan civilians since it came to power in 1996. In one four-day massacre in January 2001, Taliban forces killed about three hundred people, including a group of seventy-three women, children, and elderly men who had been hiding in a mosque. Worse, the Taliban armed and trained foreign terrorists. By the time of the U.S.-led campaign to oust the Taliban, U.S. intelligence agencies had identified at least twenty-three terrorist training camps in Afghanistan. Bin Laden and his al Qaeda network used a total of fifty-five facilities in Afghanistan, which became the central training ground for this shadowy terrorist group.

But for the Chinese, the Taliban was merely another customer.

And they offer their clients far more than telephone systems. Communist China is today one of the most dangerous suppliers of advanced conventional arms, dual-use products, and materials for weapons of mass destruction. Almost all Chinese arms merchants are government or military officials, but officially the Beijing government denies any role in proliferation. Still, China shows no sign of curtailing its illicit-arms trading.

Why would the Chinese be so willing to aid groups like Afghanistan's Taliban, Saddam Hussein's Iraqi dictatorship, and Iran's radical Islamist clerical regime? Several years ago, when I asked a Chinese military official why his country sold missiles and other high-technology weapons with little or no regard for who the buyer was, the official answered, with a look of incredulity, "Why, for money, of course."

BIN LADEN AND CHINA

When pressed about reports of the Afghanistan telephone contract, China did what virtually every other proliferator does when confronted: It dismissed the reports as unfounded rumors, as lies put out by its enemies. Chinese government officials feigned ignorance about the activities of the supposedly private companies implicated in the reports. The two companies, Huawei Technologies and Zhongxing Telecom, were major Chinese companies. Zhongxing had done similar work outside of Afghanistan, including for hard-line Serbian leader Slobodan Milosevic. Huawei had been founded by at least one official of the Chinese People's Liberation Army and had helped build communications networks for the Chinese military.

On September 18, 2001, Chinese Foreign Ministry spokesman Zhu Bangzao told reporters in Beijing that China's contacts with the Taliban were limited to "working level" contacts. "China does not have any kind of formal relations with the Taliban," he said. But intelligence reports revealed that the Chinese were lying. On September 11, the day of the terrorist attacks, a group of Chinese government officials was in Kabul and concluded an agreement with the Taliban covering economic and technical assistance. This was just one of many agreements the Chinese reached with the Taliban. For example, according to U.S. intelligence officials, in December 1998 China had concluded another

agreement with the Afghan regime after the Taliban had provided Beijing with an intelligence windfall: unexploded Tomahawk land-attack cruise missiles that U.S. forces had launched during the Clinton administration's weak attempt to blow up al Qaeda terrorist camps following the August 1998 bombings of U.S. embassies in Kenya and Tanzania.

Chinese government officials vehemently deny their connections to terrorism. But bin Laden himself announced in August 2001 that there should be "good relations" between Taliban-ruled Afghanistan and China. The terrorist leader urged China to help the Taliban as a way of reducing U.S. military and economic influence in Asia—something that Beijing is keen to see happen. (One sure sign that China views America as hostile came in early October 2001, just prior to the U.S. military action in Afghanistan, when the Chinese moved their military forces to the western border region to prepare for a possible U.S. invasion of China, something no American military planner was even close to contemplating.)

China's cooperation with the al Qaeda terrorist network was not all indirect. Intelligence reports obtained by the Pentagon in December 2001 revealed that China had supplied arms to al Qaeda *after* the September 11 terrorist attacks on America. Just a week after the attacks, the ruling Taliban and the al Qaeda fighters embedded among them took delivery of a shipment of Chinese-made surface-to-air missiles known as HN-5s, which was China's designation for the Soviet-design SA-7 missiles. So much for the Chinese government's claims to be cooperating with the United States in the global war on terrorism. In reality, the Chinese were and are playing a double game of pretending to support U.S. goals while covertly undermining U.S. objectives in the war on terrorism and on other issues as well.

In December 2001, after toppling the Taliban, U.S. forces found large quantities of Chinese-made weapons in Afghanistan, including rocket launchers and rocket-propelled grenades. Intelligence officials believed that the Chinese arms had been smuggled into Afghanistan from western China, but U.S. government officials seemed to go out of their way to defend China's arms sales. "These are not necessarily from the Chinese government," one official said. "I'm not sure the Chinese are very comfortable with having that kind of terrorism on their border.

But this could have been from people just selling weapons to make money." The Chinese arms might also have come from Pakistan, which had close ties to the Taliban and Beijing.

Chinese weapons kept turning up in Afghanistan. In May 2002, U.S. Army Special Forces discovered thirty HN-5 missiles. One Taliban commander publicly praised China for its assistance to the Taliban, telling an Urdu-language newspaper in Pakistan that the Taliban had close relations with China. The commander, Maulvi Jalaluddin Haqqani, said, "China is also extending support and cooperation to the Taliban government, but the shape of this cooperation cannot be disclosed."

More intelligence surfaced to reveal the "shape of this cooperation." In June 2002, classified Defense Intelligence Agency reports disclosed that China's military had provided training for the Taliban and al Qaeda. An anti-Taliban Afghan revealed the connection between the Chinese military and al Qaeda, saying that it took place before September 11 and that Pakistan's spy agency, the Inter-Services Intelligence Directorate, known as ISI, had helped coordinate matters. U.S. intelligence analysts could only speculate on why China provided military training to Islamic radicals. One argument was that it continued the Marxist-Leninist policy of backing the enemies of the world's sole superpower, the United States. It also may have been part of a Chinese effort to gain some influence over the Taliban and al Qaeda. Another theory was that the Chinese used the military training to identify some of the thousands of Uighurs, Muslims in China's western Xinjiang province, who were working with al Qaeda.

As to be expected, Beijing dismissed reports of Chinese cooperation with the Taliban as fabrications.

ENDANGERING AMERICAN PILOTS

China supported not only the terrorists in Afghanistan but also America's next opponent in the war on terror, the bloody regime of Saddam Hussein. As in Afghanistan, Huawei Technologies played a key role in Iraq. Starting in 1999, the company was deeply involved in violating United Nations sanctions against Iraq.

In May 1999, working through the United Nations oil-for-food

program, Huawei asked the UN for permission to sell Iraq a fiber-optic communications system, the state-of-the-art technology that uses light beams to carry large amounts of communications and data, along with fiber-optic cable. The UN declared the sale of the communications system "null/void," ruling that it did not involve humanitarian goods and thus was outside the scope of the program. But the United Nations permitted the sale of fiber-optic cable, according to UN records.

Huawei then made a second request to sell communications equipment, but the UN denied the Chinese again. So the company ignored the world body and transferred the equipment anyway.

Several months later, the NSA learned that Chinese telecommunications technicians were working in Iraq. Satellite photography also showed construction of a fiber-optic communications network at five locations around Baghdad, all radar and control centers. The new network included Russian-made Tall King and Volex early-warning radar. It was clear to U.S. intelligence analysts who saw the information that the Iraqis were working to integrate their air defenses—that is, to link them together so that sensor data from one part could be relayed to another part. The integration would allow the Iraqis to use radars located in one part of the country to identify, track, and shoot down U.S. aircraft from a missile battery in another part. Saddam had developed a system that would allow him to shoot down U.S. and allied aircraft patrolling the UN-mandated no-fly zone. And he had done it with Chinese technology.

As in other deals, the Chinese used the cover of a commercial transaction with apparently peaceful purposes to build a system that had direct military uses.

When informed of the new fiber-optic network in early February 2001, Defense Secretary Donald H. Rumsfeld authorized a major military strike against the five facilities that made up the network. On the afternoon of February 16, twenty-four U.S. Navy and British jets, using laser-guided and radar-guided bombs, severely damaged the five targets, which had nearly been completed.

Publicly, the Bush administration did not point the finger at China, at least initially. Marine Corps Lieutenant General Gregory Newbold, director of operations for the Joint Chiefs of Staff, acknowldriven by the misguided notion that pressuring China would not alter its pro–rogue state and pro-terrorist behavior.

John Shaw, the deputy undersecretary of defense for international echnology security, told me that the Chinese sold Iraq even more oods than did France, all in violation of UN sanctions. "Their inolvement in Iraq, to my mind, is more pervasive than that of the rench," Shaw said.

A report prepared after the Iraq war for Shaw's office stated that hina was the number-two supplier of conventional arms and dual-use ods to Saddam's regime. It identified the fiber-optic network as the ost significant high-technology transfer from China to Saddam's milry. Another key Chinese weapon transferred to the Iraqis was a laser ngefinder, which the Iraqi Republican Guard used for its tank forces.

Shaw told me that the Chinese have tried to work deals with the st-Saddam government as well. "The Chinese have already moved in d tried to cut deals with the minister of communications," he said. "It ws you that by hook or by crook, they're gonna try and get back things in Iraq." For example, in February 2004 a Russian transport ved in Baghdad with a shipment of telephone equipment; intellice officials blocked the deal when they discovered that the seller was hinese firm. Shaw revealed another Chinese attempt to work their into post-Saddam Iraq. Using Arab intermediaries in Kuwait and pt to try to hide their involvement, the Chinese tried to cut a deal in for cellular telephones, according to Shaw.

Arthur Waldron, a China specialist at the University of Pennsyl-, viewed China's aid to Iraq as a sign that Beijing was continuing to itself "with the most backward and repressive regimes in the ." Waldron said, "We see an increasing pattern, in which the Chialign themselves with states like North Korea, Iran, Syria, and ' He blamed China's Communist dictatorship for supporting states. "The dictatorship needs external enemies and is exaggeratars that foreigners are going to come in and subvert China," he

Valdron was right. Afghanistan and Iraq are just two of Amernemies that China has helped. Large numbers of classified U.S. ence reports present more details and expose Beijing's continu-

edged the threat the Iraqi air defenses had posed to U.S. aircraft, calling the air strike "essentially a self-defense measure." But he never identified China by name, saying only that some of the radars had come from "a particular country" but then carefully adding, "They can come from a variety of sources." It was the closest the Pentagon would come to publicly identifying the Chinese as a supplier to the Iraqi military.

Privately, however, Rumsfeld was angry at the Chinese, according to aides to the secretary. He knew what U.S. intelligence had uncovered. A senior defense official confirmed what Newbold had been unwilling to say, telling me that the Chinese had been helping Iraq "construct a fiber-optic connection network to better integrate the air-defense system of Iraq. These are largely buried fiber-optic cables that would protect them from a variety of things like weather—or coalition air attacks."

When reports of this military assistance got out, President George W. Bush admitted that the reports were disturbing. "We're concerned about the Chinese presence in Iraq, and my administration is sending the appropriate response to the Chinese," he told reporters. "Yes, it's troubling that they'd be involved in helping Iraq develop a system that will endanger our pilots."

To respond, China again relied on lies and deception. "This is a rumor, an excuse for the U.S. and British bombing of Iraq," said Shen Guofang, China's deputy representative to the United Nations. "China does not have any military or civilians working in Iraq."

The statement was another official lie. Huawei had maintained an office in Iraq, and Iraqi officials visited Huawei's offices in southern China and placed orders from 2000 to 2001.

China's foreign minister, Tang Jiaxuan, denied that Chinese companies were working on the Iraqi air-defense grid. Like Shen Guofang, he accused the United States of fabricating the fiber-optic case to justify bombing raids in Iraq.

During a Senate Foreign Relations Committee hearing in March 2001, Secretary of State Colin Powell contradicted China's public denials, saying that Beijing had privately acknowledged that Chinese firms were working on the fiber-optic network in Iraq. "With respect to the fiber-optics case, China has now said that they have told the companies that were in the area doing fiber-optics work to cease and desist," Powell said.

But intelligence reports revealed even those private Chinese assurances to be unreliable. Electronic communications intercepts and spy satellite photographs showed that technicians from the Chinese companies were continuing work *after* Beijing promised that it would force the companies to stop the project. "We're sure [the Chinese companies] are playing a role due to the complementary nature of the intelligence reports," a U.S. official said.

Then in December 2002, under pressure from the UN Security Council, Iraq submitted to the United Nations a 12,000-page dossier that was supposed to be a full and complete declaration of its banned arms programs. As part of the declaration, Iraq supplied detailed information on the foreign companies that helped. Among the more than 150 foreign companies were three Chinese firms. To the surprise of few in the U.S. government, Huawei was one of the three. According to officials who viewed the classified report, the Iraqis confirmed that Huawei had supplied the fiber-optics and communications-switching equipment for the Iraqi air-defense network.

Huawei spokesmen denied that the company was involved in any Iraqi military projects. The most the company would say was that in 1999 it had bid on two civilian telecommunications projects in Iraq and that the United Nations had eventually approved one.

In late 2003, another account emerged to contradict Chinese denials. The London *Sunday Telegraph* cited an Iraqi military officer who reported that Saddam's military had purchased Chinese air-defense equipment and used it against U.S. and British air strikes. The officer, identified only as Lieutenant Colonel al-Dabbagh, a former air-defense unit commander, said he had worked with a number of Chinese air-defense specialists in 2002 and the early part of 2003. Al-Dabbagh recounted how Chinese military officers had played a pivotal role in supporting Iraqi military forces in the months leading up to the conflict of 2003. "They [Chinese advisers] arrived in the spring of 2002," he said. "They were personally greeted by Saddam. A couple of them grew mustaches and wore keffiyehs [Arab scarves] around their heads so that they would look more like us."

The Chinese military support was part of a secret a
between Iraq and China that was concluded in 2001—in
United Nations sanctions. According to the former Iraqi
Chinese developed a high-technology decoy device that div
bombs dropped by U.S. and allied warplanes, forcing them
targets. "The Chinese devices only cost $25, but were ver
he said.

Predictably, the Chinese government denied the lieute
claims. "The report is groundless and irresponsible," said
eign Ministry spokesman Liu Jianchao, who insisted t
followed UN resolutions on Iraq. "The Chinese side has
tacts in any form with the Saddam [Hussein] governmen
field since 1990, when the Gulf crisis broke out."

That simply wasn't true. China's military assistanc
tensive, going beyond what Huawei provided with the
work. The two other Chinese firms that the Iraqis i
2002 United Nations dossier, China State Missile C
China Wanbao Engineering Company, assisted Sadd
his weapons program. The missile firm helped Sadda
range missile program, and the second firm was in
chemical, and conventional arms technology trans
U.S. officials. Even more details of the Chinese conn
arms program emerged in April 2003, when U.S. m
large numbers of Iraqi intelligence files shortly aft
dad. As of this writing, however, the CIA was ke
procurement network secret, reportedly to avoid o
countries, including China and Russia and other
nations.

The intelligence that was available by 2004 c
dent Bush had said in early 2001, that sanctions th
put in place against Iraq after the 1991 Persian G
tive. "A lot of goods are heading into Iraq that
[go]," Bush said at the time. Indeed, most goverr
Nations, seemed to ignore China's active sup
rogue states, preferring to accept Beijing's im
Even within the U.S. government, some pro-C

ing pattern of lies and deception. The intelligence reports, obtained by this author from U.S. officials, expose China's covert assistance to such rogue states as Iran, Syria, Libya, and Cuba—all pariah states that the U.S. government lists as supporters of international terrorism.

NUCLEAR, CHEMICAL, AND BIOLOGICAL TERROR

As seen in the previous chapter, Iran has benefited from China's military support for years. Just as it did with Iraq, Beijing helped Iran build its air defenses. In October 2001, the same month that U.S. military operations began in Afghanistan, U.S. intelligence agencies detected Chinese technicians working on an advanced radar system near Iran's border with Afghanistan. Intelligence officials identified the radar system as the JY-14, critical components of which the China National Electronics Import-Export Corporation had sold to Iran, according to an October 1996 CIA report, "Arms Transfers to State Sponsors of Terrorism." The JY-14, a sophisticated radar that forms part of an automated air-defense system, can track up to one hundred targets simultaneously and feed the data to missile-interceptor batteries. It can identify targets flying as high as 75,000 feet and as far away as 186 miles.

As in other cases of Chinese arms proliferation to terrorist-supporting states, Bush administration intelligence and national security officials played down the China-Iran radar work. One official claimed that the Chinese had been helping the Iranians with the JY-14 for many years and that therefore it was not a problem. The official also claimed that the cooperation on the JY-14 did not violate arms agreements. It was typical of the spin politics that took root during the Clinton administration, from 1993 to 2001, and continued to be standard procedure for many politicized CIA, State Department, and other national security officials under the Bush administration.

One of the world's most irresponsible weapons proliferators has been the China North Industries Corporation, or NORINCO, which is among China's largest state-run manufacturers. The Iranian regime has been a valued NORINCO customer. In May 2003, the company was slapped with economic sanctions for selling missile-related goods to Iran's Shehid Hemmat Industrial Group, the state-owned defense contractor that builds Iran's short- and medium-range missiles. In October

2002, the company was caught selling Iran specialty steel for its missile programs. Paula DeSutter, an assistant secretary of state for verification and compliance, in testifying before a congressional review commission in July 2003, singled out NORINCO for its proliferation activities and revealed that Beijing was not addressing the problem. DeSutter told the China Joint Security Review Commission, "For some time, we've been alerting the Chinese government to our concerns about the activities of NORINCO. Nevertheless, the Chinese government has taken no action to halt NORINCO's proliferant behavior." In fact, the 2002 transfer of specialty steel took place just two months after Beijing announced, with great public fanfare, that it was initiating a series of new export regulations aimed at curbing missile-technology sales. DeSutter concluded, "In the face of Chinese inaction, therefore, the administration has twice sanctioned NORINCO."

NORINCO will infiltrate virtually any market with its products. The company, which is under the control of the China International Trust & Investment Company (CITIC), is extremely active, buying and selling real estate and manufacturing everything from toys to guns. And they've taken those guns to the United States. NORINCO representatives were arrested in May 1996 attempting to smuggle two thousand AK-47 assault rifles and other weapons into the United States for sale to street gangs in Los Angeles.

Yet NORINCO is not the only problem company in China. The Bush administration concluded in its 2003 annual report to Congress on compliance with arms-control agreements that "Chinese state-owned corporations transferred missile technology to Pakistan, Iran, North Korea, and Libya, and that these transfers were clearly contrary to China's commitments to the U.S." In her congressional testimony, DeSutter said, "At the highest levels, the Chinese government has claimed that it opposes missile proliferation and that it forbids Chinese firms and entities from engaging in transfers that violate its commitments to the United States. Unfortunately, the reality has been quite different." She went on to list China's promises not to export missiles and dangerous goods to nations like Pakistan, showing how in each case the U.S. government proved that the Chinese were lying. Even when the U.S. government identified the Chinese state-run companies involved in the arms sales, Beijing refused to act to halt the transfers.

Occasionally Beijing has been motivated to make a public display of its commitment to curtailing weapons proliferation, but these public displays are empty gestures. The export regulations the Chinese announced in 2002 were just the beginning. In late 2003 China announced that for the first time it would require its state-owned and "private" companies to apply for export licenses on more than six hundred controlled goods and technologies, including nuclear materials, biological products, missiles and missiles parts, and related equipment and technologies. Unfortunately, the Chinese government's list accounted for only about half the products that need to be controlled for export, according to U.S. arms-control officials.

Paula DeSutter also testified about China's irresponsible nuclear sales abroad. She noted, for example, "It's clear that China continues to contribute to the nuclear programs of both Pakistan and Iran." China's nuclear proliferation goes on despite the fact that China's government has signed a number of nuclear nonproliferation agreements. DeSutter reported that Beijing has "structured its membership and involvement in various international nuclear regimes so that they may still 'lawfully' circumvent the basic purpose and intent of these regimes."

In addition, China contributes to the poison gas and chemical weapons programs of a number of rogue states. DeSutter reported that "the U.S. is particularly concerned about the role of Chinese entities" in providing chemical weapons–related technology to Iran. "And the U.S. has imposed sanctions on several Chinese entities for providing material assistance to Iran's [chemical weapons] program," she said. But China has, of course, lied about its biological weapons program. According to DeSutter, the United States became convinced that "despite being a member of the Biological Weapons Convention, China maintains a BW [biological weapons] program in violation of those obligations." China's consistent claims that it has never researched, produced, or possessed biological weapons "are simply not true." China "still retains its BW program," DeSutter said. The State Department official summed up the fears about China's biological weapons: "Given China's failure to enforce its stated nonproliferation goals with respect to missile technology, nuclear related items, and its chemical weapons program, we must be concerned about the possibility of undetected proliferation of dual use or actual elements of a BW program."

DeSutter bluntly and undiplomatically cast China's role as a proliferator in commonsense terms: "On the surface, China's policies appear to tackle nonproliferation issues. China avows that it's opposed to proliferation of [weapons of mass destruction] and their means of delivery. In the last decade or more, China has signed up to an impressive array of commitments. Regrettably, however, China has not delivered on many of these promises." Why hasn't Beijing curbed its weapons and missile exports? DeSutter suggested that this failure reflected the Chinese government's "inability" to fight proliferation, or perhaps its simple "unwillingness" to stop arms exports. It is obvious that the latter is more accurate.

DeSutter's testimony was eye-opening, but the major newspapers and television networks nevertheless ignored the congressional hearing. This was not unusual. Nothing about China's weapons transfers has been the subject of in-depth news reports for either television or print. The media silence can be attributed to the influence that Beijing wields with news organizations anxious to keep reporters based in China from being expelled. Using this influence, the Chinese government has been able to block stories that it perceives as negative toward China, and that includes reports about Chinese arms transfers.

But the mainstream media are not alone in almost completely ignoring the terrible problem of weapons proliferation. The Bush administration's approach to Chinese arms transfers has been an utter failure. Limiting its antiproliferation approach to economic sanctions that generally prevent Chinese companies from doing business with the U.S. government, the administration does not do much to curtail arms transfers, since many Chinese companies do not seek government contracts in the first place. Moreover, by focusing on the notion of "dialogue" with Chinese leaders, the U.S. government never gets anything from Beijing but the same vehement denials. Each time the United States brings up Chinese arms deals, Chinese officials demand to see more intelligence information backing up the charges. As DeSutter noted, however, the United States makes its determinations on sanctions "based on rock-solid evidence."

The problem was even worse under President Bill Clinton, and in fact the Clinton administration created a number of obstacles for George W. Bush's administration. Under Clinton, the U.S. government treated China as a normal, friendly nation instead of as the Communist dictatorship it is, and as a result it compromised a great deal of intelligence to the Chinese. Moreover, President Clinton severely degraded the U.S. intelligence community's ability to monitor deadly arms transfers. One senior U.S. official told me that the damage has been severe and long-lasting. "We just simply do not have the resources to be able to track these things," the official said.

"SELLING EVERYTHING TO EVERYONE"

The problem of Chinese proliferation, while posing a clear and present danger to the United States and its allies, is nothing new. China began spreading dangerous weapons technologies and equipment back in the 1960s. Robert Einhorn, a State Department arms proliferation specialist during the Clinton administration, said that "China has come a long way since the 1960s, when its declared policy was to support nuclear proliferation as a way of breaking the hegemony of the nuclear superpowers." The Chinese may have become more sophisticated in their public proclamations and strategies, and more adept at denial and deception, but they are still arming some of the worst of the world's tyrants and terrorists.

Few in public life have had the courage to challenge the Chinese on their double game. One who did was former senator Jesse Helms, a North Carolina Republican who as chairman of the Senate Foreign Relations Committee struck fear into U.S. government bureaucrats in both Republican and Democratic administrations. In July 2001, as he neared the end of his Senate career, Helms produced a devastating report on Chinese arms duplicity. The report on China's broken promises clearly indicated that China had not abandoned its strategic goal of weakening the world powers by covertly spreading deadly arms.

In releasing the report, Helms stated, "During the past twenty years, the People's Republic of China (PRC) has made fifteen formal nonproliferation pledges—seven related to the proliferation of nuclear technology, six regarding the transfer of missile technology, and two commitments undertaken at the time the PRC joined the Biological Weapons Convention in 1997. None of these pledges has been honored."

Using public and internal reports, Helms documented how China "repeatedly and massively" violated its promises to curtail arms sales and emerged as "an increasingly aggressive proliferator." Helms's staff produced a chart showing the time line of Chinese broken promises and violations that had undermined U.S. national security. The chart (see box) shows Chinese weapons sales from 1981 to 2001, including nuclear weapons goods sold to Pakistan and Iran as well as ballistic missile transfers to Pakistan, Iraq, Syria, Iran, Libya, and North Korea.

For years, this list of China's support for rogue states and unstable regions has been kept from the public, in an apparent effort to avoid offending Beijing. The classified record helps to fill in many of the blanks in China's record of proliferation.

One of the most egregious deals was China's 1995 transfer of nuclear materials to Pakistan. The Chinese exported five thousand specialized ring magnets that became the backbone of a centrifuge network that helped Islamabad produce highly enriched uranium. The Pakistanis would share the centrifuge-based enrichment technology with Libya, Iran, and North Korea.

Beijing's shipment of some fifty short-range missiles to Iran in the spring of 1990 marked the beginning of an upturn in China's missile transfers. It was the first time that China had delivered missiles to Iran since Defense Secretary Frank Carlucci appealed to Chinese leaders in 1988 to curtail arms shipments. This sale would mark the beginning of China's unrestricted missile and weapon proliferation. As the Defense Intelligence Agency learned, another shipment of short-range missiles followed at the end of the year.

Chinese technicians also were spotted in Libya in 1990 helping construct a major underground facility for the production of chemical weapons and artillery shells. The facility was located in the Libyan desert some 370 miles south of Tripoli. Intelligence analysts estimated that the plant was about two years away from completion. It could not be learned if the plant was completed.

By November 1990, U.S. intelligence agencies had uncovered evidence that Chinese military advisers were working with Saddam Hussein's forces in Iraq. North Korean advisers also were spotted there.

In January 1991, about a thousand Chinese military technicians were spotted in Saudi Arabia, working under the command of the Saudi military, to maintain the fifty CSS-2 intermediate-range ballistic missiles that Beijing had sold to the kingdom several years earlier. That sale had marked the first time that a missile of that range, 1,550 miles, had ever been transferred. The Chinese had also built a launch control center in the Saudi desert, several hundred miles south of Riyadh, where the two CSS-2 bases were located. Defense intelligence officials suspected that the missiles were nuclear-armed, although nuclear warheads were never detected at or near the desert base. Fueling the suspicions was the appearance of Chinese vans capable of carrying nuclear warheads. Moreover, U.S. officials realized that the CSS-2s were quite inaccurate and concluded that the missiles would be useful for only one thing: delivering nuclear warheads.

A U.S. intelligence report in early 1991 provided disturbing new information on China's support to North Korea. The report said that the Chinese government had helped North Koreans use the island of Macao as a place to train terrorists. One North Korean agent who had been trained in Macao, which was then a Portuguese colony, was Kim Hyun Hee, who in 1988 planted a bomb on Korean Air Lines Flight 858, killing all 115 people on board. Officials familiar with the report disclosed no other details.

In June 1991, a CIA report stated that China and North Korea had shipped missile components to Syria. The agency believed that the parts and equipment were for Scud missiles, or possibly CSS-6 or CSS-7 short-range missiles.

On December 10, 1991, the CIA identified Chinese aircraft shipments of missile equipment to Saudi Arabia. The shipments were believed to be related to the CSS-2 missiles. The agency noted that China was also shipping missile-related goods to Iran. Two months later, in February 1992, the CIA discovered that Chinese missile manufacturers had sold Iran missile guidance equipment. That same month, intelligence intercepts showed that China's NORINCO had concluded a $200 million deal with Libya to provide materials used in making solid pro-

CHINA'S BROKEN PROMISES

CHINA PROMISES

1984 • Pledges not to "help other countries develop nuclear weapons."

1989 • Concludes an agreement for safeguards with the International Atomic Energy Agency.

• Assures that it has no plans to sell any medium-range missile to any Middle East country except for a few missiles to Saudi Arabia.

1992 • Pledges not to proliferate nuclear weapons technology.

• Joins the Nuclear Nonproliferation Treaty.

1994 • Pledges not to export ground-to-ground missiles featuring controlled technology.

1995 • Pledges not to sell nuclear reactors to Iran.

1998 • Pledges not to "engage in proliferation of nuclear weapons."

• Pledges not to transfer antiship cruise missiles or production technology to Iran.

2000 • Pledges not to assist, in any way, any country in the development of ballistic missiles that can be used to deliver nuclear weapons.

CHINA ACTION

1985 • Signs a secret protocol for nuclear cooperation with Iran.

• Sells tritium, useful for triggering nuclear weapons, to Pakistan.

1987 • Assists Iraq in manufacturing nuclear-enrichment components.

1988 • Agrees to build a nuclear reactor in Pakistan.

1990 • Transfers M-II missiles and components to Pakistan.

• Transfers ballistic missile and nuclear-related chemicals to Iraq.

1991 • Supplies a nuclear reactor and enrichment technology to Iran.

1993 • Transfers a missile fuel precursor to Iraq.

• Agrees to sell two nuclear reactors to Iran.

1995 • Supplies nuclear-enrichment technology to Pakistan.

• Initiates the transfer of an M-11 missile production facility to Pakistan.

• Sells C-802 missiles to Iran.

1996 • Sells missile-related components to Syria.

• Sells specialized steel and aluminum, gyroscopes, accelerometers, and telemetry equipment to Iran.

1997 • China is a "key supplier" of nuclear technology to Iran and is Pakistan's "primary source of nuclear-related equipment and technology," according to a CIA report.

• Supplies chemical weapons technology to Iran.

1999 • Signs a deal to improve Iran's FL-10 antiship cruise missiles.

• Sells missile technology to North Korea.

• Provides testing equipment and training for Libya's missile program.

2000 • Steps up nuclear and missile assistance to Pakistan.

• Supplies ballistic missile–related goods, technology, and expertise to Iran.

2001 • Serves as a conduit for North Korea in sending specialty steel to Egypt, and in acquiring special equipment for missile development.

• Plans to sell missile-related guidance and test equipment to Iraq, and ships specialty metals and chemicals to Iraq for missile production.

• CIA warns of the potential for continued Chinese assistance to Pakistan's missile programs and continued Chinese-Pakistani nuclear contacts.

pellant for missiles. U.S. intelligence officials said that NORINCO and the Libyans included some small arms in the deal to provide cover for the more ominous missile-related exports.

"The PRC is selling everything to everyone" was the way one frustrated government official put it in 1992.

And when the official said "everything," he was including nuclear materials. In March 1992, a classified intelligence report showed that China had helped build the nuclear arsenals of Pakistan and India. The report noted that China had supplied Pakistan with the design for a nuclear bomb in 1978 and later with "several score" bottles of tritium gas, which boosts the yield of nuclear explosions. Intelligence analysts believed that the tritium had helped the Pakistanis double the yield of their nuclear bombs, from 15 kilotons to 30 kilotons. (A kiloton is the equivalent of a thousand tons of TNT.)

In October 1992, the CIA reported that a group of Chinese missile technicians had arrived in Iraq to help the Iraqis develop missiles—this despite the United Nations' strict ban on military cooperation with Iraq, which had recently been defeated in the Persian Gulf War. Once again, China was helping America's enemies with little regard for the consequences, and with the goal of undermining the United States.

By July 1998, China was once again shipping short-range missiles to Iran. A U.S. spy satellite detected the shipment as the missiles were being loaded on a cargo vessel in Shanghai. That same month, the Defense Intelligence Agency reported that China was selling Iran special guidance technology that would enable the Iranian military to make a version of the U.S. Stinger antiaircraft missile. The guidance equipment had originally been made by the U.S. electronics giant Motorola; China had gotten a Stinger from Pakistan's government. Later that year, the CIA reported that China had sent Iran telemetry equipment for testing missiles. The Chinese might also have provided Iran with specialty steel used to make missiles; U.S. intelligence tracked the shipment from Hong Kong and revealed that it was for a customer in the Middle East but did not identify the customer.

Chapter 5 showed how active the Chinese were in 1999 in supporting Iran's clerical regime. Indeed, in January, U.S. intelligence learned that Chinese companies were assisting Iran's nuclear program by selling zirconium tubes. In March, Chinese titanium-stabilized duplex steel, an ultralight, ultrastrong metal, arrived at an Iranian missile-manufacturing facility, and according to the NSA, ten Iranian engineers went to Beijing University to be trained in manufacturing missile guidance components. In April, the NSA, relying on intercepted communications, revealed that a Chinese company was ready to sell Iran chemical weapons protective suits. On June 29, the Defense Intelligence Agency reported that China was selling Iran gyroscopes, accelerometers, and special milling equipment to make missiles and missile components. The next month the Chinese sold the Iranians an upgraded version of the C-801 cruise missile known as the FL-10, and the NSA discovered that China and Iran were negotiating the sale of Chinese specialty steel and components used in missiles. The NSA also picked up signs that China was providing Iran with even more zirconium. On November 19, the NSA reported that a Chinese firm had sold guidance and telemetry equipment for Iran's missile program.

And Iran was just one customer for the Chinese during that busy year. North Korea was another rogue state that benefited from China's hyperactive arms trading in 1999. U.S. intelligence agencies believed that a large amount of special wire that China shipped through Macao ended up at a North Korean missile-manufacturing plant. A March 8 NSA report, based on communications intercepts, said that China had sent the North Koreans specialty steel with applications for missiles. In May, the Chinese began shipping missile components and specialty steel to North Korea; a Chinese ship delivered the last of four shipments of specialty steel in July.

China helped Pakistan in 1999 as well. In April, intelligence reports indicated that China had transferred U.S. missile production equipment to Pakistan for a facility with the nondescript name of the National Development Complex. The equipment included U.S. metalworking presses and a special metal-making furnace. The Chinese disguised the shipment as "Masada Cookware."

It also seemed that the Chinese were working to improve their own weapons capabilities, if only to give them new products to shop on the black market. On October 20, 1999, the NSA reported that China was negotiating with Russia for the purchase of fiber-optic gyroscopes that could be used in missiles. An earlier purchase of Russian gyroscopes had been reexported to North Korea.

According to the NSA, China was using Hong Kong–based front companies to acquire U.S. technology, which it would then reverse-engineer for Chinese military and civilian products. A key target of the front companies was U.S. aerospace technology. The NSA identified the Chinese company, the China Precision Machinery Import-Export Corporation, and the Hong Kong firm, the Autosoft Jitong International Ltd., but domestic intelligence-gathering restrictions prevented the agency from naming the U.S. high-technology firm that the Chinese had targeted. According to the report, however, the U.S. company was "known by NSA to be involved in [China's] Institute of High Energy Physics," which engages in nuclear weapons development.

In late December 1999, China provided Libya with what one U.S. official noted wryly was a "Christmas present." According to the NSA, China sold Libya a hypersonic wind tunnel, which is used in testing missile aerodynamics. The Chinese were helping the Libyans develop the Al-Fatah ballistic missile. In June 2002, the director of the NSA, Lieutenant General Michael Hayden, sent a top-secret report to senior Clinton administration officials revealing that the director of the Al-Fatah missile would visit China later that month. The Libyan made the trip and visited China's University of Aeronautics and Astronautics in Beijing, China's premier training center for missile scientists and technicians, where Libyan missile specialists were being trained. In April 2000, after details of China's aid to Libya's missile program were reported by this author in the *Washington Times,* Secretary of State Madeleine K. Albright told a Senate hearing that the United States had formally protested the China-Libya missile cooperation.

Unfortunately, the protests did nothing, and China kept up its weapons sales. In June 2001, the NSA reported that a Chinese company known as CMEC had provided missile components for Pakistan's Shaheen-1 and Shaheen-2 missiles. In August, the NSA revealed that China had supplied Iran's missile program with electrical components that came from the United States.

In May 2002, the Bush administration slapped sanctions on Chinese companies for selling Iran cruise missile goods and glass-lined equipment that could boost Iran's chemical weapons capabilities. Then in April 2004 the U.S. government again imposed sanctions against companies that were helping Iran's nuclear, biological, or chemical weapons programs, or its ballistic and cruise missile efforts. Of the thirteen companies hit with sanctions, five were Chinese, including three that had been sanctioned earlier: NORINCO, the China Precision Machinery Import-Export Corporation, and Zibo Equipment Plant. (The other sanctioned firms included two in Macedonia, two in Russia, and one each in North Korea, Taiwan, Belarus, and the United Arab Emirates.)

Chinese weapons sales to Iraq would continue to hurt the United States even after the fall of Baghdad to U.S. and allied forces. In late 2003, a young Iraqi boy exposed a group of pro-Saddam Iraqis, including his father, a former Iraqi colonel, that was carrying out attacks on U.S. and allied troops. The boy led U.S. soldiers to an arms cache that included two Chinese rockets, a rocket-propelled grenade, and other weapons. One of the artillery rockets had been doctored so it could be fired from the shoulder. "It was one of the first times we've found Chinese rockets," Army Staff Sergeant Matthew Guetschow told the *Philadelphia Inquirer.* "That's what's been getting the tanks. Every one of those we can get off the streets, the better."

"That's what's been getting the tanks": Sergeant Guetschow neatly summed up the high price we pay for letting other nations arm our enemies.

A VAST NETWORK

One of the most frightening aspects of weapons proliferation is that almost as soon as a nation obtains a weapons capability, it can turn around and supply that capability to someone else. That is, the buyer quickly becomes a seller.

China's proliferation clearly illustrates this uncomfortable truth. The Chinese played a fundamental role in one of the most extensive nuclear networks in recent memory. U.S. intelligence made a major breakthrough in understanding the spread of dangerous weapons when it discovered the extent of Pakistan's covert nuclear supplier network. As we will see in the next chapter, that network helped Libya build nuclear arms. But intelligence officials learned that the nuclear design

information had originated in China, and that the Chinese had supplied it to Pakistan before it ended up in Libya.

The most dramatic evidence of China's links to a much broader proliferation network came in November 2003, when Libya supplied Western officials with a cache of documents. Among the documents was a detailed how-to primer, printed in Chinese, for making a thousand-pound implosion-type nuclear bomb small enough to fit in the warhead of a ballistic missile. (An implosion-based nuclear bomb is one that involves conventional explosives wrapped around fissile material to create a nuclear blast.) According to U.S. government officials who have examined the documents, Libya also received Chinese instructions for making components for the device. The documents revealed that Chinese nuclear weapons experts continued collaborating with Pakistani nuclear scientists for years after first supplying the design information in the early 1970s.

LIBYA AND SYRIA: THE NEW "AXIS OF EVIL"

CHAPTER 7

MUSA KUSA, THE HEAD OF LIBYAN INTELLIGENCE, contacted officials Britain's Foreign Office and the MI6 intelligence service in March 2003. Kusa was a man with blood on his hands. He had been deputy chief of the Libyan spy service when the agency dispatched two agents to blow up Pan Am Flight 103 in December 1988, killing 271 people on board. Yet when Kusa informed the British officials that he had an offer from Libyan dictator Moammar Qadhafi, they heard him out.

Kusa said Libya would agree to rid the country of all nuclear and chemical weapons and materials, along with its longer-range missile delivery systems, if Britain and the United States would help the regime get sanctions removed and normalize relations with the officially designated state sponsor of terrorism.

The CIA, when informed of the offer, was skeptical. "You're talking to the most suspicious organization in the world," said one intelligence official who was closely involved in the talks. Still, a decision was made at the highest levels of both governments—by President George W. Bush and Prime Minister Tony Blair—to pursue the talks. Over the next several months, CIA officers and British diplomatic and intelligence officials held secret meetings with Libyan representatives in London. In May, Qadhafi himself met with U.S. and British officials in Tunisia, and in October, a CIA and MI6 team visited Libya.

A second visit to Libya was planned, but before it could take place, an event occurred that exposed a clandestine network of nuclear suppliers headed by scientist Abdul Qadeer Khan, the father of Pakistan's nuclear weapons program. The event also called into question the Libyans' sincerity in wanting to dismantle their nuclear and chemical arms.

A CIA official said the event was a "breakthrough" in the secret arms talks with Libya.

The breakthrough came as a result of electronic eavesdropping conducted by the supersecret National Security Agency (NSA). Back in 2000, U.S. intelligence agencies had put Khan under clandestine electronic surveillance, and the surveillance soon confirmed U.S. intelligence officials' long-held suspicions that Khan represented a major nuclear proliferation problem. Indeed, the intercepts revealed that Khan's network of companies and contacts stretched from Southeast Asia to Europe.

The intercept that reached NSA headquarters in early October 2003 would have a profound impact on Western efforts to halt the spread of nuclear weapons technology. That intercept involved Khan and a key associate, Buhary Seyed Abu Tahir, a Sri Lankan businessman who, having married a Malaysian in 1998, was a permanent resident of Malaysia. According to U.S. officials, Tahir and his brother owned SMB Group, a company based in the Persian Gulf state of Dubai. Tahir did work with SCOMI Precision Engineering, known as SCOPE, which was a subsidiary of a petroleum services company that produced centrifuge parts for Libya's growing nuclear weapons program. SCOPE had a plant in Shah Alam, Malaysia, about ninety-five miles southeast of the capital of Kuala Lumpur, where it worked on centrifuge components for Qadhafi.

The evidence revealed in this NSA intercept would lead investigators directly to Tahir, who would reveal the extent of his involvement with Khan and the reach of Khan's network. As investigators later concluded, Tahir's company served as a front for numerous black-market deals for nuclear technology; he was a key player in building Libya's nuclear weapons program.

Tahir's first contact with A. Q. Khan occurred in 1985, when Tahir visited Pakistan and won a contract to supply air-conditioning equipment to the Khan Research Laboratory. That would be just the first of many deals he did with Khan, according to investigators. In fact, U.S. officials concluded that he played a critical role in Khan's covert nuclear weapons network, which would sell equipment—specifically centrifuge components—to Libya, Iran, North Korea, and other rogue states. The network cleverly disguised its nuclear parts network by also selling commercial equipment used in oil drilling, water treatment, and other endeavors unrelated to nuclear weapons development.

Investigators reveal that around 1995, Khan asked Tahir to send two containers of centrifuge parts from Dubai to Iran aboard an Iranian merchant ship. Iran paid Tahir and Khan about $3 million for the centrifuge components. The cash was delivered in suitcases to a guesthouse in Dubai that Khan used during his frequent visits to the Gulf.

In 1997, Libyan intelligence agents reportedly contacted Khan and requested help in developing a uranium-enrichment system with centrifuges. Several meetings between Khan and the Libyans were held, including a meeting in Istanbul, Turkey, in 1997. Among those present were Khan, Tahir, and two Libyan arms procurement officials, Mohamad Matuq Mohamad and another man identified only as Karim. The Libyans said they wanted to build a centrifuge and were willing to pay for it, whatever the cost.

Khan, Tahir, and Mohamad met several times from 1998 to 2002—at least once in Dubai and once in Casablanca, Morocco, according to Tahir. In 2001 Khan notified Tahir that Pakistan had sent Libya a shipment of uranium hexafluoride, the gas necessary to produce highly enriched uranium for bombs. By 2001 and 2002, Khan was sending centrifuge components for complete machines aboard Pakistani cargo flights from Pakistan to Libya. Tahir told Malaysian investigators that he believed the centrifuge design had been copied from the P1 model, which Pakistan had adapted from the centrifuge plan stolen from the European conglomerate Urenco.

The Libyans put the centrifuges in their nuclear facility code-named Project Machine Shop 1001. According to Tahir, Libya used middlemen to set up the facility and to obtain equipment for it—for example, a lathe to make centrifuge components and a furnace used to temper the components. Tahir identified one key middleman as Peter Griffin, a British national who was retired and living in France, but whose company, Gulf Technical Industries, was now headed by his son.

Tahir disclosed the names of several other nuclear agents. One agent he named was the late Heinz Mebus, an engineer who helped Khan smuggle centrifuge designs to Iran in 1984 and 1985. Another supplier was Gotthard Lerch, a German who lived in Switzerland and at one time worked for the German company Leybold Heraeus, which produced vacuum technology equipment. Lerch tried to help the Libyans obtain specialty pipes for the Machine Shop 1001 project from South Africa but was unable to conclude the deal, even after Libya paid for the tubes in advance. Tahir also fingered Gunas Jireh, a Turkish national whom Khan had hired to supply aluminum casting and a centrifuge dynamo for the Libyan nuclear program. Another Turk, engineer Selim Alguadis, supplied the Libyan nuclear program with electrical cabinets and power supply voltage regulator equipment.

According to Tahir, some of the most important contributors to the Libyan nuclear program came from one Swiss family, the Tinners. Friedrich Tinner, a Swiss mechanical engineer, had worked covertly with Khan since the 1980s and was able to provide safety valves for centrifuges that had been obtained from European manufacturers. Tinner arranged for the goods to be shipped to Libya by way of Dubai. Meanwhile, Tinner's son Urs worked for Tahir and helped set up the SCOPE factory in Shah Alam in December 2001. Urs was also in charge of setting up Libya's machine shop. At one point he coordinated with his brother Marco, the owner of Switzerland's Traco Company, to import key machines into Libya. Urs procured machines from Britain, France, and Taiwan as well.

In all, the Khan network helped Libya purchase more than a hundred machine tools for the plant. Libya's goal was to produce a cascade of ten thousand centrifuges in order to make highly enriched uranium for nuclear bombs.

In addition to using middlemen, the Libyans made other efforts to hide their nuclear procurement efforts. For example, when purchasing the raw materials for centrifuge components, Libya chose a special grade of aluminum tubes that was not controlled for export and thus would not raise suspicions among intelligence agencies. After Libya purchased 300 metric tons of the tubes from a Singapore-based company that was a subsidiary of the German company Bikar Metalle, Tahir arranged for the tubes to be machined at the SCOPE plant in Malaysia. Between December 2002 and August 2003, Tahir sent the tubes to Libya in four shipments; first the tubes went to Dubai, where a trading company sent them along to Libya.

The Khan network enabled the Libyans to make major nuclear advances, but everything changed on October 4, 2003. On that date, the CIA alerted German and Italian authorities to the fact that the German-flagged ship *BBC China* was bound for Libya with parts for Libya's nuclear program. The vessel had set sail from Dubai to Libya, but it never reached its destination.

The U.S. government contacted the ship's owner, the German company BBC Chartering and Logistic GmbH, and asked for help in blocking the shipment. With assistance from the company, the United States diverted the ship to a port in Italy. A U.S. warship took part in the effort; this is considered the very first action of what has become known as the Proliferation Security Initiative, the Bush administration's program for halting illegal-weapons sales.

When investigators boarded the boat and seized the cargo, they confirmed that the five shipping containers contained parts that could have helped Moammar Qadhafi build nuclear bombs. The containers were filled with wooden boxes bearing the SCOPE logo. All the goods were made of the high-quality aluminum used to make high-speed centrifuges for enriching uranium. Also on board the *BBC China* were the aluminum casting goods and the dynamo that nuclear agent Gunas Jireh had procured for Libya.

Before the *BBC China* discovery, U.S. intelligence agencies had not known the full extent of Libya's nuclear arms program. But soon the United States would receive further confirmation of Libya's covert nuclear buildup. Two weeks after the *BBC China* cargo was seized, investigators discovered that Tahir had arranged to ship electrical components to Libya for its machine plant.

Caught in the act, Libya was forced to reveal that it had been secretly working to build nuclear weapons, as well as chemical and biological weapons. Libya ultimately admitted that it had spent some $500 million since the late 1990s in developing nuclear weapons. Qadhafi, concerned about his legacy and an economy hit hard by sanctions, announced in December 2003 that Libya would abandon its nuclear and chemical arms program, limit the range of its missiles, and comply with numerous international treaties. He declared that Libya would comply with the standards of the Missile Technology Control Regime, which limits missiles to ranges below 186 miles, and with the Nuclear Nonproliferation Treaty, the Biological Weapons Convention, the Chemical Weapons Convention, and the International Atomic Energy Agency's Additional Protocol—all international efforts to curb the spread of weapons of mass destruction.

The announced disarmament was widely hailed as a victory in the effort to stem the flow of weapons technology to rogue states. Douglas Feith, the undersecretary of defense for policy, was more cautious, but he acknowledged that Libya's pledge to disarm could be an important step in nonproliferation efforts. The undersecretary suggested that Qadhafi adopted this new approach after the ouster of the Taliban in Afghanistan and Saddam Hussein in Iraq, which were sobering for Qadhafi, he said. "At that point Qadhafi, having tried for years to get off the 'bad list' by means short of opening up, decided that he had to open up," Feith remarked. "Now, what does one infer from that? I suppose it seems as if he came to the conclusion that it was too risky being coy, it was too risky trying these lesser means to get off the bad list, and it became more urgent for him to get off the bad list when he saw the fate of the Taliban regime and the Saddam Hussein regime."

To Feith, Qadhafi's decision to "open up" reflected a victory in President Bush's global war on terrorism, which has focused on the connection between terrorist organizations, weapons of mass destruction, and state sponsors of terrorism. Qadhafi understood that "he lived at that intersection which turns out to be a dangerous place to live," Feith said. For many years, Qadhafi tried to remain there while attempting to buy his way off the rogue state list, but according to Feith, "When President Bush made it clear that living at that intersection is really dangerous, Qadhafi decided he was going to come clean."

In March 2004, Energy Secretary Spencer Abraham announced another step forward in the disarmament of Libya. Abraham declared that the United States had retrieved 55,000 pounds of nuclear material and goods from Libya, including uranium hexafluoride and centrifuge equipment. "This 55,000 pounds of nuclear materials and equipment constitutes the largest recovery, by weight, ever conducted under U.S. nonproliferation efforts," Abraham said. The energy secretary acknowledged that this was "only the tip of the iceberg," however. "What we retrieved in January," he explained, "represents less than 5 percent, by weight, of the total amount of equipment and materials that we are recovering from Libya."

The dismantling of Libya's nuclear program and the unraveling of the Khan network are positive developments. But Libya has a long history of deception, terrorism, and repression, and that record should not be easily dismissed or forgotten. Before we take the Libyans at their word, we must remember, for starters, that they have continued to deny the existence of a biological weapons program, even though numerous intelligence reports indicate that they have such a program.

Douglas Feith himself told me that we should be cautious when assessing Qadhafi's disarmament pledge. "Let's not jump to conclusions," Feith said. "I mean, it's a good news story so far, but let's be sober. The Libyans for many years were looking for ways to get off the bad list. They put out all kinds of feelers. They tried different types of actions that were more or less in the nature of bribes."

Feith and other U.S. officials were right to be skeptical of Libya's disarmament. In May 2004, the United Nations' International Atomic Energy Agency (IAEA) produced a report that confirmed their suspicions. The confidential report did praise the Libyan government for allowing inspectors to examine nuclear facilities (and it disclosed for the first time the exact locations of those nuclear weapons sites; the list can be found in this book's appendix). But on the whole the report was a sobering reminder that much remained unknown about the Libyan nuclear weapons program.

The report stated, for example, that Libya had failed to provide all the documents needed to confirm that the program had been dismantled. And according to U.S. officials, the Libyans could not account for major portions of the components and equipment for their nuclear weapons. The IAEA report stated that a container of centrifuge components "actually arrived in Libya in March 2004, having escaped the attention of the [Libyan] state authorities that had seized the cargo ship *BBC China* in October 2003."

The IAEA's report confirmed the foreign support for Libya's nuclear weapons program. It concluded that "nearly all of the technology involved in Libya's past nuclear activities was obtained from foreign sources, often through intermediaries." The report did not identify the countries or individuals who had cooperated with Libya, but those involved included at least one declared nuclear weapons state, probably Russia or China; an Eastern European nation; a Western European company; a Far Eastern country; and a "supplier state," believed to be Pakistan. "Libya has stated that centrifuge-related training had been provided by foreign experts at locations in Africa, Asia, Europe, the Middle East and Southeast Asia," the report said.

The stark conclusion was that a state known to be involved in supporting international terrorism had received assistance in building the most deadly weapons known to man.

The report's most alarming section related to whether the Libyans had tried to make a nuclear warhead for missiles. Libyan government officials claimed that in January 2004 they had turned over to the United States all documents and drawings related to nuclear weapons design and manufacturing. They also asserted that the weapons data had never been transferred in electronic form. But, highlighting just how much remained unknown about the Libyan program—and the difficulty of weapons monitoring and verification in general—the IAEA reported, "It is practically impossible for the Agency to prove or disprove such statements."

Libya received nuclear warhead design data in late 2001 or early

2002, but the Libyans claimed they did not act on the information or even check whether it was credible or practical. The IAEA doubted this claim. "This is surprising," the report said, "given the substantial effort that was being devoted to uranium enrichment. It would have been logical for the Libyan authorities to review Libya's indigenous capabilities in the necessary technical areas and to consider other resources that might be needed to make use of the nuclear-weapons related information." U.S. officials familiar with the Libya program said the nuclear design information had originated in China and had probably been reexported from Pakistan through Abdul Qadeer Khan's nuclear supplier network.

As it did in Iran, the IAEA discovered trace amounts of weapons-grade uranium on centrifuge components in Libya. The highly enriched uranium may have come from the equipment sent from Pakistan, or it could have been produced in Libya. Whatever the case, the discovery raised serious questions about how far along the Libyan nuclear program was and whether Libya's promises could be trusted.

The political euphoria over Libya's supposed disarmament faded even more in June 2004, when officials learned that Libya had apparently violated its promise to renounce terrorism—a promise that had prompted the United Nations to lift economic sanctions in 2003. Moammar Qadhafi was accused of plotting to assassinate the head of the Saudi government, Crown Prince Abdullah. The details of the plot emerged from two participants in the alleged conspiracy, former Libyan intelligence official Colonel Mohamed Ismael, who had defected and been arrested, and Abdurahman Alamoudi, an American Muslim radical who was caught trying to take $340,000 from Libya in violation of U.S. economic sanctions. According to U.S. officials familiar with intelligence reports of the assassination plot, the plan apparently grew out of a dispute between the Libyan dictator and Abdullah at an Arab summit meeting in early 2003 in the weeks before the U.S. invasion of Iraq. Ismael reported that he had traveled to Saudi Arabia to try to organize a group of four al Qaeda–linked Islamists to investigate an attack on Abdullah, and Alamoudi claimed that he had met with Qadhafi personally.

Before he resigned as CIA director, George Tenet pointed to Libya's disarmament as one of the major intelligence successes of his tenure. But based on the IAEA report and other evidence, it would be foolish to accept Libya's promises uncritically.

It also would be foolish to overlook the fact that for years Qadhafi was getting away with his illicit nuclear buildup. In fact, the story of Libya's covert nuclear weapons development offers yet another example of how the threats to America have only multiplied in the post–Cold War world. The question remains: How could a dictatorship that for decades had been deeply involved in supporting terrorism have so easily gotten deadly nuclear, chemical, and biological arms?

REIGN OF TERROR

On December 21, 1988, a group of travelers, most of them Americans, boarded Pan Am Flight 103 at London's Heathrow Airport to head to New York for the Christmas holiday. The passengers had no idea they were on a doomed aircraft. Thirty-one minutes after takeoff, the Boeing 747 reached its cruising altitude over Lockerbie, Scotland. Suddenly a bomb hidden in a Toshiba portable radio packed inside a Samsonite suitcase blew up. The bomb, which contained the Czech-made plastic explosive Semtex, had been wired with a detonator set to go off at 31,000 feet. The jet broke into pieces and crashed into the village, killing all 259 passengers and crew and 11 people on the ground. Debris and the bodies of many victims were strewn over a wide area of Scotland.

The terrorist attack had been ordered by Libyan dictator Moammar Qadhafi, in retaliation for the U.S. bombing raid on the Libyan cities of Tripoli and Benghazi in 1986. That raid had been a response to another terrorist attack the Libyan government had ordered, the April 5, 1986, bombing of a discotheque in Berlin that killed two U.S. soldiers and a Turkish woman, and wounded more than two hundred other people. The NSA intercepted diplomatic communications from Tripoli ordering its embassy in East Berlin, the Libyan People's Bureau, to use agents to carry out the bombing. The Berlin prosecutor who ultimately tried the bombers revealed that "the instruction from Libya read: 'Kill as many people as possible.'" He affirmed that "the telex messages exist and are with us."

Although the Lockerbie bombing was more devastating than the Berlin attack, the United States took no further military action against

Libya. Instead the U.S. government pursued a legalistic approach, seeking to put the two Libyan intelligence officers whom investigators had linked to the Flight 103 bombing on trial, but not Qadhafi or senior Libyan intelligence officials. The United States did appeal to the United Nations, which led to sanctions against Libya beginning in 1992. Eventually, many years later, the two Libyans, Abdelbaset Ali Mohmed al-Megrahi and Al Amin Khalifa Fhimah, went to trial in Scotland. The court acquitted Fhimah of all charges, and although Megrahi was found guilty of murder on January 31, 2001, he did not suffer much for the crime of killing 270 innocent people. He is now serving twenty-seven years in a Glasgow prison that provides him with a private four-room suite, a color TV, a VCR, a stereo, a personal computer, a kitchen, floral curtains, framed art, and unlimited telephone access.

The Libyan government had turned over Megrahi and Fhimah in 1998, but that was part of Qadhafi's carefully crafted strategy to get the United Nations and the U.S. government to lift sanctions against his country. The UN cooperated, suspending the sanctions in 1999. But the United States remained wary of Qadhafi's Libya. The U.S. government kept in place its rules prohibiting American companies from doing business in Libya, even though U.S. oil companies were anxious to develop the oil concessions they held there. Also, the State Department kept Libya on its list of state sponsors of international terrorism.

The U.S. government had good reason not to bargain with the Libyans. CIA Director George Tenet pointed out the Libyan threat while briefing Congress in February 2003: "I want to mention our renewed concern over Libya's interest in WMD," Tenet said. "Since the suspension of sanctions against Libya in 1999, Tripoli has been able to increase its access to dual-use nuclear technologies." Tenet also noted that "Libya clearly intends to reestablish its offensive chemical weapons capability and has produced at least 100 tons of chemical agents at its Rabta facility, which ostensibly reopened as a pharmaceutical plant in 1995."

Qadhafi had made that intention clear several years earlier. On February 20, 1995, speaking at a religious festival in Tajura honoring the conquest of Mecca, he spoke of Libya's "right" to have weapons of mass destruction. "When they [the West] colonized Palestine we paid the price, so that until now we have had to live in the shadow of the terror of Israel," Qadhafi said. "They say Israel has . . . 200 nuclear bombs. . . . The whole world got obsessed with our factory in Rabta. . . . Our waters in the Gulf of Sirte are threatened and our regional waters are threatened, we are threatened from the north and the south by imperialist ambitions. So we have the right, like the Israelis, to have nuclear, biological, and chemical weapons if we can find a way to get them." The comments sparked chants from the supportive crowd.

Qadhafi repeated the claim that Arabs have the right to possess weapons of mass destruction in an interview with the satellite television network Al-Jazeera in 2002, as George Tenet noted in his 2003 congressional testimony.

And Libya was exercising its supposed right. The Libyans were covertly developing deadly nuclear arms and missiles to carry them, as well as the chemical weapons it had already been producing. Senior Bush administration officials worried that the Libyans were digging an underground nuclear facility. The United Nations accelerated Libya's program when the world organization suspended sanctions in 1999, because that action granted Libya legitimacy in the marketplace, which in turn gave Tripoli more leeway to conduct black-market transactions. As one U.S. official told me, the Libyans went on a major buying spree. "Since the suspension of UN sanctions," the official said, "the Libyans have been out around the world aggressively seeking [chemical weapons, biological weapons], and nuclear capabilities, no question about it." According to intelligence, the support came from Iran, North Korea, China, India, and Russia. The Russians, for instance, announced plans to upgrade and maintain Libya's two Russian-made nuclear reactors.

Matters only got worse in the fall of 2003, when the UN lifted sanctions altogether. This was the fulfillment of Qadhafi's strategy. He appeared to be making amends to the world community when he agreed to pay out $2.7 billion in reparations for the Lockerbie bombing—$10 million for each of the 270 Flight 103 victims. Later he agreed to a similar, $170 million deal for the victims of the 1989 bombing of a French airliner that killed 170 people. He had already muted his anti-U.S. rhetoric and pretended to support the international war on terrorism.

The U.S. government still refused to lift its own sanctions on Libya, however. And in the United Nations, the United States did not vote to lift sanctions, choosing instead to abstain. The U.S. deputy representative to the United Nations, James B. Cunningham, was careful to explain that the decision to go along with the UN action "must not be misconstrued by Libya or by the world community as tacit U.S. acceptance that the government of Libya has rehabilitated itself." He cited serious concerns about Libyan human rights violations. Qadhafi has ruled Libya with an iron fist since he took over in a military coup in 1969. The government routinely uses torture to silence critics or perceived enemies. Libyans disappear without a trace, victims of the same political police service that was behind the Lockerbie bombing. Political prisoners number in the hundreds, according to human rights organizations. Most have never been charged with a crime but have been behind bars for more than a decade.

Cunningham also revealed that the Libyan government threatened the rest of the world, not just its own people. "Libya is actively pursuing a broad range of WMD and is seeking ballistic missiles," Cunningham said. "In those efforts, it is receiving foreign assistance—including from countries that sponsor terrorism. Libya's continued nuclear infrastructure upgrades raise concerns. Tripoli is actively developing biological and chemical weapons. The United States will intensify its efforts to end Libya's threatening actions. This includes keeping U.S. bilateral sanctions on Libya in full force."

To the United States, if not other UN member states, it was clear that Qadhafi and Libya were still extremely dangerous.

And there was simply too much evidence of Qadhafi's active role in international terrorism. Mohammed Abdallah El-Hosck, a former Libyan diplomat, told me in an interview that the world should be concerned about the Libyan government. "Those are bloody people," said El-Hosck, who defected to the United States in 1986. Recruited as a CIA spy in September 1979, he was the number-two officer at the Libyan embassy in Lagos, Nigeria. El-Hosck helped U.S. intelligence learn about Tripoli's assassination plots and other terrorist activities. For example, he disclosed that in April 1984 his government had ordered Libyan guards at its London embassy to shoot demonstrators who had gathered to protest Qadhafi; the Libyans killed a London police officer and wounded ten bystanders in the attack.

More important, while he was a member of the Libyan Foreign Ministry's "secret department," which was responsible for sending and receiving coded embassy communications, El-Hosck gave CIA officers in Nigeria access to the machine used to code and decode all government communications. The NSA used this extraordinary ability to uncover Tripoli's role in the Berlin discotheque bombing in 1986. Also thanks to El-Hosck, U.S. and Western governments were able to avert many Libyan terror attacks during the 1980s. Said one official, "From [the intercepts] we knew how the Libyans operated."

Although El-Hosck has been in the United States for nearly two decades, he still fears for his life, he told me. "You know Qadhafi is still dangerous," he said. "They have money. If you have money, you can kill anybody." To El-Hosck, it is evident that Libya has not rehabilitated itself, despite what the United Nations would like to believe.

ARMING THE LIBYAN TYRANT

In late 2003, when investigators caught the Libyans trying to import thousands of centrifuge parts in order to produce highly enriched uranium, Tripoli was forced to reveal that it had been secretly working to build nuclear weapons, as well as chemical and biological weapons. Qadhafi went a step further, agreeing to disarm all his weapons of mass destruction. Yet to many observers, this seemed just another Libyan gambit.

No doubt the U.S. military action to oust Saddam Hussein was weighing heavily on Qadhafi's mind. As one Western diplomat put it, "The Iraqi lesson was so bitter. And so clear." According to U.S. intelligence officials, however, Libya could well continue to pursue its covert effort to develop nuclear weapons, despite the agreement to disarm. Qadhafi's regime was far too active on the international black market to suddenly cease all nuclear buildup. The Libyans have worked around sanctions and violated international law before, so it would not be a shock if they ignored the terms they agreed to at the end of 2003.

The seizure of centrifuges headed to Libya was certainly the most dramatic evidence of Tripoli's covert nuclear weapons program, but it was not the only evidence. In June 2003, several months before investigators boarded the German ship *BBC China,* a senior U.S. intelligence official told me, "Libya is moving ahead in the area of nuclear weapons." In October of that year, Israeli Prime Minister Ariel Sharon let slip some new intelligence indicating that Libya had contacted both North Korea and Pakistan to develop nuclear weapons. In a meeting with foreign ambassadors in Israel, Sharon told the diplomats that the Libyans were getting help from those countries—"not help as in buying a bomb, but help in acquiring technology and know-how to build a bomb." Sharon remarked, "One would not be surprised if Libya would be the first Arab country [to] have nuclear weapons."

Also, in February 2003, Deputy Secretary of State Richard Armitage told the Senate Foreign Relations Committee of concerns about Libya's covert nuclear weapons program. Asked about hostile nations that were developing nuclear weapons, Armitage said, "We're always looking at Libya."

The CIA concluded in a November 2003 report to Congress that during the first half of the year "Libya continued to develop its nuclear infrastructure." The report confirmed that the suspension of UN sanctions had been a boon to Libya's nuclear procurement. For instance, "Tripoli and Moscow continued talks on cooperation at the Tajura Nuclear Research Center and a potential power reactor deal," the CIA report said. "Such civil-sector work could have presented Libya with opportunities to pursue technologies also suitable for military purposes." The agency also said that Libya had taken part in technical exchanges that improved their nuclear technology. And it laid bare Qadhafi's true aims: "Although Libya made political overtures to the West in an attempt to strengthen relations, Libya's assertion that Arabs have the right to nuclear weapons in light of Israel and its nuclear program—as Qadhafi stated in a televised speech in March 2002, for example—and Tripoli's continued interest in nuclear weapons and nuclear infrastructure upgrades raised concerns."

U.S. intelligence had amassed more information about Libya's chemical arms program, which it had been tracking for more than a decade. "Libya is on the verge of succeeding in developing a weapons-of-mass-destruction capability in the form of chemical and biological weaponry and the ballistic missiles to deliver them," said Joshua Sinai, a private specialist on Libya's arms, in testimony before Congress in July 1999. According to Sinai, Libya produced a massive network of underground pipes connected to chemical arms facilities, using its "Great Man-Made River Project" as cover. Sinai also said that Saddam Hussein's government cooperated with Libya on chemical arms.

The Libyans had revealed how far they would go to throw foreign intelligence services off their trail back in 1990. In March 1990, U.S. intelligence agencies obtained satellite photographs showing severe fire damage to the Libyan chemical weapons complex at Rabta, about fifty miles south of Tripoli in the Sahara. The CIA learned from other intelligence sources that as many as five hundred people were injured in the fire, which appeared to be the work of sabotage. President George H. W. Bush expressed the satisfaction the U.S. government felt when he told reporters, "I don't lament what happened." State Department spokeswoman Margaret Tutwiler was pleased to pronounce, "Production [of chemical weapons] is clearly now impossible."

There was only one problem: The fire never took place. Within several weeks, U.S. intelligence learned that the "fire" had been an elaborate ruse by the Libyans to fool the United States and perhaps stave off a U.S. bombing raid. Working with former East German intelligence officers, some four hundred of whom had been sent to Libya to assist Qadhafi before the fall of the Berlin Wall, the Libyans had done nothing but burn tires and chemical stocks. They had transferred equipment out of the facility before setting the blaze. They also painted black markings on the sides of Rabta's buildings to make them look burned out. By May, the CIA had uncovered intelligence indicating that Rabta was at full capacity and producing large quantities of chemical weapons, including deadly nerve agent and mustard gas.

Little wonder, then, that U.S. intelligence officials do not trust Qadhafi's 2003 vow to disarm.

Qadhafi's chemical weapons threat should not be underestimated, since the Libyans have already used such weapons against an enemy. Libya used Iranian-supplied mustard gas bombs during a conflict against Chad, a neighboring country to the south, in 1987. And the Libyans have ramped up their chemical weapons program since then. In fact, just two months after the supposed fire at Rabta, satellite intelligence photographs showed a steady flow of trucks laden with chemicals entering the compound, a sign that the Libyans were getting help from other countries. Just as troubling, trucks were leaving with what appeared to be containers of poison chemicals, indicating that Libya was exporting chemical weapons as well, or at least storing them at other locations.

Intelligence officials determined that Libya was getting support from a number of countries. The Chinese government supplied Libya with more than a dozen chemical ingredients used to produce weapons. For several months Chinese ships were photographed in Libya unloading the chemicals, and the deliveries were traced to Rabta.

And once again, a supposed ally of the United States was among the key suppliers. In June 1990 a West German businessman, Jürgen Hippenstiel-Imhausen, said that his company, Imhausen-Chemie, had helped build the Rabta chemical weapons plants. He claimed he had been unaware that the plant would be used for making chemical arms, though he admitted that he had suspected that building the plant conflicted with export laws. He had gone ahead with the project, he said, because he "didn't want to lose the business."

Also in June 1990, U.S. intelligence agencies discovered that the Libyans were building a new, underground chemical weapons complex at Tarhuna, fifty miles southwest of Tripoli. "It looks exactly like what they have at Rabta," said one official familiar with satellite photographs of the complex. The plant was estimated to be fully built within two years. The discovery of this underground complex, coupled with the discovery of the fire deception at Rabta, showed that the Libyans hoped to have free rein with their chemical weapons program by fooling the world into thinking they had shut the program down.

U.S. intelligence officials said that the Tarhuna plant also included armament plants, missile launcher system runways, and command and control centers. On April 26, 1991, the CIA reported that Thailand, Malaysia, and Iran had sent technicians, chemicals, and equipment to Tarhuna; the intelligence report described the Malaysian firms as a "cutout," or surrogate, for British companies.

And U.S. intelligence believes, further, that Libya has been working on its biological weapons at the Tarhuna facility. In 1993, a German firm sold Tarhuna a labortary suitable for making deadly germ weapons, which prompted the chief of Germany's Central Customs Office for Criminal Investigations, Karl-Heinz Matthias, to remark, "According to the evidence we have, Libya is trying to develop such biological weapons."

Besides Germany, South Africa also secretly helped Qadhafi develop biological weapons, according to evidence the intelligence community has uncovered. In July 2002, U.S. officials met with Wouter Basson, a medical doctor with the South African military who became known as Doctor Death because he developed deadly anthrax and many other biological weapons agents. Basson was intimately involved in a top-secret South African arms program known as Project Coast, in which the South Africans cooperated on technology and equipment with Libya, Russia, Czechoslovakia, Croatia, China, Britain, East Germany, the United States, and Iran, according to court testimony given by former South African Defense Forces surgeon general Niel Knobel. International intelligence agencies never detected any of this cooperation, Knobel said, but in 1997, a container full of documents found at the home of an associate of Basson uncovered details of Project Coast. One of the most important discoveries among the documents was a list of clandestine weapons the South Africans had sold. U.S. officials also discovered from the documents that Basson had made at least five trips to Libya in the 1990s.

Basson ultimately went to court in South Africa facing sixty-seven charges that included murder, conspiracy, assault, and possession of classified documents. Many of the charges were dropped because of lack of evidence, and in April 2002 Basson was found not guilty on the rest of the charges. Nevertheless, much that was revealed in the trial, including what Basson himself was forced to admit, convinced U.S. intelligence that South Africa's government had been secretly helping other countries produce biological weapons. For instance, Basson admitted that he had conducted research at two front companies set up by the South African military, Delta G and Roodeplaat research laboratories, developing deadly substances like cholera and working on a formula for what he called a "super toxic substance." Basson also said that he had worked with what he termed a "chemical and biological warfare mafia" ranging from Russia and North Korea to the United States.

Of particular interest to U.S. intelligence was what the case revealed about Libya's biological warfare program. After prosecutors disclosed that Basson had worked closely with a Libyan contact named Abdul Razak, the South African doctor initially claimed that Razak did not exist but eventually admitted the truth. Testimony in the case showed that three nations with whom Basson worked, Libya, East Germany, and Russia, had purchased a Jet Star aircraft for the South African Defense Forces, and Basson acknowledged that he had flown on the Jet Star with Razak on many occasions.

Basson also told South African intelligence agents that in 1994 he had had contacts with Libya. South African authorities questioned him about a 1993 visit he made to Libya with Sol Pienar, a South African with connections to Yousef Murgham, a Libyan intelligence agent who posed as a perfume dealer. Court testimony disclosed that Basson had other contacts with the Libyans as well, including a 1997 meeting with Libyan intelligence agents in Namibia; this testimony supported what was revealed by the container of documents found in 1997. Niel Knobel testified that Basson "did not try to hide the fact that he was visiting Libya. I knew he also tried to broker contacts with Libya for other state departments. It is true that he must have built up very close ties with Libya's security forces in the twelve years of Project Coast." Lawyers for Basson actually admitted that Libya took part in buying equipment and technology for Project Coast, which Basson headed until the late 1980s.

The full story of what Libya received from South Africa's Project Coast was never disclosed, but U.S. officials remain convinced that it included biological agents.

The Libyan buying spree that followed the suspension of UN sanctions in 1999 included purchases for Qadhafi's biological weapons and chemical weapons programs. Publicly, Tripoli gave indications that it might sign up to the Chemical Weapons Convention, but the CIA reported to Congress in late 2003 that "Tripoli still appeared to be working toward an offensive [chemical weapons] capability and eventual indigenous production. Evidence suggested that Libya also sought dual-use capabilities that could be used to develop and produce [biological weapons] agents."

Intelligence officials recognize that Libya's missile program has been a priority for Qadhafi for decades and has been expanded through the efforts of an array of countries—Germany, Switzerland, Ukraine, India, Serbia, Iran, North Korea, and China. Missiles are, of course, inextricably linked to the other weapons programs, since they are means of delivery for nuclear, chemical, and biological warheads.

Libya bought short-range (186-mile) Scud-B missiles from the Soviet Union as early as the 1970s, and by the 1990s the Libyans had shown that they would not be satisfied until their missiles could hit targets much farther away. A January 1991 intelligence report, for example, indicated that two companies from famously neutral Switzerland were helping Qadhafi's deadly regime develop medium-range missiles at the Rabta plant. In March of that year the CIA's *National Intelligence Daily* revealed new activity at Rabta indicating that the Libyans were using the facility as a missile test center. A satellite photo included in the report showed a mobile transporter-erector launcher at the facility. The CIA also learned that Italian, British, Indian, and Yugoslavian companies were in Rabta with tunneling equipment to make underground missile production facilities. In addition, Libya had a new Soviet-made SA-5 surface-to-air missile battery at the plant.

In May 1991, the CIA reported that Libya, shopping for missiles that could reach Israel, approached North Korea about its 620-mile-range Nodong missile. Though the Nodong had not even been flight-tested yet, the Libyans were offering $7 million for each missile and related launchers and equipment. In February 1992, the NSA uncovered new details of Libya's efforts to buy Nodongs from North Korea. In the same report, the NSA showed that the Chinese firm NORINCO had sold the Libyans missile propellants and had tried to cover up the missile components by including a number of small arms in the deal, as noted earlier.

In July 1992, Libya tried to test-fire one of its Scud missiles, but

the test failed, with the missile blowing up on its launcher. Undeterred, Qadhafi continued to improve his missile program, finding no shortage of arms dealers willing to assist him.

In 1996, the CIA revealed in a secret report to the Pentagon that Slobodan Milosevic's Serbia was violating the UN embargo by providing technical support for Libya's medium-range ballistic missile program. It was part of a $30 million deal between the Serbian company JPL Systems, a government-run arms manufacturer, and Libyan officials. According to Pentagon estimates, Libya's Al-Fatah missile, which had been in development since the early 1990s, could have a range of up to 590 miles, enough to hit targets throughout southern Europe.

A 1996 NATO intelligence report, disclosed to the Spanish newspaper *El Mundo,* predicted that by 2006, Libya would have ballistic missiles with ranges between 620 miles and 1,860 miles and that the missiles would carry nuclear, chemical, or biological warheads. And in November 2000, Israeli intelligence reported that Libya had paid North Korea $600 million for its first shipment of fifty Nodong missiles and that Pyongyang had also sent missile technicians to Libya. U.S. intelligence could not prove or disprove the Nodong transfers, but of course the U.S. government knew that Libya had approached Pyongyang about the medium-range missiles back in 1992.

Ukraine also sold Libya ballistic missiles, according to the CIA. An October 2, 1996, CIA report, labeled "top secret," outlined three weapons agreements that Ukraine had reached with the Libyan regime. In July, the Libyans had given Ukrainian officials an initial payment of $3 million, on a deal worth $500 million, for what the CIA report said were SS-21, or Scud-B, missiles, which would be dismantled before delivery to Libya. The report also indicated a complex agreement by which Iran purchased a large shipment of unspecified Ukrainian weapons "with the intention of transferring them to Libya." The CIA report said that the Ukrainian weapons would be shipped to Sudan and transported overland to Libya. A third deal, concluded in May and worth $10 million, called for Ukraine to provide maintenance services and spare parts for Libya's four Soviet-era Foxtrot submarines and other surface ships, the CIA reported.

As seen in Chapter 6, the Libyan missile program got a major boost from Communist China, one of the world's worst proliferators. Classified U.S. intelligence reports from June 1998 revealed that China sent technicians to Libya to help with missile research and development—once again, in violation of UN sanctions. And in 1999, the NSA learned that the director of Libya's Al-Fatah program visited China's premier training center for missile scientists, and the agency also caught the Chinese trying to sell Libya a hypersonic wind tunnel for its missile-development program. That same year, a U.S. spy satellite photographed Libyan efforts to enlarge a missile test facility.

In March 2000, NSA director Michael Hayden issued a classified report to senior government officials revealing that China had transferred more missile technology to Libya. The same day that the NSA reported the missile technology transfer, Xinhua, China's official news agency, announced that Beijing had reached an agreement with the Libyan government to build a railroad system as part of "broad railway cooperation." Intelligence officials said the rail agreement would provide cover for the secret missile cooperation.

When the NSA's March 2000 report was disclosed by this author in the pages of the *Washington Times,* the news came just days after an announcement that the United States and China would resume talks on how to halt the spread of weapons of mass destruction and missiles to rogue states. It was still more evidence of a fact that too many governments—and many U.S. officials—want to deny: The public proclamations of the most dangerous weapons proliferators simply cannot be trusted.

It appeared that arms dealers were lining up to help Libya. In April 2000, Swiss authorities arrested a Taiwanese businessman who was caught trying to smuggle Scud missile components to Libya. The previous November, authorities in Britain had stopped a shipment of missile parts bound for Libya. U.S. officials concluded that the parts had originated in North Korea. Iran, too, helped Libya upgrade its missile program. A U.S. intelligence report from October 30, 2000, reported that Iranian missile technicians were installing equipment at a Libyan Al-Fatah missile factory.

As with Libya's nuclear, chemical, and biological weapons purchasing, the suspension of United Nations sanctions in 1999 allowed

Tripoli to improve its missile technology. Russia's government announced that it would resume arms sales to Libya, hoping to sell up to $500 million a year in arms and service contracts. Ukraine also stepped up military and technology cooperation with Libya, intelligence officials made clear, though they did not provide more details.

In December 2001, the CIA issued a public version of its highly classified intelligence assessment of missile threats to the United States through 2015. The report left no doubt that Qadhafi remained an enemy of the United States. "Even if Libya were to obtain a Nodong-class [medium-range ballistic missile], Tripoli would be likely to continue to try for longer-range systems to increase the number of U.S. and NATO targets it can hold at risk," the CIA report said. "If a missile were offered with range sufficient to strike 2,500 kilometers into Europe, Libya would try to obtain it." Libya could also directly threaten the United States if it obtained a longer-range missile, an intercontinental ballistic missile. The CIA believed that Libya could not develop its own intercontinental ballistic missile by 2015, but Qadhafi could purchase one or "set up a foreign assistance arrangement where foreign scientists and technicians design, develop, and produce a missile and the necessary infrastructure in Libya."

In presenting this information to the Senate Governmental Affairs Committee in 2002, CIA official Robert Walpole summed up the state of Moammar Qadhafi's missile program: "Libya's missile program depends on foreign support, without which the program eventually would grind to a halt." The same could be said for the weapons programs of many rogue states and terrorist groups, which only underscores the dangers arms dealers have created by cavalierly selling weapons to dictators and terrorists. As time goes on, America's enemies grow more deadly. This is certainly true of Syria, which along with Libya forms a new "Axis of Evil."

SYRIA: GETTING WEAPONS ANYWHERE, ANYTIME

Like Libya, Syria represents the ultimate proliferation danger: a state that supports terrorism and is developing nuclear, chemical, and biological weapons, as well as missile systems to deliver them.

Syrian dictator Bashar Assad stated in early 2004 that his country would not give up its drive for weapons unless Israel abandoned its nuclear arms. "We are a country which is occupied and from time to time, we are exposed to Israeli aggression," Assad said in an interview with a British newspaper. "It is natural for us to look for means to defend ourselves."

The Syrian leader also noted the sad and frightening reality about weapons proliferation in the modern world: "It is not difficult to get most of these weapons anywhere in the world and they can be obtained at any time."

The Syrian government's support for international terrorists has placed Damascus on the U.S. State Department's terrorism list for decades. In an October 2003 presentation to the Senate Foreign Relations Committee, the State Department's coordinator for counterterrorism, Cofer Black, outlined Syria's support for terrorism. "As we have said for some time," Black reported, "Syria provides safehaven and material support for several Palestinian rejectionist groups, including Hamas, Palestinian Islamic Jihad (PIJ), the Popular Front for the Liberation of Palestine General Command (PFLP-GC) and the Popular Front for the Liberation of Palestine (PFLP), the Democratic Front for the Liberation of Palestine (DFLP), the Abu Musa Organization (AMO), and the Popular Struggle Front (PSF)." Black dismissed Syria's claims the groups' offices in Syria played no role in terrorist attacks, saying that the U.S. government had seen ample evidence "that some of these offices are, in fact, used for operational purposes." He also noted that "the Syrian military presence in Lebanon supports Hezbollah actions there."

By providing physical sanctuary and political support to terrorist groups around the world, Syria's government is, in essence, complicit in the murder of thousands of people.

Syria poses a particular threat to the United States and its friends because it has revealed a fiercely anti-American strategy. It is, in fact, waging proxy warfare against the United States.

Nothing captures Syria's anti-American strategy better than the overwhelming support it gave Saddam Hussein's Iraq and continued to give to Saddam's loyalists long after U.S. and coalition forces had captured Baghdad. With the demise of Saddam and his Ba'ath Party in Iraq, Syria's Ba'ath Party, a pan-Arabist, socialist political party, became the last refuge for Saddam's henchmen.

On April 15, 2003, just after the fall of Baghdad, a key Iraqi official fled to Syria, where he hoped to find sanctuary. Faruq Hijazi, then Iraq's ambassador to Tunisia—and a senior intelligence officer in the Mukhabarat, Iraq's political police and intelligence agency—flew from Tunis to Damascus. Hijazi had been head of external operations for the Mukhabarat in 1993, when Saddam's regime attempted to assassinate former president George H. W. Bush during his visit to Kuwait. The Syrian government publicly denied that Hijazi was in its country, despite the fact that he was only one of many fleeing Iraqis who were given safe passage and sanctuary in Syria. Sure enough, nine days after Hijazi arrived in Damascus, U.S. military forces captured him at the main border crossing from Syria to Iraq.

Hijazi provided U.S. officials with new evidence supporting what earlier intelligence reports had indicated about Iraq's links to terrorists. Before the Iraqi war, intelligence reports showed that as Mukhabarat operations chief, Hijazi had met with al Qaeda leader Osama bin Laden in Sudan and Afghanistan in the 1990s. A top-secret Pentagon intelligence report from 2003 revealed that after his capture, Hijazi confirmed his contact with bin Laden. "During a May 2003 custodial interview," said the report, Hijazi disclosed that the al Qaeda leader had asked him for Iraqi help in procuring "Chinese-manufactured antiship limpet mines" and in establishing "al Qaeda training camps inside Iraq." The information about Hijazi and bin Laden was just one of fifty separate pieces of evidence of Iraq's connections to terrorist groups contained in the top-secret Pentagon report, which the conservative magazine the *Weekly Standard* uncovered in November 2003. Liberals within the media and government sought to discredit the intelligence, claiming that the Pentagon was guilty of "cherry picking"—taking intelligence reports out of context. But the document made a strong case for Iraqi links to al Qaeda, a case first made by this author based on earlier intelligence reports.

Syria had been linked to Iraq back in 1990, before the first Persian Gulf War. Hijazi was in charge of setting up the Iraqi government's major operation to covertly break United Nations sanctions, and Syria was intimately involved in the operation. Under Hijazi's program, Syria secretly received Iraqi oil and in exchange set up front companies and other outlets that would permit Iraq to obtain the weapons, spare parts, and dual-use products it needed to build up its military. Jordan and Turkey were involved in the covert Iraqi program as well. Despite this involvement, Syria joined the 1991 coalition that ousted Saddam's forces from Kuwait.

Syria did not oppose Iraq long, however. A classified report obtained by the author in 1998 showed that Syria and Iraq were working to cement an anti-U.S. alliance. In November 1997, a group of Syrian government, military, and intelligence officials visited Baghdad to propose the alliance, according to the secret intelligence report. The call for rapprochement came directly from Syria's president at the time, Bashar Assad's predecessor and father, Hafez Assad. A letter from Assad to Saddam Hussein called for the "formation of a Syrian-Iraqi alliance against the United States," the report stated. Also outlined in the letter was a call for "extensive Syrian assistance to Iraq, including troop support in the event of military conflict between the United States and Iraq on Iraqi territory." Later that month, the classified report revealed, Iraqi deputy prime minister Tariq Aziz visited Damascus to propose reopening an oil pipeline with Syria and opening up border gates between the two countries.

And the countries carried through on this alliance right up to the second Gulf War, intelligence indicated. In early March, just weeks before the war began, U.S. intelligence agencies detected large shipments of pentolite, an explosive, moving into Iraq from Syria. "Recent information revealed that Iraq has received twenty-four railroad boxcars full of pentolite explosives," the Pentagon said in a statement. Intelligence officials believed that the Iraqis wanted the explosives for blowing up their oil wells before U.S. troops could seize them. Some of the explosives were eventually found in oil fields in southern Iraq, though the Iraqis blew up only a few oil wells.

A dissident Syrian journalist disclosed in early 2004 that the Syrian military had helped Iraq hide weapons of mass destruction before the U.S. military began its assault on Iraq. The journalist, Nizar Najoef, who defected from Syria to Western Europe, alerted a Dutch newspaper to the location of three hiding places the Syrian military had used. According to Najoef, the Syrians had spirited Iraqi chemical weapons, long-range missiles, and other weapons components to underground tunnels beneath the town of al-Baida in northern Syria, to a Syrian air base in the village of Tal Snan, and to another site in the city of Sjinsjar, on the Syrian border with Lebanon. One of the key coordinators of Syrian cooperation with Saddam's military, according to Najoef, was Syrian dictator Bashar Assad's cousin Assif Shoakat, the chief executive officer of a trading company linked to the Assad family. David Kay, the former CIA weapons inspector, said intelligence reports of Iraqi weapons in Syria could not be investigated because of the Syrian government's refusal to cooperate.

John Shaw, the deputy undersecretary of defense for international technology security, told me that based on intelligence reports, he believes that Iraq's weapons of mass destruction were moved to Syria. "I began to get a sense from my sources in Iraq that there was a huge transportation trail, if you will, going from Baghdad and central Iraq, first toward the Syrian border, but in to Syria and Lebanon," he said. "One of my people who was out there said there were three reports in a single day of caravans, of trucks, going fully loaded with tarps over them to the main Baghdad-to-Syria border road, coming back empty. And these are caravans of ten and twelve trucks at a time. The point is, they were moving something, and if it was conventional stuff, that's interesting by itself. If it was a mixture of things, that's interesting too. But I have some people, in short, who are out there following both in Syria, and in Lebanon."

The U.S. government believed that Syria was helping Saddam even after coalition forces had entered Iraq. On March 28, 2003, Defense Secretary Donald Rumsfeld told reporters, "We have information that shipments of military supplies have been crossing the border from Syria into Iraq, including night-vision goggles. These deliveries pose a direct threat to the lives of coalition forces. We consider such trafficking as hostile acts and will hold the Syrian government accountable for such shipments." Rumsfeld was making a blunt threat, clearly signaling that the U.S. military would not stop in Iraq if it became clear that Syria had taken up the fight against the United States.

Most U.S. government officials were not as direct as the defense secretary. In fact, in August 2003, officials from the U.S. intelligence community and the State Department blocked John Bolton, the undersecretary of state for arms control, from publicly presenting damning information about Syria's weapons programs and its aid to Iraq. These officials wanted to avoid offending Damascus, because Syria had established a limited liaison program with the CIA. Bashar Assad's government understood all too well the leverage it had, and the Syrians attempted to pressure the Bush administration into muting its criticism of their pro-Saddam regime.

Bolton pushed ahead nonetheless. A month later, in September, he took his case to a House International Relations subcommittee. Bolton spoke of Syria's active support for terrorist organizations like Hamas, Hezbollah, and Islamic Jihad. He also testified about how Syria had directly attacked American service members. "Syria allowed military equipment to flow into Iraq on the eve of and during the war," Bolton revealed. "Syria permitted volunteers to pass into Iraq to attack and kill our service members during the war, and is still doing so." Damascus stepped up its cooperation after the fall of Saddam, he said, noting that "its behavior during Operation Iraqi Freedom underscores the importance of taking seriously reports and information on Syria's weapons-of-mass-destruction capabilities."

And Bolton laid bare those capabilities, and the support the Syrians were receiving from foreign arms dealers. On the nuclear arms front, Bolton outlined Syria's troubling research-and-development program. "We are aware of Syrian efforts to acquire dual-use technologies—some, through the International Atomic Energy Agency (IAEA) Technical Cooperation Program—that could be applied to a nuclear weapons program," the undersecretary said. Among the nations helping Syria develop its nuclear program, ostensibly for civilian purposes, were Russia and China, Bolton noted. Syria is a member of the Nuclear Non-Proliferation Treaty—as are Iran, Libya, North Korea, and other rogue states that have covertly developed nuclear weapons programs.

Syria already has one of the most advanced chemical weapons stockpiles in the Arab world. Bolton told Congress, "It has a stockpile of the nerve agent sarin that can be delivered by aircraft or ballistic missiles, and has engaged in the research and development of more toxic and persistent nerve agents such as VX." The threat is not theoretical. A classified Defense Intelligence Agency report from November 1999 revealed that in late October of that year Syrian military forces conducted a live chemical weapons bombing test, with a Syrian MiG-23 jet dropping a chemical weapons–laden bomb on a practice range. And the Syrians are expanding and improving their chemical warfare capability, getting assistance from China, among other countries.

Even more worrying is Syria's biological weapons capability. Bolton described the threat posed by Syria's offensive biological warfare capability by saying, "These 'poor man's nuclear weapons' do not require a large production capability, and depending on the agent and dissemination method, can be extremely lethal."

Like Libya, Syria has paid a great deal of attention to missile delivery systems. The Syrians already have several hundred short-range Scud and SS-21 missiles that are armed with chemical warheads. North Korea and Iran, Bolton said, were helping Syria develop medium-range missiles that could be fired in nerve gas attacks hundreds of miles from Syria's borders. "Syria's missiles are mobile and can reach much of Israel from positions near their peacetime garrisons and portions of Iraq, Jordan, and Turkey from launch sites well within the country," Bolton said. "Damascus is pursuing both solid- and liquid-propellant missile programs and relies extensively on foreign assistance in these endeavors. North Korean and Iranian entities have been most prominent in aiding Syria's recent ballistic missile development." And Damascus was working on a longer-range missile, known as the Scud-D, with help from North Korea.

Additionally, Bolton revealed that Syria was trying to purchase advanced SA-10 and SA-11 surface-to-air missile systems, MiG-29 and Su-27 fighters, and T-80 and T-90 main battle tanks, along with upgrades for its aircraft, armored vehicles, and air-defense systems.

John Bolton reminded Congress what was at stake with Syria. "When the world witnessed the destructive potential of terrorism on September 11, we were reminded of the need to remain steadfast in recognizing emerging threats to our security," he said. "In Syria, we see expanding [weapons of mass destruction] capabilities and continued state sponsorship of terrorism.

"We cannot allow the world's most dangerous weapons to fall into the hands of the world's most dangerous regimes, and will work tirelessly to ensure this is not the case for Syria."

Quite true. Unfortunately, the world's most dangerous weapons *already have* fallen into the hands of the world's most dangerous regimes. Syria's Bashar Assad admitted the truth that too many others avoid: These weapons can be obtained "anywhere in the world" and "at any time."

THE UNITED STATES: PROLIFERATION NEGLIGENCE

CHAPTER 8

ONE OF THE MAJOR MYTHS SPREAD BY AMERICA'S ENEMIES is that the United States is largely to blame for the rapid spread of deadly arms and dual-use goods to rogue states and unstable regions of the world. Statistics show large U.S. arms sales abroad, these opponents point out. For example, the Stockholm Peace Research Institute rated the United States as the number-one exporter of major conventional arms between 1998 and 2002, with $37.7 billion in sales. Russia came in at number two for the same period, with $20 billion in sales, followed by France with $8.3 billion, Germany with $4.9 billion, Britain with $4.8 billion, and Ukraine with $2.6 billion.

Statistics do not tell the whole story, however. U.S. arms and weapons systems are sold to allies and friends. The sales are part of a carefully crafted strategy to keep America's friends free from danger, following President Ronald Reagan's adage that the best way to keep the peace is to remain strong enough to deter aggressors and foes.

Other critics of the United States point to U.S. support for Saddam Hussein's Iraq in the 1980s as an example of how Americans arm rogue states. The U.S. government did pursue a shortsighted policy with regard to Iraq in the years before the 1991 Persian Gulf War. As we will see, however, the claims that the United States willfully armed the Iraqi dictator's military are greatly exaggerated or, in some cases, simply false.

More important, the focus on how America might have actively supported rogue regimes obscures the real danger from the United States: the cultural aversion to securing our military and technology secrets. Exports have not been the only means by which U.S. weapons technology has gotten into the hands of America's enemies; these foes have relied on espionage and illegal acquisitions. This is the true story of how America's enemies have made themselves more dangerous at the expense of the United States.

AMERICA'S SECURITY LAPSES

Defense Secretary Donald Rumsfeld told me in an interview that espionage has boosted arms proliferation. Rumsfeld spoke of the "damage that's been done by spies" and the "harm that is caused by their exposing people who help us, by spies transferring information on how enemy countries can best deny and deceive us." As a result of this espionage, the defense secretary remarked, "we don't really know what they're doing to the extent we might otherwise have [known]. That has accelerated [proliferation]."

Rumsfeld also highlighted the undeniable truth that the end of the Cold War has not brought a new era of security but has only *increased* the spread of deadly arms. "There's kind of a big gap and relaxation where everyone just sort of sat down and said, 'Well that's that, we've taken care of that problem. The biggest, most dangerous problem in the world has gone away. And so we can suddenly be friends with everybody,' " he said. "The movement of technology in that relaxed environment accelerated."

A case in point is the loss of American nuclear secrets. In the late 1990s the severe security problems at U.S. nuclear facilities finally began to draw public attention. First, in 1999, a special congressional committee released a bipartisan report documenting how Communist China had stolen U.S. secrets to advance their nuclear program. Around the same time, there emerged a spy scandal involving a nuclear scientist suspected of but never charged with selling warhead secrets to the People's Republic of China, which has been the key beneficiary of the compromise of U.S. nuclear warhead secrets.

Amazingly, despite all that attention, the security crisis at American

nuclear facilities continues. A classified Energy Department report from early 2003 made clear that a lax attitude toward security at U.S. nuclear weapons facilities allowed a host of friendly and hostile powers to steal secrets from the United States. According to the report, two of the department's weapons laboratories provided scientists from Iran, China, Russia, and other potentially hostile nations with access to unclassified research areas without checking their authorization or getting needed approvals. "We found that the [Energy] Department had not adequately controlled unclassified visits and assignments by foreign nationals at two national laboratories," said Energy Department inspector general Gregory Friedman in his report. "Neither laboratory provided sufficient information to the department's centralized tracking system, which was designed to facilitate complex-wide tracking of the status of foreign nationals."

In one case, an Energy Department science office laboratory allowed an Iranian scientist access to unclassified research areas more than two months before the Iranian had undergone the required background check. Lab officials also failed to obtain approval for the scientist's visit from Energy Secretary Spencer Abraham, as required for scientists from countries that the State Department has identified as supporting terrorism. The Iranian scientist was on site for a full five days before counterintelligence officials at the Office of Security facility realized the oversights and ordered the scientist to leave the facility. Although the Iranian was not granted access to classified areas, the inspector general's report explained that the visit nonetheless posed a security risk because national laboratories contain some of the U.S. government's most sensitive national security information, including data on nuclear weapons and key defense technology.

The Iranian case was just one of several examples that the Energy Department's inspector general outlined in his report. In fact, out of 187 foreign scientists who visited the Office of Science laboratory, Friedman's report found that 70 scientists, or almost 40 percent, received badges or were granted access to lab facilities "before their background checks or counterintelligence consultations were completed." Moreover, the Office of Science lab failed to perform passport or visa checks on 91 of the foreign scientists—nearly half. "Forty-one of the

91 had active [site] badges and could have accessed most of the site's facilities," the report said. "Thirty-four of the 91 were from sensitive countries such as the People's Republic of China, India, and Russia." All three countries devote substantial intelligence resources to obtaining nuclear information from Energy Department laboratories, according to U.S. intelligence officials.

Nor was the Office of Science the only culprit. According to the inspector general's report, procedures were also lax at the National Nuclear Security Administration facility, where officials failed to check visa or passport information for 37 out of 188 visiting foreign scientists. Of those 37 scientists, 17 were from sensitive countries.

Why has security at nuclear and other Energy facilities been such a major problem? A major reason is that scientists and security officials often have competing interests. Scientists are more interested in international exchanges, whereas security officials are concerned with preventing nuclear weapons information from leaking out to rogue states or those that support terrorism. And the problem is not going away, as the inspector general's report pointed out. "Thousands of foreign nationals from institutions around the world interact with laboratory employees at department facilities," the report said. "These interactions are taking place in an environment in which threats to our national security have become more complex and sophisticated. Accordingly, appropriate protection of national security interests requires increased vigilance and increased threat awareness on the part of the department and its laboratories."

Notra Trulock, a former director of intelligence for the Energy Department, responded to the inspector general's report by saying, "For the laboratories, which are the repositories of our nuclear secrets and all of our most sensitive military technologies, not to even bother checking the currency or the accuracy of passports and visas, to me, is just astonishing."

The 2003 inspector general's report brought bad news, but it merely confirmed what had been going on for years in U.S. nuclear laboratories. In 1998, a classified U.S. intelligence report that I obtained spelled out numerous U.S. security failures and attempts by foreign governments to acquire nuclear weapons secrets. "The U.S. Department of

Energy (DOE) is under attack by foreign collectors—intelligence officers, as well as scientists, academics, engineers, and businessmen—who are aggressively targeting DOE nuclear, sensitive, proprietary, and unclassified information," the secret report warned. "The losses are extensive and include highly classified nuclear weapon design information to the Chinese."

Indeed, the Chinese were actively engaged in nuclear espionage and benefited the most from U.S. weapons secrets. This is particularly frightening because Chinese missiles developed using U.S. information and technology are currently targeting American cities and U.S. troops in the Pacific. But Communist China is not the only nation that has taken advantage of stolen American nuclear secrets. According to the classified 1998 report, at least twelve nations were stealing weapons data from the United States. The intelligence report said that foreign spies viewed the Energy Department as "an inviting, diverse, and soft target that is easy to access and that employs many who are willing to share information." More than 25,000 foreign scientists visited or were assigned to work in Energy facilities in 1998 alone. Travel by Energy Department employees also creates opportunities for foreign spy services to gain useful nuclear weapons information. "DOE employees are especially vulnerable to foreign collectors trained in elicitation," the report said, noting that Chinese scientists had gained valuable nuclear data from hotel room meetings with U.S. scientists. The intelligence report also revealed that, according to Energy Department records, more than 250 known or suspected intelligence officers from twenty-seven nations had visited or been assigned to Energy sites.

The report faulted the prevailing scientific culture at Energy facilities, a culture that failed to take into account the implications of losing vital nuclear arms secrets. The data that the U.S. government failed to protect from foreign collectors "clearly demonstrate that such information saved other countries substantial time and money and has undercut U.S. policy, security, and competitiveness." For example, China's espionage from 1984 to 1988 enabled Beijing to acquire design information on the W-88 warhead, the most advanced warhead in the U.S. nuclear arsenal. The United States had needed to perform tens of nuclear tests in developing the warhead, but by stealing America's information, China was able to skip most of that long testing phase and to accelerate its nuclear weapons program "well beyond indigenous capabilities." Russia, Israel, and France also targeted American advanced nuclear weapons design data, testing-simulation techniques, and data on the long-term viability of nuclear weapons, according to U.S. intelligence.

Although the report identified twelve nations engaged in nuclear espionage, it acknowledged the disturbing reality of weapons proliferation: In the end, it matters little who actually took the secrets from the United States. "Regardless of the collector, the ultimate recipients of the information are the foreign research institutes and defense establishments, which in turn apply this knowledge to advance their own scientific and technological efforts," the report said.

Most notably, Communist China stole U.S. nuclear warhead design information and then passed the data along to Pakistan, which today maintains a nuclear standoff with rival India. More alarming, Pakistan's leaders have proclaimed that their "Islamic" bombs are meant to defend more than Pakistan. They have declared that they would use their weapons to defend any Muslim nation that called on Islamabad for nuclear protection.

Pakistan has not relied on the Chinese to obtain U.S. advanced nuclear weapons data, but rather it has put its own intelligence services and scientific programs to work. The 1998 intelligence report noted that Pakistan's main nuclear weapons entities—the AQ Khan Research Laboratories and the Pakistan Atomic Energy Commission—were looking to acquire Energy Department data. In a clear illustration of how rogue states actively subvert international nonproliferation treaties, the report revealed how Pakistani scientists gathered information from Department of Energy scientists and officials while attending international conferences on South Asian arms control and nonproliferation.

And, of course as shown earlier, Pakistan has not kept the nuclear secrets for itself. According to U.S. intelligence reports, Khan's network has shared U.S. data with dangerous regimes like North Korea, Iran, and Libya.

Meanwhile, Pakistan's nuclear rival, India, also benefited from U.S. nuclear arms data, especially data on earlier nuclear programs. A classified study conducted by Sandia National Laboratories in mid-

1998 found that Indian scientists had advanced their understanding of nuclear weapons technology by taking advantage of unclassified Energy Department data that U.S. officials considered outdated and thus not worth protecting from disclosure. The information might have seemed dated to the United States, but it was relatively easy for the Indians to obtain and it was an important building block for their nuclear program.

Likewise, rogue states have looked to the United States for basic information on what the United States would consider first-generation nuclear bombs. The classified 1998 report revealed that "prospective nuclear weapons states—such as Iran, Iraq, and North Korea—are interested in the basic parameters of first-generation nuclear explosives." According to the report, the Iranians showed their interest in nuclear weapons when their nuclear scientists visited Lawrence Livermore National Laboratory in 1996 and 1997. The visitors' questions indicated that they were seeking information for both their nuclear and biological weapons programs. The Iranians even obtained information from U.S. scientists over the Internet, including information about nuclear reactors.

Like India, Iraq took advantage of unclassified Energy Department nuclear information, according to the report. "In particular, the United States tested and abandoned electromagnetic isotope separation as inefficient and expensive," the report said. "The Iraqis, however, chose this as potentially the fastest method to produce fissile material." The report also revealed that during one inspection by the representatives of the IAEA, "a copy of an unclassified Sandia publication relating to high-precision detonations was found in Iraq." In addition, the Iraqi nuclear program "benefited from the inadvertent disclosures of information on high explosives by DOE scientists at a symposium," according to the report.

Even advanced nuclear states took advantage of unclassified U.S. data. During the 1990s, tens of thousands of foreign scientists and officials made unsolicited requests for nuclear-related data. From 1993 to 1998, for instance, Russian intelligence agents obtained data from ten Energy facilities. In another case, a Chinese scientist working at Brookhaven National Laboratory in New York sent the Chinese Academy of Science "dozens" of long technical faxes regarding silicon detectors, which are a critical component of ballistic missile guidance systems. "The information enabled the CAS to duplicate Brookhaven experiments as they were being conducted," the report said.

Some of the nuclear espionage relied on electronic intercepts. Russia set up an electronic spying station in Cuba and obtained valuable data on U.S. nuclear weapons testing and research by intercepting communications from the Westinghouse and Varian corporations. The intelligence report stated, "Intercepts of Varian communications also provided Moscow with information on dual-purpose technologies transfer from the United States to China and knowledge that Varian nuclear-related equipment was being used by China for the development of nuclear power plants and nuclear weapons."

Other nations that are supposed allies of the United States have targeted U.S. nuclear facilities. For example, a document that the U.S. embassy in Paris obtained in 1993 listed French spying targets, including two major U.S. nuclear laboratories, Los Alamos and Lawrence Livermore. The intelligence report also noted that Japan was seeking U.S. dual-use technology, "including superconductor-related research and development," through the Japan External Trade Organization, "an intelligence-gathering arm of the Japanese government located in the Japanese Ministry of International Trade and Industry." Israel, meanwhile, used its military and commercial partnerships with the United States to obtain valuable weapons data. Finally, intelligence officials believed that South Korea was taking advantage of its close ties to the U.S. nuclear arms establishment to get sensitive information.

The stolen U.S. nuclear data also helped foreign proliferators prevent U.S. and international monitors from detecting their programs. First, the data that foreign governments obtained from the United States have reduced or eliminated their nuclear tests, which the U.S. intelligence community often relies on to pick up information on foreign nuclear weapons programs. Second, the U.S. data have provided rogue states with other means to cover up their weapons development or other sensitive activities. In intelligence jargon it is known as denial and deception, or D&D. Denial programs allow governments to hide weapons programs from hostile spies or reconnaissance, while deception programs "involve attempts to provide information in order to intentionally mislead or misdirect intelligence," according to the 1998 report. "Of the countries we believe to be a threat to DOE," the report said, "an earlier National Intelligence Estimate judged that China and Russia have the most effective D&D program. In addition, Iran, Iraq, and North Korea—and also India and Pakistan—engage in D&D directed against the United States."

Foreign countries have avoided detection because, among other things, their spies have obtained information on the capabilities and limitations of U.S. intelligence. The Indian intelligence service, for example, obtained valuable data on U.S. methods for detecting evidence of plutonium production and for making sensors capable of detecting nuclear and chemical weapons signatures. Moreover, nuclear weapons states have obtained "environmental remediation" technology developed by the Energy Department that is useful in "cleaning" weapons sites, which prevents U.S. intelligence from detecting evidence of chemical, biological, and nuclear weapons research and development.

This, in the end, is one of the most disturbing aspects of weapons proliferation and the threat to the United States and its allies. It is bad enough that some of America's alleged allies have armed dangerous regimes and that the United States has failed to prevent those arms transfers, but it is even worse that the United States has failed to protect even its own military technology. America's enemies have the United States in their sights, and in some cases they're targeting Americans with U.S.-developed weaponry.

DID AMERICA ARM SADDAM?

But what about the charges that the United States has been guilty of something worse than negligence, of actively arming rogue states? Many anti-American critics have accused the United States of building up Saddam Hussein's military in the 1980s, meaning that American forces went up against U.S. weapons technology in the 1991 Persian Gulf War. But an examination of Iraq's arsenal before both the 1991 war and the 2003 war made clear that Iraq's army was mostly equipped with Russian, French, and Chinese weapons.

Anthony Cordesman, a military specialist with the Center for Strategic and International Studies in Washington, researched Iraq's weapons purchases in the years before the 1991 Persian Gulf War and found that Iraq's main military suppliers were Russia, China, and the "major West European" arms makers. From 1987 to 1990, Russia sold $500 million in arms to Iraq, while China sold $700 million in weapons. European nations combined for $1 billion in arms sales. All other countries accounted for another $1 billion. U.S. arms sales during the same period were zero. Then, in early 2003, Cordesman produced a comprehensive order of battle for Iraq showing that Iraq's army had about 1,200 Russian and Chinese tanks and up to 3,700 Russian, French, Czech, and Brazilian armored vehicles. The small number of U.S. M-48 and M-60 tanks were captured from Iran or purchased illegally from other nations. Iraq's warplanes were Russian, French, and Chinese, and included various MiGs, Mirage F-1s, and Chinese F-6s.

To be sure, though, the United States aided the Iraqis during their war with Iran in the 1980s. Officially, the Reagan administration was neutral toward both Iran and Iraq during their bitter war. But in reality the United States was never totally neutral toward Iran, which had made itself an implacable foe of the United States by seizing American hostages in 1979 and holding them for 444 days. The administration's opposition to Iran's Islamist clerical regime led the United States to adopt the pragmatic but unprincipled policy of covertly supporting Iraq in the war against Iran. The "tilt" was outlined in a 1983 memorandum by Nicholas Veliotes, the assistant secretary of state for Near East affairs. In the memo, which was declassified in 2003, Veliotes focused on the subject that always comes up with the Middle East: oil. He warned that if Iraq lost its war with Iran, the Iraqis might attack Iran's oil facilities, which in turn would lead Iran to "prevent through force all oil exports." Veliotes also warned that "sustained Iranian pressure could, over the next year, bring about Iraq's political collapse." Veliotes concluded, "It is in this context that a possible tilt toward Iraq should be considered."

The administration implemented the tilt. That did not mean the United States suddenly granted the Iraqi dictator all the weapons he wished, but it did entail a fair amount of support. To begin, the United States helped Iraq get cash for its arms purchases. At the urging of the Reagan administration, in 1987 the Export-Import Bank lent Baghdad some $200 million. The first Bush administration also helped fund Iraq. In 1992 the late Congressman Henry B. Gonzalez, Texas Democrat and chairman of the House Banking Committee, helped unravel a complex funding scheme that helped Iraq pay for arms in the years leading up to the 1991 Persian Gulf War. Gonzalez, often speaking to an empty House chamber in late-night "special order" speeches, revealed how the Atlanta-based branch of Italy's Banca Nazionale del Lavoro (BNL) funneled more than $5 billion in unauthorized loans to Iraq in the 1980s, including some $900 million in loans guaranteed by the U.S. government. The BNL Atlanta branch was the main source of credits to Iraq between 1984 and 1989.

The Bush administration also helped Saddam by granting Baghdad $1 billion in agricultural credits under the Commodity Credit Corporation. Though Iraq was supposed to use the agriculture credits to purchase American farm products, investigators would discover that the money went into Iraq's military buildup. The U.S. Customs Service uncovered information showing that BNL financed shipments of industrial machinery, military technology, controlled chemicals, and illegal missile technology to Iraq. Investigators also discovered that the program was riddled with corruption, with some of the Commodity Credit Corporation's $1 billion going to bribes and kickbacks to Iraqi officials and agencies. Even when the Iraqis did use the money to purchase food from the United States, investigators suspected that they used some of that to barter for Russian and East European military goods. The United States didn't cut the agricultural credits until May 1990, by which point half of the $1 billion had been used.

According to Kenneth Juster, an undersecretary of commerce in George W. Bush's administration, the United States agreed to sell Iraq some $1.5 billion worth of dual-use items during the 1980s. But the sales required export licenses because they could have had military applications, and "in the end only about a third of that, some $500 million in goods, was sent," Juster said.

This corresponded with what another expert determined in 1991. Gary Milhollin, director of the Wisconsin Project on Nuclear Arms Control, documented U.S. exports to Iraq in the period before the first Persian Gulf War. Milhollin obtained a document from the Commerce

Department showing that Commerce approved 771 licenses for the export of $1.5 billion worth of goods to Iraq from 1985 through 1990, but that only $500 million worth went through before sanctions were imposed after the 1990 Iraqi invasion of Kuwait.

In his 1991 report analyzing exports to Iraq before the Gulf War, Milhollin concluded that U.S. export controls broke down. He cited the same Commerce Department document, which showed that in November 1989 the department had approved Hewlett-Packard's sale of $140,000 worth of frequency synthesizers to Iraq's Salah al-Din defense facility. According to the document, the Hewlett-Packard export license entry acknowledged that "according to our information the end user is involved in military matters" and that the products would be used "in calibrating, adjusting, and testing" a surveillance radar system.

Investigative reporter and author Kenneth Timmerman documented the role that U.S. companies played in boosting Saddam Hussein's weapons programs. A 1990 report he produced in cooperation with the Simon Wiesenthal Center in Los Angeles showed that U.S. companies sold chemical weapons material, computers for missile development, machine tools, and high-temperature ovens with nuclear weapons applications. Timmerman identified a number of U.S. companies involved in the transfers, including Alcolac International, Nu Kraft Mercantile Corporation, United Steel and Strip Corporation, Lummus Crest, Electronic Associates, Hewlett-Packard, Scientific-Atlanta, Wiltron Company, XYZ Options, Consarc, Centrifugal Casting Machine Company, Sitco, and Tecktronix.

The tilt in policy also led to the U.S.-approved sale in late 1986 of some $500,000 in computers to the Saad 16 facility, which was making missiles. The Pentagon had opposed the sale, but probusiness officials at Commerce overruled the objections. Other sales included $290,000 worth of precision electronic and photographic equipment and $850,000 worth of high-performance testing equipment to Iraqi military or weapons-related organizations.

Still, some of the most dramatic charges made against the United States are insupportable. Some have accused the United States of knowingly helping Saddam Hussein build germ weapons. For example, in March 2003, former senator Don Riegle, a liberal Michigan Democrat

who conducted hearings on Iraq's weapons programs in the mid-1990s, told the *St. Petersburg Times,* "What is absolutely crystal clear is this: that if Saddam Hussein today has a large arsenal of biological weapons, partly it was the United States that provided the very live viruses that he needed to create those weapons."

The United States did send some anthrax samples to Iraq, but for veterinary use. On September 29, 1988, the American Type Culture Collection, a commercial firm near Manassas, Virginia, shipped eleven items to Iraq's Ministry of Trade, including several strains of anthrax bacteria. The export was meant to help in dealing with the animal cases of anthrax. Although the Iraqis revealed after the Persian Gulf War that they had diverted the American anthrax strains to a biological warfare facility, the U.S. government was not intentionally improving Saddam's biological weapons program.

Similarly, the Centers for Disease Control in Atlanta acknowledged that it had supplied Iraq with fourteen agents that could have been used in biological warfare, including West Nile virus. A spokesman for the center admitted, "We did work with Iraq's scientists along with other scientists on microbiological agents and reagents. That did occur in the mid-'80s but . . . there were no other shipments that were sent after the incident involving Iraq's invasion of Kuwait." Again, the United States was not trying to improve the Iraqis' biological warfare capabilities. Most of the materials were noninfection diagnostic reagents for detecting infections from mosquito-borne viruses.

Whatever biological weapons capabilities Saddam Hussein had, the United States was not his main supplier. Iraq's biological weapons work began in secret around 1985. And according to interviews CIA weapons inspectors conducted with Iraqi biological weapons scientists after the 2003 war, as well as documents the inspectors uncovered, the Iraqis ran a clandestine network of laboratories and facilities for developing germ warfare throughout the 1990s. The inspectors even found a vial of a biological agent precursor in an Iraqi weapons scientist's home refrigerator. Working so hard to develop and refine biological weapons, the Iraqis were clearly not relying on material they had gotten from U.S. sources.

After the Iraq war, however, U.S. officials did discover some American-made weapons that had apparently been sold illegally to Iraq. The U.S. Customs Service sent a team of investigators to Iraq, and by early 2004 the investigators, working with Defense Department officials, had identified more than twenty U.S. companies as having been involved in illegal transfers to Saddam Hussein's regime. As of this writing, at least six were facing federal indictments for illegal arms transfers.

Information gathered from some 1.7 linear miles of documents related to Iraqi arms acquisition efforts revealed that in several cases the U.S. companies, most of which U.S. officials did not identify by name, supplied arms and military-related equipment through Ukrainian traders, who in turn shipped the goods to Iraq through Syria. "The Customs people have got huge amounts of Syrian-related information," said John Shaw, the deputy undersecretary of defense for international technology security.

In October 2003, federal prosecutors indicted an Iraqi-born father-and-son team from San Diego for exporting six armored patrol boats to Saddam Hussein from November 2000 to July 2003. It was the first prosecution of U.S. arms brokers for selling goods to Saddam, but at this writing other legal action was expected against American firms.

Sabri Yakou, sixty-nine, and his son, Regard Yakou, forty-three, were charged with violating the Arms Export Control Act and International Traffic in Arms Regulations. Sabri Yakou headed a company called P. T. Gulf International, and allegedly he was to be paid $11 million for serving as a middleman in an Iraqi-run company's construction of patrol boats. According to documents released by the U.S. government, in a letter to Iraqi military officials dated November 14, 2000, Sabri Yakou stated that he had hoped to help Saddam's regime circumvent international arms and technology embargoes. "My main goal was (and there should be no doubt about this) to serve this nation which is dear and loved by me and to transfer new industry (new technology) and train the Iraqi workforce in this new technology," he wrote. His company signed a contract with the Iraqi company on April 29, 2002. The government's affidavit stated that raw materials for the boats would be purchased in Malaysia, electronics in Singapore, and engines in Germany.

Michael J. Garcia, head of U.S. Immigration and Customs Enforcement at the Department of Homeland Security, said at the time of the indictments that investigators were trying to "peel back the layers of Saddam's covert weapons procurement and track down his suppliers." Garcia noted that the indictments were intended as "a message to those U.S. companies and individuals that may have helped arm the brutal regime of Saddam Hussein." Assistant Attorney General Christopher Wray, in charge of the criminal division, reiterated that the action was aimed at U.S. arms control violators. "The illegal brokering of arms and weapons to our enemies is a serious and deadly business," Wray said.

While the most strident critiques of U.S. involvement in Iraq prior to the 1991 Gulf War are unjustified, what can be said is that the U.S. government employed a shortsighted policy based on animosity to Iran and fear for future oil supplies. It is a proliferation lesson that should not be forgotten.

But the more important lesson is the one that the United States still seems not to have learned: The greatest threats often emerge because we let proliferation continue unchecked. It is a lesson that the United Nations, too, has failed to heed.

THE UNITED NATIONS' FAILURES

CHAPTER 9

ON DECEMBER 16, 2003, HOSHYAR ZEBARI, IRAQ'S NEW foreign minister, appeared before a meeting of the United Nations Security Council in New York. Zebari, an Iraqi Kurd, began his remarks to the council by noting that three days earlier, when Saddam Hussein had been captured, was a historic day for Iraq. Decades of brutality and barbarism were finally coming to an end, and Zebari laid out a detailed plan for Iraq to become a self-governing democratic state over the next two years. Then he lowered the boom on the assembled diplomats.

"One year ago," Zebari said, "this Security Council was divided between those who wanted to appease Saddam Hussein and those who wanted to hold him accountable. The United Nations as an organization failed to help rescue the Iraqi people from a murderous tyranny that lasted over thirty-five years, and today we are unearthing thousands of victims in horrifying testament to that failure. The United Nations must not fail the Iraqi people again." He finished with an appeal to the assembled international delegates to "put aside your differences, pull together, and work with us."

It was clear to whom Zebari was referring when he spoke of "those who wanted to appease Saddam Hussein." France, Germany, Russia, and China, among others in the United Nations, sided with the Iraqis, fighting efforts to oust Saddam's bloody dictatorship.

Zebari said that the United Nations had failed the Iraqi people, but the organization's failure was far more significant than that. In fact, the UN had failed in its founding purpose: to preserve peace and international security. And the UN's failure went beyond its refusal in 2002 and 2003 to hold Iraq accountable for its actions. The United Nations was appeasing Saddam Hussein for years before the United States called for decisive action against Iraq.

Moreover, Saddam's Iraq is just one of many rogue regimes that the UN has failed to keep in check. Again and again we have seen how dangerous states have built up their militaries and weapons programs right under the UN's nose. The organization's failure to enforce sanctions and antiproliferation agreements has meant that the world has become a far more dangerous place.

APPEASEMENT

In the twelve years between the Persian Gulf War and the 2003 Iraq War, Saddam Hussein routinely flouted United Nations sanctions and in general showed that his regime would not be held accountable to any international standard of behavior. The case of Iraq provides the most dramatic example of how the UN refuses, or is unable, to protect the world from dangerous rogue states. American service members had to go to war, and many have had to give their lives, to do what the United Nations could not or would not do.

One of the biggest problems was that the UN did not block the Iraqis' repeated efforts to build up their weapons programs. In fact, in its efforts to appease Saddam, the United Nations actually *helped* the Iraqi dictator strengthen his arms programs.

On April 15, 1995, under a propaganda barrage indicating that Iraq's people were suffering not at the hands of Saddam but as a result of UN sanctions, the United Nations agreed to let Saddam sell oil so Iraq could purchase needed "humanitarian supplies." The resolution establishing the oil-for-food program gave UN Secretary General Kofi Annan the authority to supervise the sale of oil and monitor the goods Iraq bought with the revenue. Annan and the UN failed to prevent the massive corruption and abuse that began almost the moment the program started operating in December 1996. The oil-for-food program was one of Saddam's most effective deception operations. He and other Iraqi officials skimmed billions of dollars from the supposed aid program. More troubling, the UN arrangement allowed Iraq to rebuild its weapons and missile programs.

On March 31, 2004, the United Nations posted on its website a notice that received little attention in the press. The announcement stated that the UN controller had transferred to the UN Development Fund for Iraq some $7.6 billion that had been gathered from the oil-for-food program. What the announcement left out was that Saddam had skimmed off additional billions of dollars during the nearly seven years the program had operated. The oil-for-food program had been designed to help Iraq's people, but in reality, Saddam had exploited loopholes and lax United Nations oversight to steal a significant portion of the estimated $45 billion raised by the program.

A month earlier, U.S. officials had begun unraveling the corruption in the program, which involved kickbacks from companies that did business with Iraq. The firms reportedly funneled money through a network of foreign bank accounts and violated United Nations sanctions against Iraq. The corruption scandal involved oil traders from a number of countries, including France, Russia, China, and other European, Asian, and Middle Eastern nations; these traders paid off Iraqi officials with suitcases full of cash, according to U.S. officials.

Documents uncovered by the Iraqi Governing Council in the months after the fall of Saddam revealed how the operation worked. Initially, the oil-for-food program permitted Iraq to sell oil only to purchase humanitarian goods. But by 2000, the UN had eased controls and the Iraqis were selling oil to the tune of $10 billion a year. The corruption became more pronounced then. Saddam's vice president, Taha Yassin Ramadan, stated in an August 3, 2000, letter to Iraqi government ministries that Saddam wanted "extra revenues" from the oil-for-food program. The letter stated that all suppliers doing business under the program would be required to inflate proposed contracts by the largest percentage possible and then to transfer the amounts to Iraqi bank accounts in Jordan and the United Arab Emirates. Millions of dollars that were supposed to be used for medicine and food instead went to Saddam, who used much of the money to covertly build up his military. The kickbacks ranged from 3 percent to 10 percent, and at times went even higher, according to U.S. officials.

Estimates are that the Iraqis skimmed up to $2.3 billion of out of nearly $33 billion just in contracts signed after mid-2000. A March 2004 report by the General Accounting Office revealed that overall, the Iraqi government illegally skimmed some $5.7 billion through oil smuggling and another $4.4 billion through kickbacks on contracts under the UN program. This was only part of the cost of the appeasement strategy the United Nations had implemented in 1995. On April 16, 2003, a week after U.S. and coalition forces took Baghdad, Army General Tommy Franks took a dig at the UN's failed policy as he surveyed the opulent Abu Ghraib Palace, which was just one of at least forty-eight palaces Saddam had built in Iraq. The commander of Operation Iraqi Freedom, noting the gold sink fixtures, gold toilet-paper dispenser, and gold-handled toilet-bowl brush, remarked, "It's the oil-for-palace program." The Iraqi people might have been starving, but they would not benefit from the UN's misguided oil-for-food program.

"The oil-for-food program deserves to be looked at," Douglas Feith, the Bush administration's undersecretary of defense for policy, told me in an interview. "It is clear that that program was badly abused." Feith argued that Saddam's scheme had corrupted the entire system through which shipments in and out of Iraq were inspected. "It's the kind of thing that I watched because there were so many reports," he said. "And there are beginning to be people in the UN bureaucracy who realize that for the sake of the UN, this should be investigated and straightened out so that you could do something to try to shore up some integrity for the UN as an organization, because this was not a glorious enterprise for the UN."

Feith believed that it was important to correct the problems with the United Nations because "there are a lot of people, ourselves included, who want there to be options short of war when there's a problem. And you know, one of the options short of war was a kind of sanctions regime that the oil-for-food program was supposed to provide." He added, "If it's a completely corrupt program, and it doesn't

work and it's ineffective, . . . then after the fact, if nobody looks at it, nobody investigates it, nobody improves on it, nobody does lessons learned, nobody fixes it up so that it's better the next time around, then that kind of tool to deal with problems goes away, and you have fewer options short of war."

Other Iraqi skimming involved illegal surcharges imposed on companies that shipped crude oil by ship, which supplied an estimated $228 million. An additional $540 million went to Saddam's officials from surcharges slapped on overland oil transports.

The United Nations officials involved in the program claimed to be ignorant of the stealing. Still, in April 2004, Secretary General Annan appointed a three-member panel headed by Paul Volcker, the former federal Reserve chairman, to investigate corruption in the oil-for-food program.

Saddam used vouchers to reward his friends, including foreign politicians and journalists who would come to Iraq and praise Saddam and his regime. The vouchers granted permission from an Iraqi Oil Ministry entity called the State Oil Marketing Company to purchase Iraqi oil under the oil-for-food program. The vouchers would be worth hundreds of thousands of dollars to those who held them. If a voucher authorized the purchase of a million barrels of Iraqi oil, the voucher could bring in about $200,000 after it was sold to oil traders.

An Iraqi newspaper, *Al Mada,* published the long and embarrassing list of those who, according to the State Oil Marketing Company, had received vouchers. Among the 267 people and companies on the list was Bernard Guillet, a French diplomat and adviser to former French interior minister Charles Pasqua. Another was British member of Parliament George Galloway, who was one of the most outspoken supporters of Saddam Hussein. London's *Daily Telegraph* obtained Iraqi documents that linked Galloway to Iraqi intelligence, but in a statement he denied "to the best of my knowledge" ever meeting anyone from Iraqi intelligence. Galloway maintained that most of his contacts were with Iraqi deputy prime minister Tariq Aziz. He also said that he had "never solicited nor received money from Iraq for our campaign against war and sanctions." But the documents from the State Oil Marketing Company indicated that Galloway had been given a voucher for a million barrels of oil.

As noted in Chapter 3, some forty-six Russian companies and individuals received oil vouchers from Saddam's government, according to the list published in the Baghdad newspaper. Thus Russia received more grants, by far, than any other country. The fact that the list also identified the "chief of the Russian presidential office" as a major recipient of vouchers raised questions about the Russian government's involvement in the deals with Iraq.

The Iraqi documents indicated that Chinese firms and individuals received many oil vouchers as well. According to the Iraqi list, a "Mr. Wan" was granted 39.1 million barrels of oil, while the company listed as "Noresco" received 17.5 million barrels. The list identified other Chinese voucher recipients like "Zink Ronk" (13 million barrels), "Byorg" (13.5 million), and "South Holken" (1 million).

Moreover, it appears that Saddam rewarded Palestinians with oil vouchers. Among the reported recipients were Abu al-Abbas (1 million barrels), the Popular Front for the Liberation of Palestine (4 million), and the Palestine Liberation Organization (9 million).

Intelligence agencies learned almost immediately that Iraq was abusing the oil-for-food program, as Saddam's regime diverted money from the oil sales for nonhumanitarian purposes and also purchased items that could be used to help its military. The program did maintain a special watch list known as the Goods Review List to identify items that Iraq could use for military purposes. But the list did not do much to deter Iraq, in part because key products and equipment that the Iraqi military could use were left off the list. Moreover, the UN showed no desire to enforce its import regulations when it became clear that the scofflaw Saddam was working around the program's rules. Part of the problem was that the program operated in complete secrecy; even when the United Nations found that Iraq had tried to import inappropriate items, it did not identify the specific product or the supplier company. Neither Iraq nor the proliferators, of which there were many, were held accountable.

The UN's failure to prevent Iraq from illegally circumventing arms sanctions would be critical to the U.S. decision to go to war in

2003. For years, U.S. intelligence agencies catalogued numerous instances of Iraqi cheating through the oil-for-food program and through smuggling. But the United Nations continually ignored the evidence.

Saddam's military buildup began well before the oil-for-food program was instituted. It started right after the end of the Gulf War, despite the complete embargo on delivering weapons and military goods to Iraq. U.S. intelligence picked up a number of illegal arms deals involving Iraq right around the time that the UN was agreeing to the so-called humanitarian program. In 1995, Russia was caught trying to ship missile guidance components to Iraq when the components were uncovered and seized in Jordan, but the United Nations took no action against the Russians for the transfers. In 1996, a CIA report revealed that suppliers in Bulgaria or Russia were involved in a deal to sell Iraq batteries for MiG-29 aircraft. Also that year, Pentagon officials discovered that a squadron of Iraqi F-1 Mirage fighters had been outfitted with upgraded warheads and engines for Magic 2 air-to-air missiles. Many officials suspected the French government of sanctioning the sales, since the government in France tightly controls military exports from the country.

But the oil-for-food program expedited Saddam's military buildup. A secret CIA report issued in January 1997 stated that "Iraq is buying spare parts for its aircraft and armored vehicles as well as components to produce ammunition." The report did not elaborate, but it did explain that Iraq and neighboring Iran "have well-developed ties to brokers and will be the most aggressive buyers" among rogue states seeking conventional arms banned under United Nations resolutions and other international agreements.

In some instances, the U.S. government was able to use the intelligence to block deals that the United Nations had missed. For example, in the fall of 1997, the CIA uncovered a secret agreement between Iraq and Bulgarian arms dealers who were connected to Czech military officials. The $375 million deal would have sent Baghdad special high-technology electronic-warfare systems that, according to the manufacturer, could detect and target U.S. stealth jets. Czech officials denied that they had approved any illicit sales to Iraq.

Similarly, a report by the Office of Naval Intelligence issued in September 1997 disclosed that China had tried to supply Iraq with chemicals needed to produce missile fuel; the Chinese merchant ship carrying the illegal chemicals to Iraq had been detained in Saudi Arabia, the cargo seized. Another 1997 intelligence report revealed that an Iraqi front company based in Jordan was negotiating to buy German computer and communications technology. Classified U.S. intelligence reports from 1998 showed that Baghdad had successfully acquired missiles, spare parts for aircraft and armored vehicles, and components needed to produce ammunition.

Also in 1998, Saddam Hussein banned all UN weapons inspectors from Iraq. The Iraqis would not let the inspectors return until late 2002, four years later, when they were trying to forestall a war with the United States. Because the Iraqi dictator was defying UN resolutions calling for weapons inspections, the United States had to rely on intelligence to assess the status of Iraq's illicit-arms program. And in early 2002, U.S. intelligence agencies discovered stunning evidence that Iraq was using the supposed humanitarian relief program for military purposes. Satellite photographs showed Russian and German trucks being unloaded at an Iraqi port.

The United States took its intelligence to the United Nations. On March 6, 2002, during a closed-door briefing to the UN Security Council committee in charge of monitoring sanctions on Iraq and of the UN weapons inspection agency for Iraq, senior State Department officials presented intelligence revealing that the Iraqi military was using about a thousand trucks that Iraq had imported from Germany and Russia under the oil-for-food program since July 2001. The United States had satellite photographs that showed trucks at military bases hauling artillery and heavy weapons; converted to carry surface-to-air missiles; with hydraulic systems for raising and lowering missiles; and painted in military camouflage colors. The briefers also showed video footage of an Iraqi military parade from December 31, 2001, in which the same trucks were towing artillery guns. Converting the trucks for military use violated UN sanctions. As one British diplomat put it, "Though this may not be the highest technology equipment, it is equipment that allows them to project power more effectively."

But the United Nations remained unmoved by the U.S. government's presentation. UN officials said simply that the sanctions-monitoring committee would attempt to verify the information. Syria, which at the time was a member of the UN Security Council, tried to defend its fellow rogue state. Syria's deputy UN ambassador, Fayssal Mekdad, said that committee members questioned whether the trucks arrived in Iraq before the oil-for-food program started, in 1996, or whether the trucks were smuggled into the country.

By late 2002, as war with Iraq was rapidly approaching, it was clear that the Iraqis were purchasing almost anything they wanted from the UN program. The CIA stated in a report made public in October 2002 that "Iraq has been able to import dual-use, WMD-relevant equipment and material through procurements both within and outside the UN sanctions regime." According to the report, "Baghdad diverts some of the $10 billion worth of goods now entering Iraq every year for humanitarian needs to support the military and WMD programs instead." One of the major problems, the CIA revealed, was the UN's failure to monitor material going into Iraq. United Nations officials posted at Iraq's borders "do not inspect the cargo—worth hundreds of millions of dollars—that enters Iraq every year outside of the oil-for-food program. Some of these goods clearly support Iraq's military and WMD programs. For example, Baghdad imports fiber-optic communication systems outside of UN auspices to support the Iraqi military." As seen in Chapter 6, the fiber-optic system came from China.

"Even within the UN-authorized oil-for-food program," the CIA reported, "Iraq does not hide that it wants to purchase military and WMD-related goods." In addition to the trucks, the Iraqis were using construction equipment and other goods "designed to rehabilitate facilities—such as the Al Qa'im phosphate plant and Fallujah—that in the past were used to support both industrial and WMD programs."

The United States insisted that the United Nations enforce its own rules, but the UN refused to act. At least in some cases, the UN appeared to be at odds with its own weapons inspectors over the oil-for-food program. The UN Monitoring, Verification, and Inspection Commission (UNMOVIC) recognized that Iraq was trying to buy goods, such as neutron generators and servo valves, that could be used in prohibited Iraqi military programs, even when, as the CIA said, "it easily could substitute items that could not be used for WMD." At one point in December 1999, UNMOVIC began screening the contracts under the program and spotted more than one hundred deals that had allowed militarily useful products to go to Iraq.

One of the most alarming deals made under the oil-for-food program came when Baghdad purchased a specialty chemical that could enhance its chemical or biological weapons. U.S. intelligence officials revealed that in August 2001 the Iraqis had ordered a large shipment of a chemical known as colloidal silicon dioxide from an unidentified supplier. The chemical, which was not on the UN's Goods Review List, was just the kind of dual-use product that Iraq could buy without arousing too many suspicions. Colloidal silicon dioxide can be used to make commercial products like glass and electronic-circuit boards. But that was not what worried the CIA. The real danger was that the substance could be used to create what are called "dusty" chemical or biological agents. Mixing the fine powder with anthrax or a chemical agent produces what the military calls a "persistent" weapon, an agent that can penetrate protective gear.

Chemical and biological weapons specialist Eric Croddy, a researcher with the Center for Nonproliferation Studies in Monterey, California, told me that colloidal silicon dioxide's particles are so small that they are largely unaffected by gravity, meaning that the chemical is easy to disperse and "can get everywhere." Croddy said that the chemical could greatly enhance nerve or toxin weapons. He summed up colloidal silicon dioxide's appeal to the Iraqis: "In the desert, where temperatures reach 104 degrees, they want to make sure their agents dissipate in the breeze."

In 2002, the U.S. State Department appealed to the United Nations not to send the shipment to Iraq. But the UN ultimately disregarded that request. A United Nations spokeswoman, Hasmik Egin, said that the United States had asked to put the contract on hold and that the UN had done so. But in October 2002, when the special sanctions committee received additional information on the sale, "that hold was lifted," she said.

One intelligence official familiar with reports of the chemical sale remarked, "The UN is helping the Iraqis to enhance their biological and chemical weapons."

Other evidence surfaced to indicate that Iraq was using the oil-for-food program to prepare for war. Intelligence reports indicated that Iraq had imported hundreds of atropine injectors, which are an antidote for chemical weapons. The injectors were not on the UN's list of goods banned for export, but John Negroponte, the U.S. ambassador to the United Nations, observed that the injectors "have no possible civilian use and would only be used, or could only be used, in a chemical warfare kind of situation." Iraq was also importing Russian-made jammers of the global positioning system (GPS), as seen in Chapter 3. These deals, combined with the dusty agent purchase, caused the Pentagon to step up efforts to close the loopholes in the Iraqi oil-for-food program. Defense officials appealed to the State Department, which is in charge of dealing with the United Nations.

The United States forced a vote within the United Nations Security Council to expand the Goods Review List. As Negroponte put it, the United States wanted to prevent the Iraqi government from importing "items for military purpose under civilian guise." On December 30, 2002, the Security Council approved the expanded Goods Review List.

The new resolution prevented the Iraqis from purchasing a number of items they had previously been able to acquire. U.S. intelligence officials helped draft the additions to the list. Among the items that the resolution banned, or at least limited, were trucks like those that Iraq was converting to missile launchers and artillery transports, atropine injectors, certain pesticides and chemicals, centrifuges and related equipment that could be used in chemical and biological arms, rocket motor cases and missile-related test equipment that sellers disguised as dual-use items, milling gear that could be used to make germ weapons, GPS jammers and receivers, special telecommunications equipment with military applications, armored trucks, electromagnetic pulse defenses, military-grade tires, fast work boats, and radar with military applications.

But by that point, the United States was just weeks from war with Iraq. The damage had been done. Indeed, it was the UN's failure to curb the Iraqi threat in the first place that forced the United States and coalition forces to launch a military assault against the Iraqi regime.

The UN's failure to halt the corruption of the oil-for-food program would haunt U.S. efforts to rebuild postwar Iraq. In May 2004, the Pentagon's Directorate of International Armament and Technology Trade, a special unit set up to track arms and technology transfers, began investigating an Iraqi-born Briton whom U.S. investigators had linked to the oil-for-food scandal. U.S. officials saw billionaire financier Nadhmi Auchi, a former Ba'ath Party member, as a key figure in the emerging scandal because of his close ties to officials in Saddam Hussein's regime. Moreover, most of the billions of dollars from the eight-year oil-for-food program had been deposited in the Paris bank BNP Paribas, in which Auchi was a major shareholder until 2001.

A report by the Directorate of International Armament and Technology Trade stated that Auchi had used his influence in the Iraqi regime, and in the international business community, to rig it so that the Middle Eastern and European cellular phone companies he favored edged out American firms for lucrative contracts to provide wireless phone service in Iraq. The contracts were worth as much as $500 million annually. Said one defense official, "The winners of the Iraqi cellular tender were Saddam's most senior financiers, their Egyptian, Kuwaiti, and Iraqi supporters, the bank BNP Paribas, European cellular corporations . . . , and Chinese telecom interests, such as Huawei, which had been active in breaking the Iraqi embargo. The losers were American bidders."

According to the report, "significant and credible evidence" indicated that "a conspiracy was organized by Auchi to offer bribes to 'fix' the awarding of cellular-licensing contracts covering three geographic areas of Iraq." Auchi thus gained access to the entire cellular phone system in postwar Iraq by using contacts and front companies to design the phone network's architecture and to make sure that he owned or controlled the components.

As the report pointed out, however, the problem with this alleged fixing was not simply that it cut American firms out of the contracts. More troubling, the official said, was that "it put in control of Iraqi telecommunications a man with an anti-American, anticoalition mindset and a history of illegal international arms traffic. That control could allow him to compromise the entire Iraqi telecommunications system and undermine the Iraqi security system on an ongoing basis."

If Auchi did fix the contracts in Iraq, it would not be the first time he practiced shady business dealings. In November 2003 he was convicted in a French court of accepting illegal payments from the oil company Elf-Aquitaine. He received a fifteen-month suspended prison sentence and a $2.4 million fine.

CONTINUAL FAILURES

The UN's refusal to deal with the Iraqi threat, as well its enabling of Saddam's military buildup, is a clear example of how the United Nations has failed to deal with threats to international peace and security. But it is just one of many examples we have seen in recent years.

The United Nations has shown itself to be a failure when it comes to monitoring nuclear weapons development by rogue states. Three times the UN's international nuclear watchdog agency missed the covert nuclear arms programs of rogue regimes, allowing those dangerous states to build up deadly weapons programs under the guise of generating nuclear power. If the UN's IAEA did not detect the nuclear weapons programs of North Korea, Libya, and Iran, one must wonder what purpose it serves.

The IAEA was established in 1957 to help countries build nuclear facilities for generating electricity. Its initial program, Atoms for Peace, quickly became "Atoms for Bombs." And not much has changed in the past five decades except the size of the program. Today the IAEA has some 2,200 staff members at its headquarters in Vienna and at four regional offices in Geneva, New York, Toronto, and Tokyo; its budget for 2004 was $268.5 million.

The IAEA's statute calls for the agency to assist in the transfer of expertise and equipment for the "peaceful" use of nuclear power. It also charges the IAEA with making sure that nations do not divert equipment or material for nuclear energy development into weapons programs. Specifically, Section 5 of the statute calls on the IAEA to "establish and administer safeguards designed to ensure that special fissionable and other materials, services, equipment, facilities, and information made available by the agency or at its request or under its supervision or control are not used in such a way as to further any military purpose."

In this function the IAEA has failed. The agency has not administered appropriate safeguards, and as a result it has been fooled again and again, by such states as North Korea, Iran, Libya, Syria, and Iraq.

The centerpiece of the IAEA's work has been the Treaty on the Nonproliferation of Nuclear Weapons (NPT), which went into effect on March 5, 1970. Rogue states generally sign international agreements only if doing so is expedient. Nothing better illustrates this point than North Korea's involvement in the NPT. The agreement provided cover for North Korea's secret nuclear weapons programs, allowing Pyongyang to purchase nuclear equipment, train technicians, and build nuclear reactors.

North Korea was one of the NPT's 188 signatories when, in the fall of 2002, it revealed that it had been secretly developing nuclear weapons. The IAEA failed to anticipate or uncover North Korea's nuclear weapons program, as the agency would admit in 2003, when it reported, "The Agency has never had the complete picture regarding [North Korean] nuclear activities." Pyongyang had frozen its plutonium production as part of the 1994 Agreed Framework. But the CIA noted in a classified 1995 "Special National Intelligence Estimate" that "based on North Korea's past behavior, the [intelligence] community agrees it would dismantle its known program [only] if it had covertly developed another source of fissile material." Sure enough, North Korea's October 2002 disclosure about its uranium enrichment confirmed that Pyongyang was trying to build bombs. In essence, the North Koreans were announcing that their membership in the NPT had been a ruse all along.

Still, the IAEA did not take a hard line on North Korea. It responded to the disclosure by sending faxes requesting "clarification." The North Koreans ignored the request. Then the IAEA issued a resolution calling on Pyongyang to cooperate. The North Koreans responded with a letter saying that they rejected the IAEA's unfair and unilateral approach. The director of North Korea's nuclear program, Ri Je-son, stated in a December 4, 2002, letter that Pyongyang would resume nuclear work if the United States resumed oil shipments to North Korea.

Then, on January 10, 2003, North Korea unceremoniously abandoned its partners in the NPT. In a broadcast on Pyongyang's Communist state radio, North Korean government commentator Jong Pong-kil stated that the decision to pull out of the NPT was a defensive measure: "The United States trampled on the NPT and the [North Korean]–US Agreed Framework and is trying to crush us by all means," he declared. "By even mobilizing the IAEA, the United States is compelling us to give up the right of self-defense. Under such conditions, it is clear to everyone that we cannot let the country's security and the nation's dignity be infringed upon by remaining in the NPT treaty." Jong then added a threat: "If the U.S. imperialists and their following forces challenge our republic's withdrawal from the NPT with new pressure and sanctions, we will respond with a stronger self-defensive measure."

In other words, the North Koreans, who had already shown that their membership in the NPT had been a ruse, were announcing that they would keep building nuclear arms.

The IAEA's response to Jong's announcement was tantamount to appeasement. North Korea, said IAEA director general Mohamed ElBaradei, must return to the NPT. Then, during a meeting with U.S. senators, the UN bureaucrat from Egypt announced, "If North Korea were to show good behavior, they need to get some assurance as to what to expect in return for good behavior, and I think that's very important in articulation of what to expect in case of compliance." It did not matter that the North Koreans had openly admitted defying the IAEA for years; ElBaradei sent the message that the IAEA would impose no penalty.

The matter was sent to the United Nations Security Council, but that body did little more than express "deep concern" for North Korea's violations. At this point, the United States picked up its diplomatic approach, but that produced no results. North Korea continues its drive for nuclear arms.

The UN also failed to deal with the nuclear threat from Iran, which, like North Korea, used the NPT to acquire its nuclear bomb–making equipment and materials. When Iran's weapons work was discovered, showing that the Iranians had knowingly ignored their obligations to their treaty partners, the IAEA essentially ignored the violations, seeking only an additional "protocol" to Iran's safeguards agreement. ElBaradei declared after Iran signed the additional protocol, "This is a good day for peace, multilateralism, and nonproliferation. . . . A good day for peace because the [IAEA] board decided to continue to make every effort to use verification and diplomacy to resolve questions about Iran's nuclear program." But "verification and diplomacy" had failed to stop Iran from developing nuclear arms in the first place. Despite pressure from security officials within the Bush administration, ElBaradei refused to cite Iran for violating its safeguards obligations.

Moreover, the IAEA did not keep careful watch over Libya's nuclear weapons program, which was further along than both U.S. intelligence and the IAEA had known. In fact, when Tripoli's weapons program was disclosed in December 2003, the IAEA knew nothing about it. In a statement, the agency said lamely that Libya should have reported its activities to the IAEA. The IAEA was happy to report Tripoli's decision to eliminate "materials, equipment, and programs which lead to the production of internationally proscribed weapons," but it tried to minimize the agency's failure to discover the program by noting that, according to a Libyan official, Libya's nuclear enrichment program was "at an early stage of development and that no industrial-scale facility had been built, nor any enriched uranium produced."

The disclosures about nuclear weapons in North Korea, Iran, and Libya came in rapid succession, all within the space of about a year. But those are not the only nuclear threats that the United Nations has failed to deal with. Algeria is another nation that appears intent on using its status as an NPT signatory to develop nuclear weapons. Reflecting how weapons proliferation only breeds further proliferation, Algeria launched its nuclear arms program in response to the military buildup by its neighbor Libya, with which relations had been tense.

U.S. intelligence agencies detected the first signs that Algeria was developing nuclear weapons back in the spring of 1991. In classified reports and briefings to Congress, the CIA revealed that China was helping Algeria build nuclear arms. A U.S. spy satellite had identified a Chinese reactor along Algeria's Mediterranean coast in the early stages of construction. Intelligence agencies also gathered evidence that Beijing was supplying technology with nuclear weapons applications and military advice on how to marry up the nuclear arms with aircraft or missile systems.

Chinese officials ignored U.S. protests over the Algerian deal.

Both the Chinese and the Algerians claimed that the reactor was strictly for "peaceful" purposes—a claim made by all rogue states that have developed nuclear weapons programs. The location of the power plant was the key indicator that it would not be used for generating electricity. "There are no electrical-power generation facilities at the reactor and no electric-power transmission lines are nearby," said a U.S. intelligence official who disclosed the cooperation between China and Algeria. "This is clearly a military nuclear reactor for weapons production." The Algerian plant also was armed with batteries of Russian-made SA-5 surface-to-air missiles. According to intelligence estimates, the nuclear reactor when fully operational could produce seventeen pounds of plutonium annually, enough for one nuclear weapon per year.

After the Chinese-Algerian nuclear ties were exposed, the IAEA inspected the facilities, a fifteen-megawatt reactor and a one-megawatt research reactor located at Ain Oussera and Draria, respectively. The facilities were then placed under IAEA "safeguards." The Algerian government also signed up to the NPT in 1995. But U.S. intelligence agencies worry that the Algerians, like the North Koreans, have used their participation in the IAEA as cover to allow them to secretly build nuclear arms, or at least the infrastructure for building those weapons in the future.

As dangerous as nuclear weapons are in the hands of rogue states, the ultimate threat to peace is nuclear weapons in the hands of international terrorists. There is a very real danger that nuclear materials could end up in the hands of terrorists who could use them in radiological attacks ("dirty bombs") or, worse, in an actual nuclear blast that could kill thousands or hundreds of thousands. To his credit, Mohamed ElBaradei has begun to worry about this future threat. "[Nuclear] source security has taken on a new urgency since 9/11," ElBaradei said in a 2003 speech. "There are millions of radiological sources used throughout the world. Most are very weak. What we are focusing on is preventing the theft or loss of control of the powerful radiological sources."

Yet with its record of failure with regard to halting nuclear arms programs, the United Nations might not be able to grapple with the threat. The fact is, the world's most lethal terrorist organizations are trying to acquire nuclear arms.

THE ULTIMATE PROLIFERATION NIGHTMARE

CHAPTER 10

The huge Saudi Arabian container ship arrived at the Red Hook Container Terminal in Brooklyn on a clear fall day. From the outside, the ship looked the same as the hundreds of other ships that docked at the terminal from Europe, Asia, and the Middle East. But the Saudi vessel was carrying a special cargo—one chosen with great care by Osama bin Laden, a Saudi national and the leader of the al Qaeda terrorist group that years before had attacked the World Trade Center, killing three thousand innocent men, women, and children. Hidden inside one of the ship's scores of blue metal shipping containers was a nuclear bomb. After years of trying, al Qaeda had succeeded in the difficult task of putting together a nuclear device, with the help of Pakistani scientists, black market equipment purchases, and, finally, a quantity of plutonium purchased from Russian organized crime figures.

At the appointed hour, a blinding white flash signaled the detonation, followed by the explosion equal to the blast made by 10,000 tons of TNT. The shock wave spread in a large circle from the Brooklyn terminal, leveling almost everything in its path—from the Statue of Liberty in New York Harbor, to the buildings in the far north of Manhattan,

to Kennedy Airport in Queens. The mushroom cloud could be seen as far away as Montauk Point, on the far tip of Long Island. Huge flames consumed everything that was left standing by the initial blast. The death toll from the immediate blast was staggering—at least 5 million people died instantly. Millions more died a slow, agonizing death from radiation sickness in the coming days.

The above scenario is fictional. But it is realistic. The truth is that terrorists are working on obtaining nuclear weapons of such destructive power that one detonation would have horrible consequences.

Defense Secretary Donald Rumsfeld told me that he sees terrorists using weapons of mass destruction as the ultimate arms-proliferation threat. "Sure it worries me," Rumsfeld said. "It has to worry me. The lethality of those kinds of capabilities is so substantial that one would be foolish not to be concerned and attentive."

The danger is real, and growing.

AL QAEDA'S NUCLEAR PUSH

On October 7, 2001, U.S. military forces moved into Afghanistan. Their targets: the Islamist Taliban regime and the terrorist organization being harbored in Afghanistan, al Qaeda. Only weeks earlier, al Qaeda terrorists had killed three thousand people in suicide airline attacks on American soil.

The war against terrorism had begun.

The military action in Afghanistan, known as Operation Enduring Freedom, did not turn up Osama bin Laden. But it did drive the Taliban out of Afghanistan, and perhaps more important, it uncovered important information about al Qaeda—information that shocked U.S. intelligence analysts. Documents found in several Afghan camps and buildings used by al Qaeda showed that the terrorist organization was developing deadly chemical, biological, and even nuclear weapons. The ultimate nightmare had come to pass. A radical Islamist group that showed no reluctance to kill people was looking for more deadly ways to attack its perceived enemies.

After the fall of Kabul, in November 2001, General Tommy

Franks, the commander of Operation Enduring Freedom, disclosed that U.S. forces had found dozens of places where the Taliban and al Qaeda might have been working on nuclear, chemical, or biological weapons. "We've identified more than forty places which represent potential for [weapons-of-mass-destruction] research or things of that sort," Franks told reporters. The goods found in Afghanistan included laboratory equipment and chemical compositions.

For example, U.S. intelligence agencies discovered an abandoned compound in the Afghan capital that had been used by bin Laden and his terrorists. The laboratory contained numerous jars of liquids as well as papers containing chemical formulas. In addition, U.S. searchers found documents relating to nuclear weapons, including a booklet offering advice on how to survive a nuclear explosion and, as the CIA later reported, a sketch of a crude nuclear device that could kill thousands or hundreds of thousands of people. The material at the laboratory convinced analysts that al Qaeda's interest in weapons of mass destruction was not theoretical. Officials believed that the terrorist group used the lab to work on chemical weapons, and perhaps even nuclear or radiological weapons.

At the same time, a reporter for the *Times* of London found more of al Qaeda's nuclear secrets in Kabul. The reporter found a number of partially burned documents in an abandoned al Qaeda safehouse in the Afghan capital. The documents, which were in Arabic, German, Urdu, and English, contained detailed missile and bomb designs. They also revealed how to use TNT to compress plutonium and create, ultimately, a thermonuclear blast. One set of notes, which were on letterhead from the Hotel Grand in Peshawar, Pakistan, and were dated April 26, 1998, stated, "Naturally the explosive liquid has a very high mechanical energy which is translated into destructive force. But it can be tamed, controlled and can be used as a useful propulsive fuel if certain methods are applied to it. A supersonic moving missile has a shock wave. That shock wave can be used to contain an external combustion behind the missile."

Osama bin Laden had already stated that his followers had a religious duty to acquire a nuclear bomb, telling an interviewer in 1999, "It would be a sin for Muslims not to try to possess the weapons that would prevent the infidels from inflicting harm on Muslims." Now here was evidence that he was actively pursuing nuclear weapons. Homeland Security Director Tom Ridge confirmed that this al Qaeda safehouse "had some materials relative to a nuclear threat," which, he said, would be consistent with bin Laden's "statements that he would like to acquire that capacity." Ridge played down the threat, saying that the evidence didn't necessarily mean that al Qaeda already possessed nuclear arms, but rather it simply indicated that "we have to be prepared for all eventualities, including a nuclear threat."

Investigators found still other documents in al Qaeda's four facilities in Kabul. Among the documents were papers showing research into a kinetic energy supergun capable of firing chemical or nuclear warheads; studies of external propulsion missiles; preliminary research into thermonuclear devices; and detailed instructions for making smaller bombs. The al Qaeda safehouses also had studies of how Western special forces carry out hostage rescue missions, the phone numbers for industrial chemical and synthetic material producers, flight manuals, aerodynamic research, and advanced physics and chemistry manuals.

The Kabul discoveries were not the first indication that bin Laden was going after weapons of mass destruction. In September 2001, two months before the Kabul laboratory was found, U.S. intelligence officials disclosed new evidence that the Russian mafia was working closely with al Qaeda to supply the terrorist group with components for weapons of mass destruction. "There are signs they have been supplying [bin Laden] with chemical and biological materials and nuclear components," said a U.S. official familiar with the intelligence reports. Long before that, in 1998, an FBI court document made public in New York stated that al Qaeda had tried since 1983 to purchase enriched uranium "for the purpose of developing nuclear weapons." Subsequent State Department reports on international terrorism noted that al Qaeda "continued" to seek chemical, biological, radiological, and nuclear capabilities.

It appeared that if bin Laden couldn't build nuclear weapons, he would buy them. With so many unscrupulous arms traders in the world, and with ineffective antiproliferation mechanisms in place, al Qaeda and many other terrorist groups could get their hands on the world's most dangerous weapons.

In September 2001, China's intelligence service, in one of its rare cases of sharing information with the United States, supplied the CIA with information indicating that al Qaeda had already obtained some type of nuclear device. U.S. intelligence officials said they could not confirm that report, but it was clear that bin Laden and his terrorist group would not rest until they had weapons of mass destruction. U.S. intelligence and security officials recognized this reality and upgraded their efforts to counter the threat. One intelligence official told me, "All the indicators are that the next big al Qaeda attack will involve weapons of mass destruction. We are preparing for that eventuality."

In April 2003, the CIA warned for the first time in a report that the danger of a chemical, biological, or nuclear attack by terrorists had grown since September 11. The CIA noted that diagrams found in Afghanistan, "while crude, describe essential components—uranium and high explosives—common to nuclear weapons." The report stated, "Bin Laden and his organization continue to make public statements about unconventional weapons, which could be an attempt to justify the use of such weapons." The CIA also stipulated that al Qaeda was not the only terrorist group pursuing weapons of mass destruction. The agency's report said that several of the thirty terrorist groups from around the world "have expressed interest" in obtaining biological, chemical, and nuclear arms. The CIA noted, however, that most groups would continue to favor "proven conventional tactics such as bombings and shootings."

"DIRTY BOMBS" AND POISONS

In the weeks, months, and years after the September 11, 2001, terrorist attacks, the United States learned a great deal about al Qaeda and its offshoots. Both the U.S. government and the public at large wanted to know what motivated these terrorists to kill thousands of innocent people in the name of religion. In 2003, the Defense Department produced a report arguing that the extremists of al Qaeda and other Islamist terrorist groups have adopted a twisted religious doctrine to support almost any kind of killing in what they perceive as the defense of Islam. According to the Pentagon report, the ideological fervor justifies suicide bombings and war, all in the name of jihad, or holy war.

And certainly the suicide bomber believes that, as the Defense Department report put it, he will secure "salvation and the pleasures of paradise" and will "find favor with God" as a result of his actions.

But other questions about these terrorist groups emerge after the larger question of their motivations has been answered. Indeed, in discussing the forces driving Islamist terrorists, the Defense Department could not ignore the important question of how these terrorists are executing their strategy. Motive is one thing, but the Pentagon discussed means and opportunity as well. And, the report said, "the means consists of the final development or arrival of, or access to, technologies and skills necessary to fabricate a variety of command detonated explosives."

Terrorists are working hard to make sure they have these means. In a report made public in June 2003, the CIA revealed that al Qaeda terrorists consider unconventional weapons to be an important part of their global strategy. "Al Qaeda's end goal is the use of [chemical, biological, radiological, or nuclear weapons] to cause mass casualties," the CIA stated in the report. Several groups linked to al Qaeda had already attempted, but failed to execute, poison attacks in Europe. Those attacks appeared to be small-scale, but toxins and nerve agents could cause hundreds of casualties and widespread panic if used in simultaneous attacks.

The CIA's report also noted that al Qaeda had shown interest in using biological weapons. September 11 attack leader Mohammad Atta and plot suspect Zacarias Moussaoui had looked into agricultural crop dusters, which raised "our concern that al Qaeda has considered using aircraft to disseminate [biological weapons] agents," the CIA said.

In addition, the CIA report discussed how a document recovered from Afghanistan in the summer of 2002 revealed that al Qaeda "has crude procedures for making mustard agent, sarin, and VX." The report listed the various types of weapons that al Qaeda and other terrorists are planning to use or develop, including

- **Cyanides:** Sodium or potassium cyanides are white-to-pale-yellow salts that can easily be used to poison food or drinks, while hydrogen cyanide and cyanogen chloride are colorless-to-pale-yellow liquids that turn into gas as the temperature rises to room temperature or slightly below it. Exposure to cyanide can produce nausea, vomiting, palpitations, confusion, hyperventilation, anxiety, and vertigo that can progress into agitation, stupor, coma, and death. At high doses, cyanide causes immediate collapse.

• **Mustard agent:** This blistering agent can be produced with relative ease. Inhalation damages the lungs and causes breathing problems; death by suffocation can follow. Contact with mustard agent causes skin blisters to appear within six to twenty-four hours.

• **Nerve agents:** Sarin, tabun, and VX are highly toxic military agents that kill by disrupting a person's nervous system. Significant chemical expertise is required to make a nerve agent, but exposure to small amounts is deadly. Intelligence officials say that classified analysis of the types of chemicals and toxins al Qaeda has sought indicate that the group is probably trying to produce sarin.

• **Anthrax:** The bacterium that causes anthrax, *Bacillus anthracis,* can produce mass casualties. The disease is nearly always fatal unless antibiotic treatment is administered within hours of a person's inhaling anthrax spores. Anthrax can be spread by aerosol or can be used to contaminate food and water supplies. The disease can also infect people by skin contact, but this form is rarely fatal and can be treated with antibiotics.

• **Botulinum toxin:** Terrorist training manuals have shown ways to make small quantities of botulinum toxin, which is produced by a bacterium found in soil. The toxin can cause vomiting, abdominal pain, muscular weakness, and impaired sight. Terrorists can use botulinum toxin in small-scale poisonings or aerosol attacks in enclosed spaces like movie theaters.

• **Ricin:** Ricin is a plant toxin that is thirty times more powerful than the nerve agent VX by weight and that is easy to extract from castor beans. There is no treatment for ricin poisoning after it has entered the bloodstream. Signs of ricin poisoning can appear within hours. Terrorists have explored spreading ricin in foods and as a contact poison.

• **Radiological dispersal device:** This device, also known as a "dirty bomb," is made up of conventional explosives and radioactive material. It is designed to cause destruction, contamination, and injury from radiation, and also to generate fear and panic. A simple dirty bomb combines a lead-shielded container with about a kilogram of explosive; it could easily fit inside a backpack. Another dirty bomb is an atmospheric device that spreads radioactive material on air currents. The CIA noted that dirty bombs are "well within [al Qaeda's] capabilities as radiological materials are relatively easy to acquire from industrial or medical sources."

• **Improvised nuclear device:** The ultimate terror weapon, this bomb is designed to cause a yield-producing nuclear explosion. The bomb could be made up of diverted nuclear weapons components, could be a modified nuclear weapon, or could be device designed from scratch. To create such a bomb, terrorists first need highly enriched uranium or plutonium.

For all the discussion of unconventional weapons, the CIA did not ignore the damage Osama bin Laden and his fanatics could do with conventional attacks "against the nuclear industrial infrastructure of the United States in a bid to cause contamination, disruption, and terror." In fact, according to a special report that a senior Defense Intelligence Agency analyst produced in 2003, in the weeks leading up to the September 11 terrorist attacks, al Qaeda terrorist Mohammad Atta rented a small plane and flew over the Indian Point nuclear power plant, which is located about twenty-four miles north of New York City. Atta was planning to fly a hijacked commercial airliner into the plant as part of an al Qaeda plot to create a radiological disaster, but according to U.S. intelligence officials, al Qaeda leader Ayman al Zawahiri rejected the plan as too dangerous.

Two other al Qaeda officials, Khalid Sheikh Mohammed and Ramzi Binalshibh, confirmed this nuclear plot in June 2002, telling Al-Jazeera television that the initial plan had been to crash the hijacked jets into nuclear power plants. Mohammed told Al-Jazeera reporter Yosri Fouda, "When we began to examine the targets, the idea of attacking nuclear reactors began to crystallize." But ultimately, he said, al Qaeda scrapped the plan because of fears that "it would go out of control." Perhaps the terrorists feared nuclear debris would reach the Middle East.

Nevertheless, the terrorists did not rule out the idea of targeting nuclear plants for future operations. Authorities in Manchester, England, searched an al Qaeda member's home and uncovered an al Qaeda training manual. The eleven-volume manual identified nuclear facilities as good targets for attacks that would spread fear in the United States and Europe. Other targets mentioned included skyscrapers, crowded football stadiums, and sites that have "sentimental value," such as the Statue of Liberty, London's Big Ben, and Paris's Eiffel Tower.

BOMBS FOR THE ASKING

Al Qaeda and other terrorist organizations are clearly eager to make their attacks as deadly as possible, so it is troubling how easy it might be for them to get components for advanced weapons. Russia probably poses the biggest threat when it comes to arming terrorists, because it has stockpiles of biological and nuclear weapons that are not well protected.

At its height during the Cold War, the Soviet biological weapons program employed some 65,000 people, and U.S. officials have feared for years that some of these out-of-work biological weapons scientists will sell their expertise to terrorists like bin Laden. Also, as noted, Russian crime groups could well be providing bin Laden's Islamic extremists with components for advanced weapons. That would not be surprising, for they have already established a close partnership with al Qaeda, according to U.S. intelligence officials. The Russian mafia has reportedly provided al Qaeda with small arms and helped bin Laden launder money from drug trafficking. A boat that the U.S. Navy seized in the Strait of Hormuz in December 2003 confirmed that al Qaeda was still earning money from drug trafficking. The forty-foot dhow was carrying forty-five bags of hashish, each weighing seventy pounds. The street value of the drugs was about $10 million. Four of the small vessel's twelve crew members had ties to al Qaeda.

One of the biggest fears of intelligence and security officials is that bin Laden or other terrorists will manage to covertly buy special atomic demolition munitions (SADMs). The Soviet Union produced these tactical nuclear weapons for its special operations commandos toward the end of the Cold War, to be used against bridges, command posts, and similar targets. The chilling prospect of the bombs getting loose on the international black market was raised in September 1997. Alexander Lebed, a retired Russian general and former national security adviser to

Russian president Boris Yeltsin, announced that as many as one hundred of the "suitcase nukes" were lost, were "not under the control of the armed forces of Russia." (The term "suitcase bombs" is somewhat misleading, since these weapons are actually the size of small steamer trunks. Still, the bombs are portable.)

Lebed, who was killed in a helicopter crash in 2002, sounded the alarm about this missing inventory. "Can you imagine what would happen psychologically, morally, if this weapon is detonated in a city?" the general asked. "No government would want to see such a situation. About 50,000 to 70,000 people, up to 100,000 people would be killed." Indeed, these nuclear weapons have the blast power of one kiloton—the equivalent of a thousand tons of TNT.

The Russian government denied that any of the suitcase nuclear bombs even existed and did not list them as part of its nuclear arsenal. Shortly after Lebed went public with his claims, however, Alexei Yablokov, a former member of the Russian National Security Council, confirmed in testimony before the House of Representatives that the small nuclear devices existed. The KGB had directed the development of the SADMs, Yablokov said.

A U.S. intelligence official told me that a Russian defector provided detailed information that the KGB and its military counterpart, the GRU, had covertly hidden several of these tactical nuclear weapons in the United States. The FBI dismissed the intelligence as not credible, but other officials were not so sure. In any case, the possibility that the bombs are in the country has never been investigated. Meanwhile, U.S. intelligence agencies have never been able to confirm the numerous intelligence reports that some of the small nuclear bombs were lost, stolen, or sold on the black market.

The CIA and other intelligence agencies did not have much confidence in the intelligence regarding al Qaeda's acquisition of portable tactical nuclear weapons. The only fact arguing against the idea that the terrorist group has gotten such weapons is that it has never used any. And intelligence reports continued to surface that the group has obtained portable nuclear weapons on the Russian black market.

As for nuclear material that could be used as fuel for a nuclear bomb, the International Atomic Energy Agency (IAEA) does not rule out that al Qaeda has some weapons-grade fissile material. The agency stated in a 2001 report that several kilograms of plutonium or several times that amount of highly enriched uranium is enough to make a bomb. And a terrorist could build a bomb within weeks of getting hold of bomb-grade material, if the right preparations had been made. "The international community could be faced with a new threat with virtually no warning—and virtually no time to dissuade the proliferator from building a bomb," the report said. "Reactor-grade plutonium poses nearly as great a proliferation threat as weapons-grade plutonium, as crude nuclear explosives can be made from reactor-grade material with no greater technology or sophistication than would be required for making explosives from weapons-grade material."

Unirradiated mixed materials such as uranium-plutonium mixed oxide, also known as MOX fuel, are also a danger. "Any group capable of making a nuclear weapon from plutonium metal would likely be capable of accomplishing the less difficult task of separating plutonium from fresh MOX and reducing it to metal," the IAEA report said. "Those seeking to acquire nuclear material will go wherever it is easiest to steal, and buy it from anyone willing to sell—and the terrorists of September 11 have demonstrated global reach. Hence, vulnerable weapons-usable nuclear material anywhere is a threat to everyone everywhere."

As the IAEA report indicated, there is no shortage of weapons-grade material, with the worldwide supply of separated plutonium estimated at 450 tons and of highly enriched uranium at more than 1,700 tons. These stockpiles, both military and civilian, are concentrated in the five nuclear weapons states of the United States, Russia, China, Britain, and France. Other plutonium stocks are located in India, Israel, Belgium, Germany, Japan, and Switzerland.

"Most of these weapons and materials are reasonably well secured and accounted for," the IAEA said. "But this is by no means universally the case. Levels of security and accounting for both the military and civilian material vary widely, with no binding international standards in place. Some weapons-usable material is dangerously insecure and so poorly accounted for that if it were stolen, no one might ever know."

And the people involved in making nuclear weapons are showing up in rogue states. In 1998, for instance, one Russian nuclear weapons specialist was caught spying for Iraq and Afghanistan, and in October 2000, Russia blocked the Taliban's effort to recruit a former Soviet nuclear weapons scientist. The IAEA report noted the real risk: "A knowledgeable expert from a major state weapons-of-mass-destruction program could substantially accelerate a proliferator's weapons-of-mass-destruction program, or make it possible for a terrorist group to achieve a nuclear, chemical, or biological capability that would otherwise be beyond their reach."

The IAEA has linked al Qaeda to nuclear trafficking. Jamal Ahmed al-Fadl, who defected from al Qaeda and helped convict former colleagues for the 1998 U.S. embassy bombings in East Africa, claimed that he had bought $1 million worth of enriched uranium in Sudan. He said that bin Laden paid him $10,661 as part of the scheme to acquire nuclear goods. Al-Fadl did not know if the material was genuine, but he maintained that it was sent to a terrorist training facility in Afghanistan.

Also, in 2001, a Bulgarian businessman claimed that he had met bin Laden after being asked by al Qaeda to establish a front company to help acquire highly radioactive material. The businessman, a former intelligence officer, said that al Qaeda offered him $243,000 but that he turned down the offer. The next day, the Bulgarian said he met with a Pakistani scientist who wanted help in buying spent nuclear fuel rods from Bulgaria's Kozlodui nuclear electricity plant. The Pakistani was one of several scientists detained in Pakistan and questioned by authorities regarding links to bin Laden and al Qaeda's nuclear program in Afghanistan.

In another instance, in September 1998, Mamdouh Mahmud Salim, a senior associate of bin Laden, attempted to purchase nuclear reactor fuel. He was arrested by German authorities.

Al Qaeda might have been thwarted in that attempt and at other times, but radical terrorist groups have shown that they will not be deterred. It is not hard to imagine a scenario in which terrorists procure weapons of mass destruction—that is, if they haven't already. The question then becomes, How and when will they use those weapons? That is the ultimate proliferation nightmare.

CONCLUSION

THE WAY AHEAD

The team of U.S. Special Forces commandos silently streamed out of the back of a U.S. Army MH-60 Pave Hawk helicopter on the deck of a U.S. Navy troop-carrying ship. The mission: Destroy North Korea's uranium-enrichment facility hidden deep underground, beneath yards of solid rock. Inside the facility was a centrifuge cascade—used to produce highly enriched uranium, the key ingredient for nuclear bombs. The North Koreans had obtained the centrifuge design from Pakistan, which had stolen a European design.

North Korea's covert nuclear operation had become more advanced since October 2002, when the North Koreans revealed to a U.S. diplomat that they had been secretly developing nuclear weapons in violation of their 1994 agreement with the United States. In fact, ever since the 2003 U.S. military operation in Iraq that ousted Saddam Hussein, North Korean dictator Kim Jong-il had been desperate to produce at least five reliable nuclear bombs—that is, five bombs in addition to the four or five devices that North Korea had kept in pieces since the mid-1990s but had never tested in an underground blast. The covert uranium-enrichment facility was the key to that effort.

Intelligence officials had discovered the North Koreans' underground nuclear plant only months earlier. Now, however, the Special Forces troops knew the exact location of the secret facility, which U.S. intelligence had code-named Mayflower. The commandos had swung into action in a matter of hours, after U.S. officials received a simple message from an allied penetration agent in Pyongyang, one of the most difficult security environments for agents. "Mayflower has bloomed," the message said.

From the Navy vessel, the Special Forces commandos swam to a deserted North Korean beach some thirty miles south of the port of Hungnam. Once ashore, they jumped aboard the vintage Russian-made military transport trucks that were waiting for them. The trucks were identical to those used by the Korean People's Army. The drivers were Korean-American Special Forces sergeants who spoke Korean fluently and with a North Korean accent. The team sped down the road toward the mountains and the underground uranium plant.

After several hours of winding their way in total darkness, with the drivers using the most advanced night-vision goggles, the trucks reached their objective. The sign, written in Hangul, the Korean alphabet, read "Soap Plant No. 142." Yet the small dilapidated building in front of them was no soap plant. The North Koreans used it to hide their nuclear weapons plant from U.S. reconnaissance satellites and aircraft.

The guards at the North Korean facility were expecting the trucks, but they had no idea of the true purpose of the visit. An hour earlier, the commando team had sent a message to the plant saying that the trucks were bringing an important visitor to the facility. The plant had accepted the message because the Special Forces had known the exact method, wording, and channel for North Korean secret communications related to the nuclear program.

Once inside, the elite U.S. military team quickly killed the guards and cut off the facility's communications with high military and industrial headquarters before any alerts could be sent out. The team was inside the 100-square-foot centrifuge room within minutes of arriving. Emptying the facility of workers, the commandos photographed the complex and then dismantled one of the centrifuges, packing it in boxes. Then they set explosive charges and detonated them, leaving the room a charred mess of metal and equipment.

The entire operation lasted seventy-five minutes. The commandos had the time they needed to carry out the sabotage and escape because South Korea had created a diversion. South Korean gunboats had engaged several North Korean patrol boats in waters off the western side of the peninsula.

Thanks to U.S. intelligence, the U.S. military, and the cooperation of an American ally, a rogue regime had suddenly lost its ability to threaten the world with the most dangerous weapons.

This fictional scenario is something that the U.S. government is working on as part of its efforts to stop the spread of deadly weapons and technology to rogue states and terrorists. In many cases the United States and the United Nations have failed to prevent our friends or our foes from arming the greatest threats to global security, so the challenge will be to counter the threats that treacherous arms traders have created.

A PLAN OF ACTION

The transfer of dangerous weapons and related technology is the most significant threat to U.S. national security for the foreseeable future. The global war against terrorism is making progress at rooting out Islamist and other terrorist groups, and it has also forced some rogue regimes to change their approach. Simply put, these regimes saw what happened to Saddam Hussein, and they do not want to be the next target.

The successes of the war on terrorism have come largely because the U.S. military has projected its power and, to a lesser extent, because of achievements of the American intelligence community. The arms-

control regimes and policies of the past will not be able to provide the framework for keeping arms and weapons technologies out of the hands of terrorists and rogue states. Unless new systems are established to deal effectively with the spread of nuclear, biological, and chemical weapons and missiles, the danger will grow. A strike against the United States with these horrendous mass-casualty weapons will be inevitable.

In addition to instituting policies and structures that deter arms proliferation, the United States needs to take action, either military or intelligence, when nonproliferation agreements fail.

The centerpiece of the Bush administration's efforts to stop arms proliferation has been the Proliferation Security Initiative. The program was the brainchild of John Bolton, undersecretary of state for arms control. With the Proliferation Security Initiative, the conservative policymaker has put together a core group of nations that have agreed to take the first steps in actually fighting arms transfers on the seas and ultimately in the air and on the ground.

President George W. Bush announced the initiative in May 2003 during a visit to Krakow, Poland. "The greatest threat to peace is the spread of nuclear, chemical, and biological weapons," the president said. "And we must work together to stop proliferation." The initiative called for taking steps to stop arms sales at the source. "When weapons of mass destruction or their components are in transit, we must have the means and authority to seize them," Bush said. The plan called for working with allies to set up new agreements that would give initiative members the power to "search planes and ships carrying suspect cargo and to seize illegal weapons or missile technologies." President Bush declared, "Over time, we will extend this partnership as broadly as possible to keep the world's most destructive weapons away from our shores and out of the hands of our common enemies."

Eleven nations signed on to the Proliferation Security Initiative: the United States, Australia, Canada, France, Germany, Italy, Japan, the Netherlands, Poland, Portugal, and Spain. The participation of France and Germany, which U.S. security officials consider to be two of the most irresponsible arms proliferators, is viewed as a sign that Paris and Berlin will change their past behavior. In the early going, the program was limited to exercises by PSI members' military and security agencies. For example, in late 2003, they conducted a military exercise that simulated the boarding of a North Korea ship in waters off Australia.

Although headed by a State Department arms official, the initiative was also the work of Defense Secretary Donald Rumsfeld, Deputy Defense Secretary Paul Wolfowitz, and Undersecretary of Defense for Policy Douglas Feith. In an exclusive interview, Rumsfeld told me that the Proliferation Security Initiative is essential, saying, "There does not seem to be any other way." The defense secretary acknowledged, however, that the initiative will require "a lot of diplomatic effort around the world to see that we get the capability, the authorization, the legal right, if you will, to interdict the transfer of these weapons, if they're going to end up in the hands of terrorists or terrorist states, or states that cooperate with terrorist states."

Prior to the announcement of the initiative, Rumsfeld told a group of unofficial advisers that it was time for the United States to "get serious about WMD and the axis of evil." One of those whom Rumsfeld tasked with looking at ways to stop arms transfers was Pentagon consultant Michael Pillsbury. In 1986, as a Defense Department official, Pillsbury played a key role in the success of one of the U.S. government's most important covert operations, one that offers an important lesson in the need for action-oriented policies. Pillsbury helped push through a joint Pentagon-CIA effort to send Stinger antiaircraft missiles to Afghanistan's anti-Soviet resistance fighters. The program helped the lightly armed Afghan rebels defeat the Soviet army in Afghanistan, a defeat that has been credited with pushing the Soviet empire into the ash heap of history.

The 1980s Stinger operation offers another important lesson for today: It shows how, to achieve these successes, U.S. officials might need to push their programs through an entrenched and overly cautious government bureaucracy. This is precisely what Pillsbury and his boss at the time, Fred Ikle, the undersecretary of defense for policy, did with the Stinger program. A CIA-sponsored study produced by Harvard University's John F. Kennedy School of Government in 2000 revealed that the Stinger operation succeeded despite the efforts of CIA bureaucrats who opposed the program on political grounds. In the unusually candid study, Thomas Twetten, the CIA's Near East operations chief from 1983 to 1986, was quoted describing the Reagan political appointees who favored the Stinger transfers as "strange people developing strange ideas" and as "the rabid right." In contrast, Twetten considered himself and his colleagues who opposed the transfers to be "sensible bureaucrats." Indeed, Twetten had lots of like-minded thinkers with him in the CIA bureaucracy. The CIA's station chief in Pakistan, William Piekney, worried that sending the missiles to Afghanistan would expose the CIA's support for the Afghan fighters, even though it was known throughout the world that the agency was backing the rebels. And according to the Harvard report, the CIA feared that sending the Stingers "would risk provoking retaliation from the Soviets against host country Pakistan—and such an attack could plausibly escalate into World War III."

But the Pentagon pushed the plan through, and it worked. Thus, when Rumsfeld asked Pillsbury to address the issue of stopping weapons proliferation, the Pentagon consultant outlined a new policy that called on the U.S. government's experiences with Afghanistan and the Soviets. In a memorandum sent to senior policymakers within the U.S. government in late 2003, Pillsbury presented sound ideas for an action-oriented approach to counterproliferation.

Specifically, the new policy called for using U.S. Special Forces troops in the covert war against arms proliferation. According to Pillsbury's plan, the Pentagon would create three Special Operations Joint Task Forces, one within the U.S. European Command, one within the U.S. Pacific Command, and one within the U.S. Central Command, which covers the Middle East and South Asia. The Special Forces units, which would be part of the military-intelligence component of the Proliferation Security Initiative, would conduct intensive operational training designed to deal specifically with threats from terrorists and rogue states equipped with nuclear, chemical, and biological weapons and with missile delivery systems.

Just as special operations commandos carefully prepared for prisoner-of-war raids in North Vietnam in the 1980s and for the hostage-rescue operation in Iran in 1979, the task forces would undergo realistic training based on what intelligence knew about weapons-of-mass-destruction facilities and missile sites. The forces would train for their missions using exact replicas of weapons facilities like North Korea's nuclear reprocessing plants and Iran's underground nuclear sites.

The key to the entire concept is for the task forces to be ready to conduct rapid-response missions based on "actionable intelligence." Intelligence might arrive at any time and can be perishable, and only by rigorously training Special Forces for interdiction missions can the United States be prepared to seize the opportunity to shut down or stop a weapons program. Soldiers and their equipment must be ready to go just hours from receipt of intelligence that, say, a terrorist group has acquired a nuclear weapon and is planning to set it off, or a rogue state has transferred weapons-related goods to terrorists bent on killing innocent people.

Pillsbury's specific plan has six key steps. First, the CIA and other U.S. intelligence agencies need to get actionable intelligence on weapons-of-mass-destruction and missile programs. To provide this sort of intelligence, the intelligence agencies will require substantial restructuring and additional resources.

Second, the Pentagon must set up the two Joint Task Forces, which should be prepared to conduct covert action operations against weapons and missiles within twelve hours of being notified to deploy.

Third, before any covert actions can be launched, the government needs to work out the authorization for such operations. Specifically, the operations would require presidential "findings," or authorizations from the president, that the activities are in America's national security interest. Securing presidential findings, which are necessary to triggering action, often requires pushing and shoving among various government agencies and can be a cumbersome process. As a result, specialists within the military, the civilian defense agencies, and the intelligence and law enforcement communities need to establish presidential findings in advance of the operations.

A fourth element is to make detailed arrangements with allied special operations forces to conduct joint training on full-scale mockups of weapons-of-mass-destruction and missile facilities of target countries and groups.

Fifth, the government needs to work out an approval process for various specific scenarios in advance. Because getting approval for action from State, Defense, Justice, and the military and intelligence agencies can be a slow process, such interagency approval should be "on the shelf." This would allow the U.S. government to act promptly on intelligence when it comes in, and while the intelligence is still valid. The government agencies would, in advance, approve action based on intelligence indicating, for example, that a terrorist group will receive a nuclear, chemical, or biological weapons transfer or that a rogue state plans to use such arms. "If the moment of a [nuclear] transfer is coming quickly," Pillsbury said, "there would be no time to go back and call together the National Security Council."

Sixth, the joint task forces need to cooperate with foreign special operations forces to conduct some of the higher-risk operations, such as the use of commandos to board and stop ships carrying weapons cargo at sea.

Pillsbury noted in the memorandum that the Special Operations Command has been responsible for countering the spread of nuclear, chemical, and biological weapons since 1998. But the command has not been funded to conduct missions. It needs several hundred million dollars to build mockups of nuclear facilities in North Korea and Iran, for example. For counterproliferation operations, the Special Operations Command needs at least double its current number of AC-130 gunships, which can train their cannons on specific targets while in flight. U.S. military forces also urgently need better sensors to be able to detect shield nuclear weapons. Rogue states that are building nuclear arms are using concealment techniques, such as venting radioactive gas into closed containers to avoid detection.

If anything has become clear in recent years, it is that dangerous regimes and terrorist groups will go to any lengths to get weapons of mass destruction, and that they will find no shortage of willing suppliers. The U.S. government urgently needs an action plan to deal with this national security threat.

OVERCOMING OPPOSITION AND TAKING ACTION

The Pillsbury plan seemed to be precisely the sort of proactive approach to the proliferation threat that the United States needed. It's possible that the mere potential for such an approach can rein in rogue regimes. For example, U.S. intelligence officials say they have evidence that North Korean leader Kim Jong-il believes that the United States already has a plan for dealing with his hidden arms programs. Kim ducked out of public sight for months after U.S. forces invaded Iraq, which intelligence officials viewed as a clear sign that the erratic North Korean dictator, whose nation President Bush labeled as part of the "Axis of Evil," saw his regime as next after Saddam Hussein's Iraqi regime and the Islamist regime in Iran. In nuclear talks, North Korea appeared desperate to gain some kind of assurance from the United States that it would not be attacked.

Nevertheless, the Pillsbury plan has met with bureaucratic resistance. Such resistance is typical of government bureaucrats when high-risk initiatives are proposed. Bureaucrats often oppose new policies that upset the status quo, and many reflexively object to ideas that infringe on their own areas of responsibility. The State Department is especially guilty of this. The department's Foreign Service bureaucracy—which has been given great authority under Secretary of State Colin Powell—generally opposes any activities that would undermine its culture of diplomacy. Thus, diplomats tend to favor negotiations and agreements over military action and intelligence operations.

An example was the CIA–State Department fight over China's delivery of short-range missiles to Pakistan in the 1990s. Gordon Oehler, who headed the CIA's Nonproliferation Center before retiring in 1997, testified to Congress that Clinton administration policymakers used "almost any measure" to block intelligence judgments confirming that China had delivered thirty-four M-11 missiles to Pakistan in November 1992 (a deployment first disclosed by this author in the *Washington Times*). According to U.S. antiproliferation laws, the weapons sale should have automatically triggered stiff economic sanctions against China. But Oehler told the Senate Foreign Relations Committee of how Clinton administration officials had "summarily dismissed" solid intelligence on the weapons transfer in order to protect the Chinese from sanctions. The Clinton administration, Oehler said, was using "loopholes" in U.S. law and requiring unrealistic standards of proof.

The administration levied only minor penalties against China—for selling missile components, not for selling missiles. And the U.S.

government lifted those minor sanctions after a short time, when the Chinese government promised to abide by the terms of the Missile Technology Control Regime, an export control agreement aimed at preventing the spread of missiles and related technology. The Clinton administration did not divert from its appeasement strategy despite the fact that this was the second time China had been caught transferring missile equipment to Pakistan in the space of two years—and the second time the Chinese government had promised to honor its nonproliferation agreements.

The lesson was not lost on proliferators like China and Russia, which saw that the U.S. government ignored proliferation intelligence and did not act to stop transfers of weapons of mass destruction.

The intelligence agencies themselves can be a problem as well. More often than not, the CIA has appeared more concerned with protecting the agency from criticism than with pursuing its mission. This proclivity at times has bordered on criminal negligence. A case in point was when the CIA protected an official who in 1998 improperly tipped off a U.S. defense contractor, Hughes Space and Communications International, that the U.S. Senate was investigating the company for illegal missile technology transfers to China. The Senate Intelligence Committee had specifically directed the CIA not to alert Hughes to the inquiry, and the tipoff undermined the Senate probe. A classified 1998 Pentagon report concluded that the Hughes technology transfer probably gave China a "significant" boost in its long-range missiles, more than a dozen of which are targeted at U.S. cities. Still, the CIA defended the official's action, claiming that the officer had notified Hughes only so it would cooperate with the investigation. The Justice Department in 2000 declined to prosecute the intelligence official on obstruction-of-justice charges. The CIA quietly covered up the matter, taking no punitive action against the official, whose identity was not revealed.

The CIA, as it did during the Stinger debate of 1986, has opposed working with the military on active counterproliferation measures. U.S. officials told me that the CIA has been reluctant to support the Proliferation Security Initiative because agency bureaucrats believe it will undermine the authority of the CIA-led Nonproliferation Center, which is now known as the Director of Central Intelligence Center for Weapons

Intelligence, Nonproliferation, and Arms Control, or WINPAC. The center is made up of analysts and operations officers from the CIA and other agencies. It also employs engineers in nuclear, chem/bio, mechanical, and aerospace affairs; mathematicians; physicists; economists; political scientists; computer specialists; and physical scientists.

The bureaucrats who have argued against setting up the Special Forces task forces on counterproliferation have sounded the themes of most bureaucratic opposition—mainly, that it cannot be done and that even if it is done, it will cause more problems instead of leading to solutions.

First, intelligence bureaucrats and some Bush administration policymakers have argued that the kind of actionable intelligence needed for such operations is impossible to gather. This is very similar to the defeatist approach to terrorism intelligence that, despite the intelligence failures of September 11, continues to dog U.S. spy agencies. The general cultural view within the intelligence community is that terrorist attacks cannot be predicted by analysts, or stopped by intelligence operators, in advance. As one intelligence specialist put it, that view is like training to win an Olympic medal by telling yourself it is impossible to win one. This mindset must be overcome if the more than $30 billion in taxpayers' money spent each year on intelligence is ever to produce real results.

The kind of actionable intelligence needed for the Special Forces counterproliferation task forces can be acquired, but it will require vastly improving U.S. human intelligence-gathering capabilities. This is the most difficult intelligence work, for it involves planting or recruiting agents inside governments and organizations. But these agents also learn the most important secrets.

Another objection to the counterproliferation plan has been that it will weaken efforts to promote the Proliferation Security Initiative. The solution to this would be to wait until the initiative is established after a year or two—but no longer—before beginning the military action component.

Also, some government officials have objected to the counterproliferation task forces on international legal grounds, claiming that the program needs to be under the United Nations charter. But the U.S. government could solve this problem by going to the United Nations in advance of instituting the program. Dealing with the UN would be a major challenge. Nevertheless, the UN Security Council could issue resolutions supporting the Proliferation Security Initiative and authorizing the United States and other countries to act against proliferators if they face a "clear and present danger," such as when a terrorist group procures a weapon of mass destruction. The resolutions could clarify in advance that no further Security Council action would be needed when the proliferation danger emerges. Although some UN members might oppose this, a sustained U.S. diplomatic effort to support the plan would eventually produce useful results at the world body.

The last objection has been that the CIA could do the job by itself, that the United States doesn't need to use special military forces. In short, the problem is that the CIA is reluctant to cooperate with the Pentagon, seeing the military as an interloper into its area of covert operations. Opponents of the plan point to problems with the Stinger decision in 1986, when a risk-averse CIA had to be dragged kicking and screaming into supporting the effort by Pentagon officials. They also claim that the CIA played the major role in the ouster of Afghanistan's Taliban militia in 2001, even though the agency had been caught without a covert-action capability and had to cobble one together from special operations commandos.

It is true that the CIA could do the job, but only by detailing large numbers of Special Forces troops to augment its depleted covert-action ranks, something the agency was forced to do after the September 11, 2001, terrorist attacks. The process is known in the intelligence world as "sheep dipping"—taking soldiers and making them intelligence personnel. Special Forces will be essential to the success of the counterproliferation initiative, because most foreign special operations troops, who would work with the task forces, do not trust the CIA and prefer to work with fellow special operations soldiers. Also, should a CIA-led special operations action escalate to the point that the target enemy responded with force, who could be sent in to rescue the CIA team members? The military is best equipped and trained for the job.

Perhaps the biggest challenge for the new counterproliferation action program will be dealing with the United Nations. The actions of France, Germany, Russia, and China during debate on Iraq in 2003 showed that gaining support will be difficult. Undoubtedly many would oppose a hard-line U.S.-led counterproliferation action program. But the challenge can be met if the United States takes a leadership role, and it must be met if the United States is to address this most dangerous threat to our national security.

One way the United States could overcome UN objections would be to point to the international support already given to the idea of setting up a counterproliferation task force. In fact, NATO has already set up the first element of a counterproliferation force. The NATO Response Force eventually will have 20,000 troops that can be deployed on short notice to any location in the world. The forces are currently focused on countering terrorism and conducting embargo enforcement, both of which are important to countering weapons proliferation. The idea was first proposed by Defense Secretary Donald Rumsfeld in 2001.

THE ULTIMATE WEAPON

The use of covert-action forces should be only one of several tools used to stop weapons proliferation.

One new weapon in development might in the future offer the single biggest deterrent to groups that want to covertly build weapons of mass destruction. It would be the ultimate precision-guided weapon: a nuclear weapon capable of penetrating through rock before detonating a high-yield blast.

The Pentagon has been working on the new weapon, called Robust Nuclear Earth Penetrator, since 2002. The bomb would be the first usable nuclear weapon, for by going through rock and earth and exploding underground, it would limit the effects of radioactive fallout. So far, work has been limited to research, but the weapon would prove critical to the war on arms proliferation. It would be a powerful deterrent to states like North Korea, Iran, Syria, and Libya; they could forget about hiding weapons facilities in rock-hardened, blastproof shelters. The penetrating nuke would also put Russia, China, and other nuclear states on notice that they could not protect hardened silos or cave missile complexes. Russian underwater submarine caves also could be taken out with the bomb. Finally, the penetrator would be the right weapon to combat terrorists hiding in caves or developing nuclear, chemical, and biological weapons underground.

Little has been said in public about the new weapon, whose development so far has been couched in utmost secrecy. Linton Brooks, director of the National Nuclear Security Administration, which is working on the bomb, told a Senate hearing in early 2003 that the plan called for using an existing B-61 or B-83 nuclear warhead on a new guided aerial bomb with a special nose cone that can burrow through solid rock. Each warhead has 350 kilotons or more of explosive power—the equivalent of 350,000 tons of TNT. The Pentagon is building the bomb so that it can go through thirty to sixty feet of solid rock before detonating. And that is the real challenge, said Brooks. "It's not just that you have to be able to penetrate," he told the Senate. "We know how to make things that will penetrate. You have to be able to penetrate and still have nuclear weapons, which are actually quite intricate machines, to work right."

If the United States can develop the penetrating nuke, this bomb would become what the Chinese call a "trump card" weapon. It would provide the world's sole superpower unrivaled power to apply other forms of pressure short of resorting to nuclear arms.

THE TASK IN FRONT OF US

Preparing for swift military action, continuing to develop advanced weapons technology, and improving intelligence capabilities will go a long way toward stopping illicit weapons transfers that make our enemies more dangerous. But there is another component of any antiproliferation program that cannot be overlooked.

The United States needs to conduct an ideological war against weapons transfers, educating friendly nations about the dangers of proliferation and deterring arms dealers from continuing selling to rogue states and terrorist groups. The war of words should be nothing less than the kind of ideological effort launched against expansionist Communism during the Cold War. This might be the most challenging component of the counterproliferation effort. Certainly fighting an ideological war could prove difficult for George W. Bush's administration, whose agencies favor secrecy and have an unshielded aversion to the press and to informing the public. But in an information age, it is essential to communicate properly with the public on the need to stop proliferation.

The reason is simple: The United States cannot stop illicit-weapons transfers on its own. In his interview with me, Rumsfeld talked about how the international community needs to be vigilant about the proliferation threat. Contrary to the view of him as a unilateralist, Rumsfeld said, "The reality is that no one country can deal with proliferation; it requires the cooperation of many countries."

And, of course, convincing other governments of the severity of the proliferation problem could help counter what is probably the most disturbing aspect of arms proliferation today: Our supposed allies are among the worst scofflaws. The United States cannot reasonably expect to educate tyrants and terrorists about the dangers of arms transfers to get them to halt their pursuit of deadly weapons or their own sales to other dangerous groups; that is why deterrence and power projection are so critical. But we might hope that educating ostensibly friendly governments would lead them finally to address a crisis to which they have turned a blind eye for so long.

Whenever weapons proliferation is discussed, attention is invariably focused on the end users—dictatorial regimes, global terrorists, and other enemies who threaten the United States and our friends around the world. Certainly these groups pose the greatest threat to our national security. Still, we must always remember that the situation today would not be so dangerous if it had not been for unconscionable weapons sales by some of our supposed allies. Their actions have been treacherous, and they cannot be allowed to get away with further transgressions.

The task of making the world safe from weapons of mass destruction will not be easy. But the likelihood of suffering an attack from nuclear, chemical, and biological weapons has never been higher. The work, therefore, is urgent. The task must not be shirked.

APPENDIX

TREACHERY EXPOSED

The following pages present stark evidence that some of America's supposed friends are among those arming the world's most dangerous regimes. The documents shown here—most of which are classified U.S. intelligence reports—highlight the pervasiveness of the weapons-proliferation problem and the threat to America's national security. These documents are, of course, only a tiny sampling of what U.S. intelligence has learned about the world's unscrupulous arms traders. And given that America's intelligence services have been caught off-guard by arms proliferation before, there could be quite a bit that the intelligence community *doesn't* know about the extent of the threat.

FOR OFFICIAL USE ONLY

Table 1: Countries, Types and Total Items

Country	Types	Total
U.S.S.R.	122	12,878,291
China	19	377,885
France	12	115,005
Italy	5	99,592
Yugoslavia	13	72,629
US	19	49,416
Bulgaria	5	40,237
Belgium	2	40,131
South Africa	6	36,574
Romania	3	20,372
Sweden	3	2,785
Egypt	1	144
Spain	3	119
Iran	1	38
Brazil	1	13

Information listed in the second source, while not including number of items, shows 9 additional countries (Austria, Canada, Chile, Czechoslovakia, Germany, North Korea, Pakistan, Singapore, and Switzerland). Of these 5 had only one type of munition, two had 2, one had 3 and the last, Germany, had 4. A list of acronyms used in the data received is at Appendix G. Details on ammunition by individual countries is at Appendix H.

Although the countries involved in transfers are important, it is instructive to see the types of munitions acquired, too. While major weapons systems may be important during a war, small arms may be more critical in the aftermath of conflict as insurgents use explosives to make improvised explosive devices. Munitions were analyzed by class (based on Federal Supply Class) to see the cumulative affect of transfers and are summarized in Table 2 below. A more detailed table of specific ammunition items found, by class, is at Appendix I.

9

FOR OFFICAL USE ONLY

This chart from a 2003 Pentagon report makes clear a fundamental truth about weapons proliferation: Deadly arms merchants operate in every corner of the globe. The chart shows that some twenty-four different nations provided Saddam Hussein's rogue regime with a staggering array of weaponry.

UNCLASSIFIED

Attachment A

Unclassified Report to Congress on the Acquisition of Technology Relating to Weapons of Mass Destruction and Advanced Conventional Munitions, 1 January Through 30 June 2003

The Director of Central Intelligence (DCI) hereby submits this report in response to a Congressionally directed action in Section 721 of the FY 1997 Intelligence Authorization Act, which requires:

"(a) Not later than 6 months after the date of the enactment of this Act, and every 6 months thereafter, the Director of Central Intelligence shall submit to Congress a report on

(1) the acquisition by foreign countries during the preceding 6 months of dual-use and other technology useful for the development or production of weapons of mass destruction (including nuclear weapons, chemical weapons, and biological weapons) and advanced conventional munitions; and

(2) trends in the acquisition of such technology by such countries."

At the DCI's request, the DCI Weapons Intelligence, Nonproliferation, and Arms Control Center (WINPAC) drafted this report and coordinated it throughout the Intelligence Community. As directed by Section 721, subsection (b) of the Act, it is unclassified. As such, the report does not present the details of the Intelligence Community's assessments of weapons of mass destruction and advanced conventional munitions programs that are available in other classified reports and briefings for the Congress.

UNCLASSIFIED
1

A November 2003 CIA report to Congress, portions of which are shown here, reveals that weapons proliferation is not going away. The report identifies Russia, China, and North Korea as "key suppliers" and emphasizes that Western Europe remains an "important source" of weaponry. It also shows that rogue states like North Korea, Iran, Libya, and Syria continue to pursue advanced weapons programs. *(pp. 235–244)*

Acquisition by Country

As required by Section 721 of the FY 1997 Intelligence Authorization Act, the following are country summaries of acquisition activities (solicitations, negotiations, contracts, and deliveries) related to weapons of mass destruction (WMD) and advanced conventional weapons (ACW) that occurred from 1 January through 30 June 2003. We have excluded countries that already have established WMD programs, as well as countries that demonstrated little WMD acquisition activity of concern.

Iran

Iran continued to vigorously pursue indigenous programs to produce WMD—nuclear, chemical, and biological—and their delivery systems as well as ACW. To this end, Iran continued to seek foreign materials, training, equipment, and know-how. During the reporting period, Iran still focused particularly on entities in Russia, China, North Korea, and Europe.

Nuclear. The United States remains convinced that Tehran has been pursuing a clandestine nuclear weapons program, in violation of its obligations as a party to the Nuclear Nonproliferation Treaty (NPT). To bolster its efforts to establish domestic nuclear fuel-cycle capabilities, Iran sought technology that can support fissile material production for a nuclear weapons program.

Iran tried to use its civilian nuclear energy program to justify its efforts to establish domestically or otherwise acquire assorted nuclear fuel-cycle capabilities. In August 2002, an Iranian opposition group disclosed that Iran was secretly building a heavy water production plant and a "nuclear fuel" plant. Press reports later in the year confirmed these two facilities using commercial imagery and clarified that the "fuel" plant was most likely a large uranium centrifuge enrichment facility located at Natanz. Commercial imagery showed that Iran was burying the enrichment facility presumably to hide it and harden it against military attack. Following the press disclosures, Iran announced at the International Atomic Energy Agency (IAEA) September 2002 General Conference that it had "ambitious" nuclear fuel cycle plans and intended to develop all aspects of the entire fuel cycle. By the end of 2002, the IAEA had requested access to the enrichment facility at Natanz, and the IAEA Director General (DG) for the first time visited the facility in February 2003. The IAEA is investigating the newly disclosed facilities, and previously undisclosed nuclear material imports to determine whether Iran has violated its NPT-required IAEA safeguards agreement in developing these facilities and their related technologies. At the June 2003 Board of Governors meeting, the IAEA DG presented a report on the Iranian program noting Tehran had failed to meet its safeguards obligations in a number of areas. The DG's report described a pattern of Iranian safeguards failures related to the undeclared import and processing of uranium compounds in the early 1990s, expressed concern over the lack of cooperation from Iran with IAEA inspections, and identified a number of unresolved concerns in Iran's program that the IAEA will continue to investigate. The IAEA Board on 19 June welcomed the report and called on Iran to answer all IAEA questions, cooperate fully with IAEA inspectors, and sign and implement an Additional Protocol immediately and unconditionally.

UNCLASSIFIED

Although Iran claims that its nascent enrichment plant is to produce fuel for the Russian-assisted construction projects at Bushehr and other possible future power reactors, we remain concerned that Iran is developing enrichment technology to produce fissile material for nuclear weapons under the cover of legitimate fuel cycle activities. Iran appears to be embarking on acquiring nuclear weapons material via both acquisition paths--highly enriched uranium and low burn-up plutonium. Even with intrusive IAEA safeguards inspections at Natanz, there is a serious risk that Iran could use its enrichment technology in covert activities. Of specific proliferation concern are the uranium centrifuges discovered at Natanz, which are capable of enriching uranium for use in nuclear weapons. Iran claims its heavy water plant is for peaceful purposes. In June, Iran informed the IAEA that it is pursuing a heavy water research reactor that we believe could produce plutonium for nuclear weapons. We also suspect that Tehran is interested in acquiring fissile material and technology from foreign suppliers to support its overall nuclear weapons program.

Ballistic Missile. Ballistic missile-related cooperation from entities in the former Soviet Union, North Korea, and China over the years has helped Iran move toward its goal of becoming self-sufficient in the production of ballistic missiles. Such assistance during the first half of 2003 continued to include equipment, technology, and expertise. Iran's ballistic missile inventory is among the largest in the Middle East and includes some 1,300-km-range Shahab-3 medium-range ballistic missiles (MRBMs) and a few hundred short-range ballistic missiles (SRBMs)--including the Shahab-1 (Scud-B), Shahab-2 (Scud C), and Tondar-69 (CSS-8)--as well as a variety of large unguided rockets. Already producing Scud SRBMs, Iran announced that it had begun production of the Shahab-3 MRBM and a new solid-propellant SRBM, the Fateh-110. In addition, Iran publicly acknowledged the development of follow-on versions of the Shahab-3. It originally said that another version, the Shahab-4, was a more capable ballistic missile than its predecessor but later characterized it as solely a space launch vehicle with no military applications. Iran is also pursuing longer-range ballistic missiles.

Chemical. Iran is a party to the Chemical Weapons Convention (CWC). Nevertheless, during the reporting period it continued to seek production technology, training, and expertise from Chinese entities that could further Tehran's efforts to achieve an indigenous capability to produce nerve agents. Iran likely has already stockpiled blister, blood, choking, and probably nerve agents—and the bombs and artillery shells to deliver them—which it previously had manufactured.

Biological. Even though Iran is part of the Biological Weapons Convention (BWC), Tehran probably maintained an offensive BW program. Iran continued to seek dual-use biotechnical materials, equipment, and expertise. While such materials had legitimate uses, Iran's biological warfare (BW) program also could have benefited from them. It is likely that Iran has capabilities to produce small quantities of BW agents, but has a limited ability to weaponize them.

Advanced Conventional Weapons. Iran continued to seek and acquire conventional weapons and production technologies, primarily from Russia, China, and North Korea. Tehran also sought high-quality products, particularly weapons components and dual-use items, or products that proved difficult to acquire through normal governmental channels.

Iraq

During the period covered by this report, coalition forces took action under Operation Iraqi Freedom to remove the Saddam Hussein regime from power in Iraq. A large-scale effort is currently underway to find the answers to the many outstanding questions about Iraq's WMD and delivery systems.

North Korea

Nuclear. In December 2002, North Korea announced its intention to resume operation of nuclear facilities at Yongbyon, which had been frozen under the terms of the 1994 US-North Korea Agreed Framework. IAEA seals and monitoring equipment were removed and disabled, and IAEA inspectors expelled from the country.

On 10 January 2003, North Korea announced its intention to withdraw from the Treaty on Non-Proliferation of Nuclear Weapons (the NPT Treaty). In late February 2003, North Korea restarted its 5 Mwe reactor which could produce spent fuel rods containing plutonium.

In late April 2003, North Korea told US officials that it possessed nuclear weapons, and signaled its intent to reprocess the 1994 canned spent fuel for more nuclear weapons. On 9 June, North Korea openly threatened to build a nuclear deterrent force. We continued to monitor and assess North Korea's nuclear weapons efforts.

Ballistic Missile. North Korea also has continued procurement of raw materials and components for its extensive ballistic missile programs from various foreign sources. In the first half of 2003, North Korea continued to abide by its voluntary moratorium on flight tests adopted in 1998, but announced it may reconsider its September 2002 offer to extend the moratorium beyond 2003. The multiple-stage Taepo Dong-2—capable of reaching parts of the United States with a nuclear weapon-sized payload—may be ready for flight-testing. North Korea is nearly self-sufficient in developing and producing ballistic missiles, and has demonstrated a willingness to sell complete systems and components that have enabled other states to acquire longer range capabilities earlier than would otherwise have been possible and to acquire the basis for domestic development efforts.

Chemical. North Korea is not a party to the Chemical Weapons Convention (CWC). During the reporting period, Pyongyang continued to acquire dual-use chemicals that could potentially be used to support Pyongyang's long-standing chemical warfare program. North Korea's chemical warfare capabilities included the ability to produce bulk quantities of nerve, blister, choking and blood agent, using its sizeable, although aging, chemical industry. North Korea possesses a stockpile of unknown size of these agents and weapons, which it could employ in a variety of delivery means.

UNCLASSIFIED

Biological. North Korea has acceded to the Biological and Toxin Weapons Convention, but nonetheless has pursued biological warfare (BW) capabilities since the 1960s. Pyongyang acquired dual-use biotechnical equipment, supplies, and reagents that could be used to support North Korea's BW efforts. As of the first half of 2003, North Korea was believed to have possessed a munitions production infrastructure that would have allowed it to weaponize BW agents, and may have such weapons available for use.

Libya

Nuclear. An NPT party with full-scope IAEA safeguards, Libya continued to develop its nuclear infrastructure. The suspension of UN sanctions provided Libya the means to enhance its nuclear infrastructure through foreign cooperation and procurement efforts. Tripoli and Moscow continued talks on cooperation at the Tajura Nuclear Research Center and a potential power reactor deal. Such civil-sector work could have presented Libya with opportunities to pursue technologies also suitable for military purposes. In addition, Libya participated in various technical exchanges through which it could have tried to obtain dual-use equipment and technology that could have enhanced its overall technical capabilities in the nuclear area. Although Libya made political overtures to the West in an attempt to strengthen relations, Libya's assertion that Arabs have the right to nuclear weapons in light of Israel and its nuclear program--as Qadhafi stated in a televised speech in March 2002, for example--and Tripoli's continued interest in nuclear weapons and nuclear infrastructure upgrades raised concerns.

Ballistic Missile. The suspension of UN sanctions in 1999 allowed Libya to expand its efforts to obtain ballistic missile–related equipment, materials, technology, and expertise from foreign sources. During the first half of 2003, Libya continued to depend on foreign assistance—particularly from Serbian, Indian, Iranian, North Korean, and Chinese entities—for its ballistic missile development programs. Libya's capability therefore may not still be limited to its Soviet-origin Scud-B missiles. With continued foreign assistance, Libya will likely achieve an MRBM capability—a long-desired goal—probably through direct purchase from North Korea or Iran.

Chemical and Biological. Libya also remained heavily dependent on foreign suppliers for CW precursor chemicals and other key related equipment. Following the suspension of UN sanctions, Tripoli reestablished contacts with sources of expertise, parts, and precursor chemicals abroad, primarily in Western Europe. Libya has indicated--as evidenced by its observer status at the April 2003 Chemical Weapons Convention Review Conference and previous Convention Conferences of States Parties--a willingness to accede to the CWC. Such efforts are consistent with steps that Tripoli is taking to improve its international standing. Tripoli still appeared to be working toward an offensive CW capability and eventual indigenous production. Evidence suggested that Libya also sought dual-use capabilities that could be used to develop and produce BW agents.

UNCLASSIFIED

UNCLASSIFIED

Advanced Conventional Weapons. Libya continued to seek new advanced conventional weapons and received assistance from other countries in maintaining its inventory of Soviet-era weapons.

Syria

Nuclear. Syria—an NPT signatory with full-scope IAEA safeguards—has a nuclear research center at Dayr Al Hajar. Russia and Syria have continued their long-standing agreements on cooperation regarding nuclear energy, although specific assistance has not yet materialized. Broader access to foreign expertise provides opportunities to expand its indigenous capabilities and we are looking at Syrian nuclear intentions with growing concern.

Ballistic Missile. During the first half of 2003, Damascus continued to seek help from abroad to establish a solid-propellant rocket motor development and production capability. Syria's liquid-propellant missile program continued to depend on essential foreign equipment and assistance—primarily from North Korean entities. Damascus also continued to manufacture liquid-propellant Scud missiles. In addition, Syria was developing longer-range missile programs such as a Scud D and possibly other variants with assistance from North Korea and Iran.

Chemical and Biological. Syria continued to seek CW-related expertise from foreign sources during the reporting period. Damascus already held a stockpile of the nerve agent sarin, but apparently tried to develop more toxic and persistent nerve agents. Syria remained dependent on foreign sources for key elements of its CW program, including precursor chemicals and key production equipment. It is highly probable that Syria also continued to develop an offensive BW capability.

Advanced Conventional Weapons. Syria continued to acquire limited quantities of ACW, mainly from Russia. Damascus's Soviet-era debt to Moscow and inability to fund large purchases continued to hamper efforts to purchase the large quantity of equipment Syria requires to replace its aging weapons inventory.

Sudan

Chemical and Biological. Although Sudan has aspired to a CW program, the US is working with Sudan to reconcile concerns about its past attempts to seek capabilities from abroad.

Advanced Conventional Weapons. During the reporting period, Sudan sought a variety of military equipment from various sources and received Mi-24 attack helicopters from Russia. In the long-running civil war, as well as for a general military modernization campaign, Khartoum has generally sought older, less expensive ACW and conventional weapons that nonetheless offered more advanced capabilities than the weapons of its opponents and their supporters in neighboring countries. We continued to remain concerned that Sudan might seek a ballistic missile capability in the future.

UNCLASSIFIED

6

Key Suppliers

Russia

During the first half of 2003, Russia's cash-strapped defense, biotechnology, chemical, aerospace, and nuclear industries continued to be eager to raise funds via exports and transfers. Some Russian universities and scientific institutes also showed a willingness to earn much-needed funds by providing WMD or missile-related teaching and training for foreign students. Given the large potential proliferation impact of such exports, transfers, and training, monitoring the activities of specific entities as well as the overall effectiveness of the Russian Government's nonproliferation regime remained an important element of the US bilateral dialogue with Russia on nonproliferation.

Nuclear. During the first half of 2003, Russia continued to play a key role in constructing the Bushehr Nuclear Power Plant project in Iran. However, President Putin has insisted that all Iranian programs in the nuclear field be placed under IAEA control.

President Putin in May 2000 amended the presidential decree on nuclear exports to allow Russia in exceptional cases to export nuclear materials, technology, and equipment to countries that do not have full-scope IAEA safeguards. For example, Russia supplied India with material for its civilian nuclear program in 2001.

Ballistic Missile. Russian entities during the reporting period continued to supply a variety of ballistic missile-related goods and technical know-how to countries such as Iran, India, and China. Iran's earlier success in gaining technology and materials from Russian entities helped to accelerate Iranian development of the Shahab-3 MRBM, and continuing Russian entity assistance has supported Iranian efforts to develop new missiles and increase Tehran's self-sufficiency in missile production.

Chemical and Biological. During the first half of 2003, Russian entities remained a key source of dual-use biotechnology equipment, chemicals and related expertise for countries of concern with active CBW programs. Russia's well-known biological and chemical expertise made it an attractive target for countries seeking assistance in areas with CBW applications.

Advanced Conventional Weapons. Russia continued to be a major supplier of conventional arms. Following Moscow's abrogation of the Gore-Chernomyrdin agreement in November 2000, Russian officials stated that they saw Iran as a significant source of potential revenue from arms sales and believed that Tehran could become Russia's third-largest conventional arms customer after China and India. In 2001, Russia was the primary source of ACW for China, Iran, Libya, and Sudan, and one of the largest sources for India. As an example, Russia actively marketed its thermobaric weapons at international arms shows, which likely increases the availability of this type of weapon in the open market.

Russia continued to be the main supplier of technology and equipment to India's and China's naval nuclear propulsion programs. In addition, Russia discussed leasing nuclear-powered attack submarines to India.

Export Controls. The Duma enacted new export control legislation in 1999, and Putin in 2000 and 2001 reorganized the export control bureaucracy to establish an interdepartmental export control coordinating body, the Export Control Commission of the Russian Federation. This organization was to establish federal oversight over export control, including compliance with international export control standards. Further, in 2001, Putin signed into effect several of the new law's implementing decrees, which updated export control lists for biological pathogens, chemicals, missiles, and related dual-use technologies and equipment. In May 2002, Russia amended its criminal code to allow for stricter punishment for violations involving the illegal export of material, equipment, and scientific-technical information that may be used in creating WMD or military equipment. The Code of Administrative Violations was also updated and became law as of July 2002. This enactment provided the Department for Export Control (under the Ministry of Economic Development and Trade) with significant administrative enforcement authority. In May 2003, President Putin signed the new Customs Code of the Russian Federation that simplifies customs rules and procedures with the ultimate goal of reducing red tape and arbitrary actions of customs officers. The Code also brings Russia in compliance with the Kyoto Convention on Simplification and Harmonization of Customs Procedures.

Despite progress in creating a legal and bureaucratic framework for Russia's export controls, lax enforcement remained a serious concern. To reduce the outward flow of WMD and missile-related materials, technology, and expertise, top officials must make a sustained effort to convince exporting entities—as well as the bureaucracy whose job it is to oversee them—that nonproliferation is a top priority and that those who violate the law will be prosecuted.

North Korea

Nuclear. In late April 2003 during the Beijing talks, North Korea privately threatened to export nuclear weapons.

Ballistic Missile. Throughout the first half of 2003, North Korea continued to export significant ballistic missile–related equipment, components, materials, and technical expertise to the Middle East, South Asia, and North Africa. Pyongyang attached high priority to the development and sale of ballistic missiles, equipment, and related technology. Exports of ballistic missiles and related technology were one of the North's major sources of hard currency, which supported ongoing missile development and production.

China

Over the past several years, Beijing improved its nonproliferation posture through commitments to multilateral arms control regimes, promulgation of export controls, and strengthened oversight mechanisms, but the proliferation behavior of Chinese companies remains of great concern.

Nuclear. In October 1997, China agreed to end cooperation with Iran on supplying a uranium conversion facility (UCF), not to enter into any new nuclear cooperation with Iran, and to bring to conclusion within a reasonable period of time the two existing projects. We remained concerned that some interactions of concern between Chinese and Iranian entities were continuing. China also made bilateral pledges to the United States that go beyond its 1992 NPT commitment not to assist any country in the acquisition or development of nuclear weapons. For example, in May 1996, Beijing pledged that it would not provide assistance to unsafeguarded nuclear facilities. We cannot rule out, however, some continued contacts subsequent to the pledge between Chinese entities and entities associated with Pakistan's nuclear weapons program.

Ballistic Missile. In November 2000, China committed not to assist, in any way, any country in the development of ballistic missiles that could be used to deliver nuclear weapons, and in August 2002, as part of its commitment, promulgated a comprehensive missile-related export control system, similar in scope to the Missile Technology Control Regime (MTCR) Annex. China is not a member of the MTCR, but on several occasions has pledged not to sell MTCR Category I systems.

Although Beijing has taken some steps to educate firms and individuals on the new missile-related export regulations--offering its first national training course on Chinese export controls in February 2003--Chinese entities continued to work with Pakistan and Iran on ballistic missile-related projects during the first half of 2003. Chinese entity assistance has helped Pakistan move toward domestic serial production of solid-propellant SRBMs and supported Pakistan's development of solid-propellant MRBMs. Chinese-entity ballistic missile-related assistance helped Iran move toward its goal of becoming self-sufficient in the production of ballistic missiles. In addition, firms in China provided dual-use missile-related items, raw materials, and/or assistance to several other countries of proliferation concern—such as Iran, Libya, and North Korea.

Chemical. Since 1997, the US imposed numerous sanctions against Chinese entities for providing material support to the Iranian CW program. Evidence during the current reporting period showed that Chinese firms still provided dual-use CW-related production equipment and technology to Iran. In October 2002, China promulgated new controls on biological items and updated chemical-related regulations, and now claims to control all major items on the Australia Group lists.

Advanced Conventional Weapons. During the first half of 2003, China remained a primary supplier of advanced conventional weapons to Pakistan and Iran. Islamabad also continued to negotiate with Beijing for China to build up to four frigates for Pakistan's navy and to develop the FC-1 fighter aircraft.

Other Countries

Countries of proliferation concern continued to approach entities in Western Europe, South Asia, and the US to provide needed acquisitions for their WMD and missile programs. Proliferators and associated networks continued to seek machine tools, spare parts for dual-use equipment, and widely available materials, scientific equipment, and specialty metals. Although western European countries strove to tighten export control regulations, Iran continued to successfully procure dual-use goods and materials from Europe. In addition, several Western European countries remained willing to negotiate ACW sales to Libya, India, Pakistan, and other countries in order to preserve their domestic defense industries. North Korea approached Western European entities to obtain acquisitions for its uranium enrichment program. A shipment of aluminum tubing--enough for 4,000 centrifuge tubes--was halted by German authorities.

Western European countries were still an important source for the proliferation of WMD- and missile-related information and training. The relatively advanced research of European institutes, the availability of relevant dual-use studies and information, the enthusiasm of scientists for sharing their research, and the availability of dual-use training and education may have shortened development time for some WMD and missile programs.

Emerging State and Non-State Suppliers

As nuclear, biological, chemical, and ballistic missile-applicable technologies continued to be more available around the world, new sources of supply emerged that made the challenge of stemming WMD and missile proliferation even more complex and difficult. Nuclear fuel-cycle and weapons-related technologies have spread to the point that, from a technical view, additional states may be able to produce sufficient fissile material and to develop the capability to weaponize it. As developing countries expanded their chemical industries into pesticide production, they also advanced toward at least latent chemical warfare capability. Likewise, additional non-state actors became more interested in the potential of using biological warfare as a relatively inexpensive way to inflict serious damage. The proliferation of increasingly capable ballistic missile designs and technology posed the threat of more countries of concern developing longer-range missiles and imposing greater risks to regional stability.

In this context, there was a growing concern that additional states that have traditionally been recipients of WMD and missile-related technology might have followed North Korea's practice of supplying specific WMD-related technology and expertise to other countries or by going one step further to supply such expertise to non-state actors. Even in cases where states took action to stem such transfers, there were growing numbers of knowledgeable individuals or non-state purveyors of WMD- and missile-related materials and technology, who were able to act outside government constraints. Such non-state actors were increasingly capable of providing technology and equipment that previously could only be supplied directly by countries with established capabilities.

March 5, 1992992

T O P S E C R E T UMBRA

[1m
****
CODEWORD CODEWORD CODEWORD CODEWORD CODEWORD CODEWORD
****

MATERIAL WITHHELD AT THE REQUEST OF THE U.S. INTELLIGENCE COMMUNITY

<DTG>
060001Z MAR 92

<FM>
FM DIRNSA

<TO>

ZEM
<CLAS>
T O P S E C R E T UMBRA
QQQQ

SIGINTDIGESTSD045-92

<SUBJ>
SUBJ: SIGINT DIGEST SD045-92 (U)
[1m<TEXT>
TEXT:
THE SIGINT DIGEST IS NSA'S DAILY REVIEW (MONDAY-FRIDAY) OF PUBLISHED SIGINT ON TOPICS OF CURRENT AND CONTINUING INTEREST WORLDWIDE.

CONTENTS

EASTERN EUROPE / EURASIA
1.
2.
MIDDLE EAST / AFRICA
3.
4.
5.
LATIN AMERICA
6.

ASIA
7.
8.

T O P S E C R E T UMBRA

This top-secret report from the National Security Agency reveals that China, one of the worst proliferators, was sending missile technology to Iran's radical Islamist clerical regime as early as 1992. The cooperation continues. *(pp. 245–246)*

March 5, 1992992

T O P S E C R E T UMBRA

MATERIAL WITHHELD AT THE REQUEST OF THE U.S. INTELLIGENCE COMMUNITY

DECL: OADR
XXHH
AU063123
NNNN
****
CODEWORD CODEWORD CODEWORD CODEWORD CODEWORD CODEWORD
****
<SECT> 03 OF 99
SECTION 03

T O P S E C R E T UMBRA

May 7, 1997

TOPSECRET UMBRA

DECL: OADR
XXHH
GC055260
NNNN
****
CODEWORD CODEWORD CODEWORD CODEWORD CODEWORD CODEWORD
****
<SECT> 08 OF 99
SECTION 08
XXMMLET08-0097127
<SERL>

MATERIAL WITHHELD AT THE REQUEST
OF THE U.S. INTELLIGENCE COMMUNITY

TOPSECRET UMBRA

In this top-secret report, the National Security Agency discloses that Iranian missile technicians went to China to observe key missile tests.

TOP SECRET UMBRA

11 June 1997

The SIGINT Digest (U)

(U) **Executive Edition**

MATERIAL WITHHELD AT THE REQUEST OF THE U.S. INTELLIGENCE COMMUNITY

(Continued on next page)

- 3 -

US ONLY
TOP SECRET UMBRA

This National Security Agency top-secret *SIGINT Digest,* headlined "Iran's Chinese-Supplied, Glass-Lined Chemical Plant Nearly Complete," reports that China supplied Iran with equipment used in making chemical weapons. Involved in the sale was Chinese broker Q. C. Chen, whom the U.S. government sanctioned in 2004 for additional proliferation-related activities. *(pp. 248–249)*

TOP SECRET UMBRA

11 June 1997

The SIGINT Digest (U)

(U) Executive Edition

MATERIAL WITHHELD AT THE REQUEST OF THE U.S. INTELLIGENCE COMMUNITY

- 4 -

US ONLY

TOP SECRET UMBRA

TOP SECRET UMBRA

NSOC DAILY INTELLIGENCE SUMMARY

Wednesday, 7 May 1997

****

* * * HIGHLIGHTS FOR DDO BRIEF (U) * * *

MATERIAL WITHHELD AT THE REQUEST OF THE U.S. INTELLIGENCE COMMUNITY

Sometimes weapons dealers compete for the same customers, as the National Security Agency documents in this top-secret report. A Kazakhstan army officer tried to sell surface-to-air missiles to Iran, but apparently China blocked the deal to protect its own markets in the Middle East.

TOP SECRET UMBRA

***SIGINT HIGHLIGHTS* (U)**

MATERIAL WITHHELD AT THE REQUEST OF THE U.S. INTELLIGENCE COMMUNITY

IRAQ: SADDAM'S GUARD DOWN; UDAY HEALS; HOLY MONTH PRECAUTIONS

CHINESE MILITARY SHIPMENTS

TOP SECRET UMBRA

Derived from: NSA/CSSM 123-2

Declassify on: Source marked "OADR"
Date of Source: 3 Sep 91

This top-secret National Security Agency report reveals that U.S. intelligence has closely monitored China's extensive military shipments.

MATERIAL WITHHELD AT THE REQUEST OF THE U.S. INTELLIGENCE COMMUNITY

This 1998 intelligence report was one of the first reports to indicate the reach of Pakistani scientist Abdul Qadeer Khan's covert nuclear procurement network. The document shows that Russia, another serial proliferator, trained Pakistani nuclear technicians in working with key nuclear-related equipment. *(pp. 252–253)*

THE CORPORATION HAS
CLOSE LINKS WITH A Q KHAN.

MATERIAL WITHHELD AT THE REQUEST
OF THE U.S. INTELLIGENCE COMMUNITY

1 May 7, 1997

S E C R E T SPOKE

CODEWORD CODEWORD CODEWORD CODEWORD CODEWORD CODEWORD

MATERIAL WITHHELD AT THE REQUEST OF THE U.S. INTELLIGENCE COMMUNITY

<SUBJ>
SUBJ: IRAN-RUSSIA/MISSILE DEVELOPMENT:

TEXT:

SUMMARY (U)

S E C R E T SPOKE

In this secret report, the director of the National Security Agency reveals that Russia sold Iran a wind tunnel to be used in testing missile aerodynamics—a critical phase of missile development. *(pp. 254–256)*

May 7, 1997

S E C R E T SPOKE

DETAILS (U)

MATERIAL WITHHELD AT THE REQUEST OF THE U.S. INTELLIGENCE COMMUNITY

DECL: OADR
XXHH
AU032507
NNNN

****

CODEWORD CODEWORD CODEWORD CODEWORD CODEWORD CODEWORD

****

S E C R E T SPOKE

May 7, 1997

S E C R E T SPOKE

<TAGS>
TAGS:
<SUBJ>
SUBJ: IRAN-RUSSIA/MISSILE DEVELOPMENT:

<TEXT>
REQS:

TEXT:

MATERIAL WITHHELD AT THE REQUEST
OF THE U.S. INTELLIGENCE COMMUNITY

XXHH
AU032507
NNNN
****
CODEWORD CODEWORD CODEWORD CODEWORD CODEWORD CODEWORD
****
<SECTION SUMMARY>

S E C R E T SPOKE

May 7, 199797

S E C R E T SPECAT NOFORN ORCON

DOI: 1997

SOURCE:

SECRET

SECRET

PAGE 03 071827Z

THIS REPORT IS CLASSIFIED SECRET US ONLY ORCON IN ITS ENTIRETY.

<TEXT>
SUMMARY: NONE.

MATERIAL WITHHELD AT THE REQUEST OF THE U.S. INTELLIGENCE COMMUNITY

S E C R E T SPECAT NOFORN ORCON

This CIA report discloses the extensive military cooperation between Russia and Iran. The report discusses the Iranian president talking about Iran's commitment to purchasing military equipment from Russia.

****

CODEWORD CODEWORD CODEWORD CODEWORD CODEWORD CODEWORD

****

<FM>
FM DIRNSA

<TO>

MATERIAL WITHHELD AT THE REQUEST
OF THE U.S. INTELLIGENCE COMMUNITY

<CLAS>
S E C R E T SPOKE
QQQQ

<SUBJ>
SUBJ: CUBA/NUCLEAR ENERGY:

<TEXT> REQS:
TEXT:

DETAILS (U)

In this report, the director of the National Security Agency discusses how Russia was providing nuclear assistance to the Communist dictatorship just off America's shores, Cuba. *(pp. 258–259)*

MATERIAL WITHHELD AT THE REQUEST
OF THE U.S. INTELLIGENCE COMMUNITY

****
CODEWORD CODEWORD CODEWORD CODEWORD CODEWORD CODEWORD
****

Top Secret

EUROPE

Germany: **Exporting Aircraft to Iran (TS NF)**

Bonn will permit the sale of five unidentified aircraft to Tehran's Defense Industries Organization—the arm of the Defense Ministry responsible for weapons production—now that the German Foreign Ministry has decided not to oppose the deal,

— The Foreign Ministry is generally a proponent of restraint in dual-use technology sales to Iran; ***its reversal of its earlier opposition may have been caused by pressure from the Economics Ministry, which is eager to increase German exports.***

— ***The sale may involve German-made Dornier transports.*** the DIO has been discussing with Dornier plans for buying and coproducing such aircraft; in 1992, Bonn permitted the export of four Dornier 228 transports, which can be used for maritime patrol and signals intelligence, although Iran has not employed them in this manner. (TS NF OC)

Bonn is generally willing to approve dual-use technology sales, even to countries of concern, such as Iran, unless the items are intended for military use. Germany might halt the sale if it had evidence that Iran would use the aircraft in military patrols or for SIGINT collection. (TS NF OC) *-CIA, DIA,*

MATERIAL WITHHELD AT THE REQUEST OF THE U.S. INTELLIGENCE COMMUNITY

Top Secret
24 July 1996

9

The CIA's top-secret *National Intelligence Daily* documents that the German government allowed German arms dealers to sell military aircraft to Iran.

MATERIAL WITHHELD AT THE REQUEST
OF THE U.S. INTELLIGENCE COMMUNITY

French Firm Ships U.S. Information System Software to Libya; Visit Planned

Iraqi Company Seeks Computer and Communications Equipment, Probably for Iraq in Violation of UN Sanctions

Here the National Security Agency reports that a French firm sent information systems to Moammar Qadhafi's Libya. The intelligence also reveals that an Iraqi company was violating United Nations sanctions by buying computer and communications equipment in the Middle East and Europe.

S E C R E T SPECAT NOFORN ORCON

ORIG:

TOR:

DTG:

SERL:

FM:

SUBJ: PLANNED VISIT OF BELARUSSIAN PRESIDENT LUKASHENKO TO TEHRAN IN MID-FEBRUARY 1998 TO DISCUSS MILITARY COOPERATION

DOI: 1998

SOURCE:
TEXT:

MATERIAL WITHHELD AT THE REQUEST
OF THE U.S. INTELLIGENCE COMMUNITY

S E C R E T SPECAT NOFORN ORCON

The CIA, in this secret report, reveals that even Belarus has helped arm America's enemies. The agency reports on the Belarussian president's planned visit to Iran to discuss military cooperation between the two countries, although it notes that the true purpose of the visit would be concealed.

1

ORIG:

TOR:

DTG:

SERL:

FM:

SUBJ: 1. PLANNING FOR "TAMARA" ELINT SALE TO IRAQ 2. BULGARIAN SOCIALIST PARTY SUPPORT FOR THE SALE

DOI: 1997

SOURCE:

TEXT:

MATERIAL WITHHELD AT THE REQUEST OF THE U.S. INTELLIGENCE COMMUNITY

This secret CIA report shows that Bulgarian arms dealers sold Saddam Hussein's regime Czech-made radar that could be used to target U.S. stealth aircraft. The Bulgarians were reportedly linked to high-level Czech officials. *(pp. 263–264)*

2

MATERIAL WITHHELD AT THE REQUEST OF THE U.S. INTELLIGENCE COMMUNITY

Top Secret

IRAQ: **Looking for Alternative Oil Export Route (U)**

In accepting UN Security Council Resolution 986 last week, Iraq noted that the Iraq-Syria-Lebanon pipeline is a potential additional vehicle for the export of oil permitted under the resolution. The mention of the ISL pipeline, repeated in several Iraqi press reports, may be part of a strategy to increase Iraq's flexibility in oil exports and to build economic ties to Damascus in the future.

— Resolution 986 allows Baghdad to use two export facilities—the Iraq-Turkey pipeline to Ceyhan, Turkey, and the Mina' al Bakr terminal in the Persian Gulf. The two acceptable approaches would have the capacity to export more than 1 million b/d.

— The resolution allows Iraq to export about 700,000 b/d—depending on price—in a 180-day period. (C NF)

A Pipeline in Disrepair (U)

According to oil industry reports, portions of the ISL pipeline have been closed for 14 years. To fully reopen it, work probably would take six months to a year, after which about 100,000 additional b/d of export capacity would become available to Iraq.

— The operational portion of the line is now used to pump oil to a point known as T-1; there oil is pumped into trucks for delivery to Jordan. Once repairs are made, the system would permit Iraqi oil to reach the Mediterranean Sea directly. (U)

Looking to Future Relations With Syria (U)

Once sanctions on Iraq are fully lifted, Baghdad will need additional capacity to export oil it is likely to obtain from newly developed oilfields. By expressing interest in the ISL pipeline, Baghdad may have signaled its interest in a closer economic relationship with Damascus.

— Syria has recently hinted at a rapprochement by publicizing the visit of an Iraqi technical delegation on water issues and by allowing the group to return overland to Iraq through a closed border crossing. (C NF) *-CIA, DIA-*

MATERIAL WITHHELD AT THE REQUEST OF THE U.S. INTELLIGENCE COMMUNITY

14

Top Secret
3 June 1996

In its top-secret *National Intelligence Daily,* the CIA discusses Saddam Hussein's oil pipeline to Syria and Lebanon. As would become clear when the United Nations "oil-for-food" scandal became public in 2004, Iraq used this pipeline to smuggle oil out of the country and evade United Nations sanctions. ***(pp. 265–266)***

Top Secret

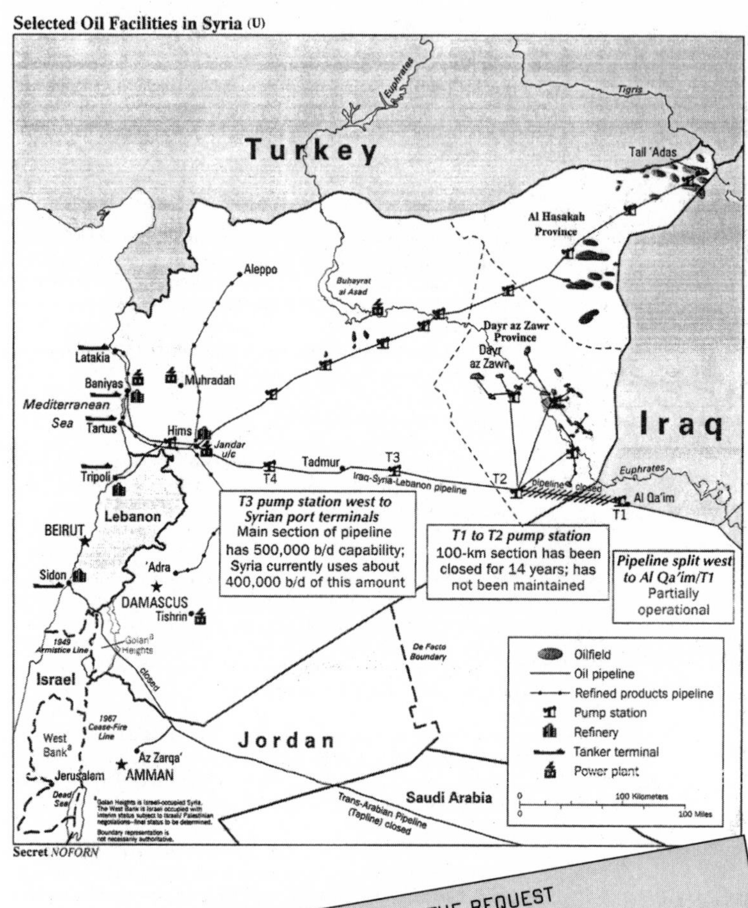
Selected Oil Facilities in Syria (U)
Turkey
Euphrates
Tigris
Tall 'Adas
Al Hasakah Province
Aleppo
Buhayrat al Asad
Dayr az Zawr Province
Dayr az Zawr
Latakia
Baniyas
Muhradah
Mediterranean Sea
Tartus
Hims
Jandar u/c
Tadmur
T3
T4
Iraq-Syria-Lebanon pipeline
T2
pipeline closed
Al Qa'im
T1
Iraq
Tripoli
Lebanon
BEIRUT
Sidon
'Adra
DAMASCUS
Tishrin
T3 pump station west to Syrian port terminals
Main section of pipeline has 500,000 b/d capability; Syria currently uses about 400,000 b/d of this amount
T1 to T2 pump station
100-km section has been closed for 14 years; has not been maintained
Pipeline split west to Al Qa'im/T1
Partially operational
1949 Armistice Line
Golan Heights[a]
closed
Israel
De Facto Boundary
1967 Cease-Fire Line
West Bank[a]
Jordan
Az Zarqa'
AMMAN
Jerusalem
Dead Sea
Saudi Arabia
Trans-Arabian Pipeline (Tapline) closed
Oilfield
Oil pipeline
Refined products pipeline
Pump station
Refinery
Tanker terminal
Power plant
100 Kilometers
100 Miles
Secret NOFORN

MATERIAL WITHHELD AT THE REQUEST OF THE U.S. INTELLIGENCE COMMUNITY

Top Secret
3 June 1996

Top Secret

MATERIAL WITHHELD AT THE REQUEST OF THE U.S. INTELLIGENCE COMMUNITY

Special Analysis

NORTH KOREA: Tough Year Ahead for Kim Chong-il (C NF)

Kim Chong-il, now entering his third year in power, will continue to face internal pressure on his regime, largely because of the floundering economy. Over the next year, North Korea will have trouble sustaining even current low levels of industrial activity and probably will be unable to adequately feed the population.

— shows that industrial operations have declined an average of more than 10 percent annually since 1992. Persistent shortages of raw materials and energy are undermining production at the regime's most modern steel and cement facilities; also shows that both were largely shut down last month.

— The North has struggled through the worst of the annual "lean season," and food aid and purchases estimated at about 200,000 tons are in the pipeline, according to US diplomats, and press reports. But even a bumper crop would leave the regime about 2 million tons short of what is needed over the next year to meet official standard rations and other grain needs, according to CIA estimates. (S NF)

Aid From Abroad (U)

Foreign assistance will determine the severity of Kim's economic problems through next summer.

— Despite occasional spot purchases, the North's primary supplies of oil will be 1 million tons of crude provided by China on concessional terms and 500,000 tons of heavy fuel oil that the Korean Peninsula Energy Development Organization must provide, according to US diplomats.

— The regime will need another several hundred thousand tons of food aid or imports next spring and summer to avoid acute shortages and cases of starvation. North Korea has relied heavily on the 650,000 tons of rice aid provided since mid-1995 by South Korea and Japan, according to press reports. (S NF)

continued

Top Secret
24 July 1996

10

The CIA's top-secret *National Intelligence Daily* assesses the totalitarian regime of North Korean leader Kim Jong-il. U.S. officials have concluded that Kim, desperate to remain in power, pushed North Korea to develop nuclear warheads at least in part to deter the United States from invading. *(pp. 267–269)*

Kim Keeping On as Before (U)

Kim most likely will continue to try to shore up his regime with external support and internal repression.

— He took extreme measures last year, including public executions for indiscipline and a crackdown on the VI Corps, according to The subsequent defections of a fighter pilot, a scientist, and a journalist suggest that discipline problems affect even elite groups—key pillars of his leadership.

— There is no indication that Kim plans to change course. His attitude toward his father's policies and legacy was reflected in a recent party newspaper article in which he said "do not expect any changes from me." (S NF) -*CIA, DIA,*

MATERIAL WITHHELD AT THE REQUEST OF THE U.S. INTELLIGENCE COMMUNITY

Top Secret

Kim Chong-il Fully in Control (C NF)

Recent media treatment of Kim Chong-il has reinforced his image as the country's ruler and sole heir to the legacy left by his charismatic father, President Kim Il-song. At the same time, the regime is trying to explain to domestic and international audiences the delay in formalizing his succession.

— An epic poem published in the party newspaper early this month implied that Kim will mourn three full years before becoming president and party general secretary. North Korean diplomats abroad have made similar remarks in recent weeks, according to press reports.

— An editorial on 7 July declared it "miraculous" that, despite the vacancies, Kim Il-song's "cause" had carried on without "any political vacuum" or "social instability." It called on North Koreans to unite around Kim Chong-il. (C NF)

There is no available evidence that Kim's lack of official trappings diminishes his status as the paramount leader. He is fully in charge, according to a wide range of intelligence reports. (S NF)

Secret *NOFORN*

MATERIAL WITHHELD AT THE REQUEST OF THE U.S. INTELLIGENCE COMMUNITY

Top Secret
24 July 1996

Terrorist CBRN: Materials and Effects

Background

Al-Qa'ida and associated extremist groups have a wide variety of potential agents and delivery means to choose from for chemical, biological, radiological, or nuclear (CBRN) attacks. Al-Qa'ida's end goal is the use of CBRN to cause mass casualties; however, most attacks by the group—and especially by associated extremists—probably will be small scale, incorporating relatively crude delivery means and easily produced or obtained chemicals, toxins, or radiological substances. The success of any al-Qa'ida attack and the number of ensuing casualties would depend on many factors, including the technical expertise of those involved, but most scenarios could cause panic and disruption.

- Several groups of mujahidin associated with al-Qa'ida have attempted to carry out "poison plot" attacks in Europe with easily produced chemicals and toxins best suited to assassination and small-scale scenarios. These agents could cause hundreds of casualties and widespread panic if used in multiple simultaneous attacks.
- Al-Qa'ida is interested in radiological dispersal devices (RDDs) or "dirty bombs." Construction of an RDD is well within its capabilities as radiological materials are relatively easy to acquire from industrial or medical sources. Usama Bin Ladin's operatives may try to launch conventional attacks against the nuclear industrial infrastructure of the United States in a bid to cause contamination, disruption, and terror.
- A document recovered from an al-Qa'ida facility in Afghanistan contained a sketch of a crude nuclear device.
- Spray devices disseminating biological warfare (BW) agents have the highest potential impact. Both 11 September attack leader Mohammad Atta and Zacharias Moussaoui expressed interest in crop dusters, raising our concern that al-Qa'ida has considered using aircraft to disseminate BW agents.
- Analysis of an al-Qa'ida document recovered in Afghanistan in summer 2002 indicates the group has crude procedures for making mustard agent, sarin, and VX.

This pamphlet contains a summary of typical agents and CBRN devices available to al-Qa'ida and other terrorist groups. It is not intended to be a summary of the overall threat from al-Qa'ida's CBRN program.

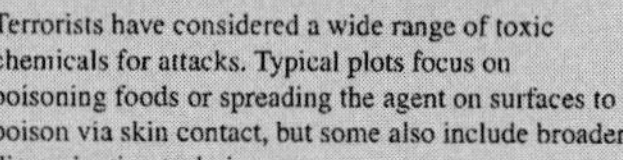

Chemical Agents

Terrorists have considered a wide range of toxic chemicals for attacks. Typical plots focus on poisoning foods or spreading the agent on surfaces to poison via skin contact, but some also include broader dissemination techniques.

Cyanides

Terrorists have considered using a number of toxic cyanide compounds.

Sodium or potassium cyanides are white-to-pale yellow salts that can be easily used to poison food or drinks. Cyanide salts can be disseminated as a contact poison when mixed with chemicals that enhance skin penetration, but may be detected since most people will notice if they touch wet or greasy surfaces contaminated with the mixture.

Hydrogen cyanide (HCN) and cyanogen chloride (ClCN) are colorless-to-pale yellow liquids that will turn into a gas near room temperature. HCN has a characteristic odor of bitter almonds, and ClCN has an acrid choking odor and causes burning pain in the victim's eyes. These signs may provide enough warning to enable evacuation or ventilation of the attack site before the agent reaches a lethal concentration.

- Both HCN and ClCN need to be released at a high concentration—only practical in an enclosed area—to be effective, therefore, leaving the area or ventilating will significantly reduce the agent's lethality.

Exposure to cyanide may produce nausea, vomiting, palpitations, confusion, hyperventilation, anxiety, and vertigo that may progress to agitation, stupor, coma,

This May 2003 CIA report highlights the ultimate proliferation nightmare: Terrorists are actively pursuing chemical, biological, and nuclear arms—and already have some deadly weapons. After the U.S. military action in Afghanistan, U.S. intelligence turned up shocking evidence that al Qaeda had made substantial progress in developing advanced weapons. *(pp. 270–271)*

Spectrum of Terrorist CBRN Threats

Castor beans, which grow on a common ornamental plant, can be processed by terrorists using crude equipment and common chemicals to produce the toxin ricin.

We believe that al-Qa'ida has explored the possibility of using agricultural aircraft for large-area dissemination of biological warfare agents such as anthrax.

Training videos found in Afghanistan show al-Qa'ida tests of easily produced chemical agents based on cyanide.

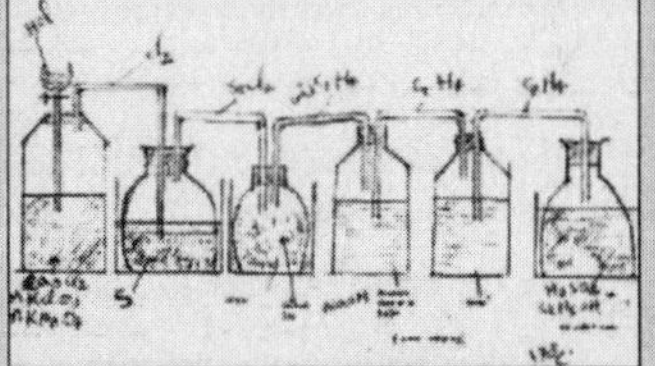

Documents found in Afghanistan highlight al-Qa'ida's interest in the production of more effective chemical agents such as mustard, sarin, and VX.

Al-Qa'ida has openly expressed its desire to produce nuclear weapons. We know that the group could easily construct a radiological dispersal device, or "dirty bomb" like the one shown here, which, while incapable of causing mass radiation-related casualties, could result in panic and enormous economic damage.

CTC 00255ID 5-03

GOV/2004/33
Annex 2

List of Nuclear Research Related Locations in Libya

Site A	The original centrifuge R&D location (Al Hashan)
Site B	The new location for centrifuge R&D, also used to store UF_6 (Al Fallah)
Site C	The original site for the Uranium Conversion Facility (UCF) (Al Khalla)
Site D	The new site for the Uranium Conversion Facility (Salah Eddin)
Site E	The machine shop for centrifuge manufacture (Project 1001, Janzour)
Site F	The yellow cake storage (Sabha)
Site G	The initial storage for the UCF and storage of centrifuge equipment from the 1980s experiments (Sawani)
Site H	The first storage location for Uranium Conversion Facility modules (Al Karamia)
Site I	The desalination production plant (Tajura)
Site J	The National Board of Scientific Research (NBSR) headquarters
Site K	The original construction materials storage location (El Ezeizia)
Site L	Tajura Nuclear Research Centre (TNRC)

Has Libya really dismantled its nuclear program? In May 2004, the International Atomic Energy Association produced a confidential report that raises serious concerns about whether Tripoli is fulfilling its promises. The report exposes how active the Libyans have been in developing nuclear weapons. Shown here are Libya's many different nuclear weapons sites. *(pp. 272–273)*

GOV/2004/33
Annex 3

Sites Inspected in the course of the Assessment of Nuclear Weapon Development Capabilities (January 2004)

1. Site J, NBSR headquarters
2. Site K, Al Ezeizia Storage Site
3. Site L, Tajura Nuclear Research Centre
4. Al Ezeizia artillery refurbishment site
5. General Company for Engineering Industries (Site 47)
6. Rabta Engineering Industrial Complex
7. Rabta Pharmaceutical Plant
8. Rabta "new service building" (adjacent to the Pharmaceutical Plant)
9. Rabta Factory 69 Bomb Filling Plant
10. Tarhuna rocket engine test stand
11. Tarhuna solid propellant pilot plant
12. Central Organization for Electronic Research (COER), Al Fajer Alga Did (Factory for SCUD Maintenance and Modification)
13. COER, Ber Osta Milad (Tripoli liquid rocket plant)
14. Centre for Remote Sensing and Space Science
15. Advanced Centre of Technology
16. Casting Institute
17. Polymer Institute
18. Welding Institute

ACKNOWLEDGMENTS

This book is the product of scores of interviews with national security specialists in and out of government. It draws on my experience as a newspaper reporter in Washington, D.C., for more than twenty years. As a defense writer, I have had the extraordinary good fortune to work with many people inside the U.S. government who helped me communicate important issues to the nation. One phenomenon of that cooperation has been my unique access to government reports of various classification levels, ranging from Confidential to Top Secret. These reports, communicated directly in hard copy and through officials who conveyed their contents, assisted me in presenting details in this book that rarely, if ever, become public. To the many officials within the U.S. national security community who helped with this project and who have asked to remain anonymous, I offer my sincerest thanks.

I have become a focus of criticism by some in government for presenting this inside information. It is my view that getting this data out to the public has made an important contribution to public debate on national security issues. This transparency is a vital part of our democratic system. I have tried to be cautious and responsible when presenting sensitive national security information. There were times when I withheld material from publication that was deemed too sensitive.

A word of special thanks goes to my employer, the *Washington Times.* The *Times,* founded in 1982 by the Reverend and Mrs. Sun Myung Moon, remains an important institution in Washington. The entire nation has benefited greatly from the news and information the *Times* presents. Three *Times* editors deserve special mention for their support: Editor-in-Chief Wesley Pruden, Managing Editor Francis B. Coombs Jr., and National Editor Ken Hanner.

I also want to thank my editor at Crown Forum, Jed Donahue, who provided great help and assistance with this book.

Finally, my deepest thanks go to my wife, Debra, who provided wonderful support for this project.

INDEX

Abdullah (Saudi Crown Prince), 146
Abraham, Spencer, 144, 172
Afghanistan, 114, 115–17, 122, 123, 205–8, 215, 221, 222. *See also* Taliban
al Qaeda, 114, 116, 162; and proliferation nightmare, 204, 205–8, 209, 210, 211–12, 213, 214, 215
Algeria, 201–2
Annan, Kofi, 187, 190
anthrax, 23, 155, 182, 210
anti-Americanism, 8, 50–51, 53. *See also specific nation*
Assad, Bashar, 85, 160–61, 163, 164, 165, 167
"Axis of Evil," 5–6, 31–33, 66, 221. *See also* Iran; Iraq; Libya; North Korea; Syria
Aziz, Tariq, 29, 30, 62, 163, 190

Baghdad International Exhibition, 41, 42–43
Banca Nazionale del Lavoro (BNL), 180
BBC China (German ship), 142–43, 145, 152
Berlin, Germany: bombing in, 147, 151
bin Laden, Osama, 61, 114, 115–17, 162, 204, 205, 206–7, 208, 211, 212, 215
biological weapons, 5, 6, 7, 45, 111, 125, 128, 143, 178; mafia for, 156, 204, 207, 212; and proliferation nightmare, 205, 206, 207, 208, 209, 212, 215; and stopping proliferation, 220, 222, 224, 229, 231; and U.N. failures, 195, 196. *See also specific nation*
BNP Paribas, 197
Bolton, John, 58–59, 83, 84, 93, 98–99, 164–65, 166–67, 220
Britain, 5, 34, 42, 138–39, 141, 150–51, 154, 155, 157, 159, 170, 214
Brooklyn terminal: fictional scenario about, 204–5
Bulgaria, 5, 192, 215
Bush, George H.W., 68, 153, 162, 180
Bush (George W.) administration: accommodationists in, 28; and nuclear weapons, 201; and Poland visit of Bush, 220; and sanctions, 121; and stopping proliferation, 142, 220–21, 222, 227, 230; and U.N. failures, 201; and U.S. support for Iraq, 180; and war on terrorism, 143–44. *See also specific nation*

Canada, 5, 33, 35, 43, 220
Carlos the Jackal, 52, 53, 68
Central Intelligence Agency (CIA): assessment of missiles threats to U.S. by, 160; and proliferation nightmare, 206, 208, 209, 211, 213; and stopping proliferation, 221–22, 223, 225, 226–27, 228; and supergun, 43; and U.N. failures, 192, 194, 195, 199, 201. *See also specific nation*
centrifuges, 45–46, 128, 196; and Iran, 90, 94, 95, 97, 98, 101–3, 107, 140, 141; and Libya, 139, 140–41, 142, 144, 145, 146, 151–52; and North Korea, 73, 74, 75, 77, 78, 79, 80, 217
chemical weapons, 5, 6, 7, 64, 110, 143, 157, 178; mafia for, 156, 204, 207, 212; and proliferation nightmare, 205, 206, 207, 208, 209, 210, 215; and stopping proliferation, 220, 222, 224, 229, 231; and U.N. failures, 192–93, 195, 196
China, 4, 7, 88, 114–36, 159; acquisition of U.S. technology by, 134; and bin Laden, 114, 115–17; and biological weapons, 125–26, 128; and Bush administration, 118–19, 123, 124, 126, 127, 134–35; and chemical weapons, 23, 121, 125, 126, 128, 130, 131, 133, 135, 192–93; and Clinton administration, 79, 127; and conventional weapons, 115, 121, 122; and dual-use technology, 70, 115, 118, 122; and how-to primer about nuclear bomb, 136; and Iraq, 5, 21, 23, 24, 25, 42–43, 60, 66–67, 69, 115, 117–23, 128, 129, 130, 131, 132, 135, 178, 179, 188, 191, 192–93, 194, 197; missile program of, 23, 116, 121, 123–24, 125, 126, 128, 129, 130, 131, 132, 133, 134–35, 157, 159, 174, 192–93; motivation of, 115, 126; nuclear program of, 70, 121, 125, 126, 128, 129, 130, 131, 132–33, 134, 135–36, 174–75, 201–2, 214; and proliferation nightmare, 208, 214; sanctions against, 124, 125, 126–27, 135, 225–26; and stopping proliferation, 225–26, 228, 229; and U.N. failures, 186, 188, 191, 192–93, 194, 197, 201–2; U.S. relations with, 17, 116, 159, 186, 208; and U.S. security lapses, 171, 172, 173, 174–75, 176–77, 178. *See also specific nation or topic*
China North Industries Corporation (NORINCO), 108, 123–24, 129, 132, 135, 157
Chirac, Jacques, 16, 17–19, 30, 35

Clinton administration, 16, 62, 76, 77, 79, 108, 116, 123, 127, 134, 225–26
Congress, U.S.: Kay's report to, 6; and U.N. failures, 201; and U.S. security lapses, 171. *See also* House of Representatives, U.S.; Senate, U.S.; *specific person or committee*
conventional weapons, 7–8, 170, 192, 211
Cordesman, Anthony, 178–79
Cuba, 68, 123, 177
Czechoslovakia, 5, 155, 179, 192

defectors, 44–45, 64, 65, 86, 146, 150–51, 213, 215
Defense Department, U.S.: and motivations of terrorists, 208; and proliferation nightmare, 208, 211; and stopping proliferation, 224; and U.N. failures, 196. *See also* Defense Intelligence Agency, U.S; *specific nation*
Defense Intelligence Agency, U.S., 14, 30, 117, 128, 129, 132, 133, 165–66, 211
DeSutter, Paula, 124–27
"dirty bombs," 202, 208–12
drug trafficking, 212
dual-use equipment/technology, 7, 31, 170, 177, 180, 194, 195. *See also specific nation*
Dubai, 139, 140, 141, 142

Egypt, 5, 61, 74, 131, 197, 200
El-Baradei, Mohamed, 200–201, 202
Energy Department, U.S., 78–79, 172–74, 175, 176, 178
espionage, 33–35, 171–78, 214–15
Ewald, Jim, 1–3, 9, 24–25

Federal Bureau of Investigation (FBI), 34, 207, 213
Feith, Douglas, 143–44, 189–90, 221
fiber optics, 118–20, 121, 122, 133–34, 194
Fischer, Joschka, 51–54
Fleischer, Ari, 51, 57–58
Foreign Relations Committee (U.S. Senate), 119–20, 127, 152, 161, 225
Foreign Service, U.S., 27, 28, 225
France, 12–36, 53, 88, 170; anti-Americanism in, 16; and biological weapons, 17, 23; and Bush administration, 13, 27, 30, 35–36; and chemical weapons, 17, 23; and China, 23, 24, 32–33; and conventional weapons, 18, 25; espionage by, 33–35; and Iran, 31–32; and Iran-Iraq War, 19; and Iraq, 1–4, 5, 12–31, 42–43, 44, 47, 48, 60, 66–67, 104, 122, 178, 188, 192; and Libya, 141; and Milosevic, 16–17; missile program of, 1–3, 15, 18, 19, 20, 23–26, 31; and North Korea, 5, 72, 74; nuclear program of, 17, 18–19, 44, 214; opposition to U.S. by, 4, 8, 16, 17, 21, 29, 36, 186; and passports for Iraqis, 12–13, 14–15, 25, 27; and Persian Gulf War, 4, 19–20; and proliferation nightmare, 214; Rumsfeld's comments about, 27–28; and Russia, 16, 22; and stopping proliferation, 220, 228; and U.N. failures, 186, 188; U.S. relations with, 13–14, 15–16, 17, 22, 27–28, 35–36; and U.S. security lapses, 175, 177. *See also specific nation or topic*
Franks, Tommy, 8, 46, 189, 205–6

Germany, 4, 38–54, 88, 184; anti-Americanism in, 50–51, 53–54; and Bush administration, 51; and conventional weapons, 47, 170; and Iran, 98; and Iraq, 3, 5, 27–28, 38–54, 66–67, 193; and Libya, 142, 155, 157; missile program of, 3, 38–39, 40, 41–43, 48, 157; and North Korea, 5, 72–73, 74, 75–76, 77–78; nuclear program of, 40, 44–46, 54; and Operation Desert Storm, 46; opposition to U.S. efforts to stop Hussein in, 8, 16, 42, 50–51, 54, 186; and Pakistan, 54; and proliferation nightmare, 214, 215; Rumsfeld's comments about, 27–28; and stopping proliferation, 220, 228; and U.N. failures, 186, 193
Gonzalez, Henry B., 180
Goods Review List, U.N., 47, 191, 195, 196

Hamas, 92, 161, 165
Hayden, Michael, 134, 159
Helms, Jesse, 127–28
Hezbollah, 105–6, 161, 165
House of Representatives, U.S., 16, 84, 165, 180, 213
Huawei Technologies, 115, 117–18, 119, 120, 121, 197
Hughes Space and Communications International, 226
human rights, 84, 87, 93, 150
Hussein, Saddam, 13, 18–19, 29–30, 48–50, 60, 101, 186, 217, 219, 225. *See also* Iraq

ideological war, 230–31
India, 69, 85, 132, 149, 157, 173, 175–76, 178, 214
inspectors, IAEA: and Iran's nuclear program, 90, 95, 96–97, 102, 103, 104, 109
inspectors, U.N., 44, 45, 48–49, 60, 62–63, 64, 65, 66, 144, 182, 193, 194–95
intelligence, Iraqi, 41, 60–61, 63–64, 68, 121, 162, 190
intelligence, Libyan, 138, 140, 146, 148, 156, 160
intelligence, Russian/Soviet, 53, 58, 60–62, 64, 68, 69, 105, 213
intelligence, U.S.: and Aziz's capture, 29;

capabilities/limitations of, 178; during Clinton administration, 127; and D&D, 177–78; and fictional scenarios, 218, 219; gathering of, 227; Kay's criticism of, 49; and oil-for-food program, 192, 193; and proliferation nightmare, 206, 208, 211, 212, 213; restructuring and resources for, 223; and stopping proliferation, 223, 224, 225, 226, 227; and supergun, 43; and U.N. failures, 192, 193, 195, 196, 201, 202; and U.S. security lapses, 173–74, 177, 178

intelligence, U.S: *See also* Central Intelligence Agency; Defense Intelligence Agency, U.S.; *specific nation*

International Atomic Energy Agency (IAEA), 130, 165, 176; and Iran, 91, 94, 95, 96–97, 98, 99, 101, 102–4, 109; and Libya, 143, 144–45, 146, 147; and North Korea, 73, 77, 80, 85; and proliferation nightmare, 213–14, 215; and U.N. failures, 198–201, 202

Iran, 32, 66, 90–111; anti-Americanism in, 5, 100, 101; biological weapons of, 94, 111, 135; and Bush administration, 98–99, 101, 123, 134–35; and chemical weapons, 94, 109, 110–11, 125, 131, 133, 135; and China, 6, 93, 94, 97, 100, 104, 106, 107–9, 110, 111, 115, 122, 123–24, 125, 128, 129, 130, 131, 132–33, 134–35; and Clinton administration, 108; concealment committee in, 101–2; and conventional weapons, 94, 111, 192; and dual-use technology, 111; human rights in, 93; and Iraq, 5, 43, 91–92, 178, 192; Kazakhstan as supplier to, 106–7; and Libya, 7, 140, 149, 153, 154, 157, 158, 159; missile program of, 5, 90, 91, 94, 99, 100, 104–5, 106–7, 108, 109, 110, 123–24, 128, 129, 130, 131, 132, 133, 134–35, 157, 166; and North Korea, 5–6, 75, 85, 93, 94, 100, 104–5, 108, 110; nuclear program of, 5, 31, 75, 90–112, 125, 128, 130, 131, 132–33, 135, 140, 141, 165, 198, 199, 200–201, 223, 224; oil in, 91, 93, 179; and stopping proliferation, 223, 224, 229; and threats to U.S., 7; and U.N. failures, 198, 199, 200–201; underground facilities in, 7, 95, 96, 108–9, 223; U.S. relations with, 17, 100, 135, 179, 184; U.S.-Russia secret agreement about, 107; and U.S. security lapses, 171, 172, 175, 176, 178. *See also specific nation*

Iran-Iraq War (1980s), 19, 63, 179–80, 184

Iraq, 88, 95; arms procurement network in, 25, 48–50; biological weapons of, 12, 17, 23, 45, 48, 49, 181–82, 195, 196; and Bush administration, 13, 27, 30, 66–67, 118–19, 121, 165, 180; and chemical weapons, 12, 17, 23, 48, 49, 64, 121, 130, 163–64, 181, 192–93, 195, 196; and China, 5, 21, 23, 24, 25, 60, 66–67, 69, 115, 117–23, 128, 129, 130, 131, 132, 135, 178, 179, 188, 191, 192–93, 194, 197; and conventional weapons, 18, 21, 25, 47, 121, 122, 192; declaration of arms to U.N. by, 40, 120, 121; and dual-use technology, 20, 23, 40, 47, 49, 58, 118, 122, 163, 165, 180, 194, 195; effects of treachery against U.S. in, 1–3; hiding/moving weapons out of, 3, 6, 12, 39, 48–49, 64, 65, 163–64; looting in, 14; military buildup in, 3–5, 191–98; missile program of, 1–3, 15, 18, 19, 20, 23–26, 31, 38–39, 40, 41–43, 45, 48, 49, 85, 86, 121, 128, 131, 132, 163–64, 180, 181, 188, 192–93, 196; no-fly zone over, 20, 118; nuclear program of, 17, 18–19, 40, 44–46, 48, 49, 78, 121, 130, 165, 175–76, 199; plot to assassinate Bush (George H. W.) by, 162; presidential palaces in, 1, 46, 63, 189; and proliferation nightmare, 215; and stopping proliferation, 228; terrorist links/support of, 68, 162; and U.N. failures, 186, 187–98, 199; U.S. air strikes in (1998), 63, 118; U.S. as supplier of arms to, 5, 170, 178–84; and U.S. security lapses, 176, 178; wireless phone service in, 197. *See also* Hussein, Saddam; oil-for-food program; *specific nation or topic*

Iraq War. *See* Operation Desert Storm; Operation Iraqi Freedom; *specific person or place*

Israel, 19, 20, 92, 100, 101, 149, 152, 157, 158, 161, 166, 175, 177, 214

Italy, 5, 42–43, 44, 97, 142, 157, 180, 220

jammers, electronic, 56–57, 58, 59, 196

Japan, 79, 80, 84, 86, 177, 214, 220

Jordan, 43, 163, 166, 188, 192, 193

Justice Department, U.S., 224, 226

Kay, David, 6, 49, 65, 85–86, 164

Kazakhstan, 93, 105, 106–7

Kelly, James, 79–80, 82

Khamenei, Ayatollah Ali, 91, 100–101, 104

Khan, Abdul Qadeer, 54, 75, 138–41, 142, 144, 146, 175

kickbacks, 63, 67, 180, 188, 189

Kim Jong-il, 73, 79, 83, 86–87, 217, 225

laser enrichment process, 70, 97, 98, 102, 107

Lebanon, 6, 106, 161, 164

Libya, 7, 64, 123, 138–60, 175, 229; and Berlin bombing, 147, 151; biological weapons of, 6, 143, 144, 149, 150, 151, 152–53, 155, 156, 157, 158; and Bush administration, 138, 142, 144, 149; and chemical weapons, 6, 64,

Libya *(continued):* 128, 138, 139, 143, 148, 149, 150, 151, 152–55, 156, 157, 158; and China, 123, 124, 128, 129, 131, 132, 134, 135–36, 145, 146, 149, 154, 157, 159; disarmament of, 143, 144–45, 146–47, 151, 153; and dual-use technology, 148, 157; human rights in, 150; and Iran, 7, 140, 149, 153, 154, 157, 158, 159; and Iraq, 143, 151, 153; and Lockerbie bombing, 147, 148; missile program of, 124, 128, 131, 132, 134, 138, 143, 149, 150, 153, 154, 157–59, 160; and North Korea, 5, 75, 85, 149, 152, 157, 158, 159; nuclear program of, 5, 6, 54, 70, 75, 102, 135–36, 138–47, 149, 150, 151–52, 158, 165, 198, 199, 201; renouncement of terrorism by, 146; and "right" to WMD, 148–49, 152; sanctions against, 138, 146, 148, 149, 150, 151, 152, 156, 159–60; as state sponsor of terrorism, 6, 138, 145, 146, 147, 148, 149; and U.N. failures, 198, 199, 201; underground facilities in, 7, 149, 154, 157; U.S. bombings in, 147; U.S./British talks with, 138–39. *See also* Qadhafi, Moammar; *specific nation*
Lockerbie, Scotland: bombing over, 138, 147, 148, 149, 150

mafia, 156, 204, 207, 212
Malaysia, 139, 140, 142, 154, 184
Milhollin, Gary, 47–48, 180–81
Milosevic, Slobodan, 16–17, 115, 158
missiles, 45, 159; CIA assessment of threats to U.S. from, 160; and how-to primer about nuclear bomb, 136; and proliferation nightmare, 206, 207; and stopping proliferation, 220, 222, 223, 225–26; and U.N. failures, 192, 193, 196, 202; and U.S. security lapses, 174, 177. *See also specific nation*

National Council of Resistance, 94, 96, 106
national laboratories, U.S., 34, 176–77
National Nuclear Security Administration, 173, 230
National Security Agency (NSA), 23, 70, 108–9, 114, 118, 133–34, 139, 147, 151, 159
National Security Council, 224
NATO, 8, 17, 28, 91, 158, 160, 229
Negroponte, John, 196
nerve agents, 47, 78, 110–11, 153, 165, 166, 195, 209, 210
NORINCO. *See* China North Industries Corporation
North Korea, 66, 72–88, 90, 222; and Agreed Framework, 73, 77, 78, 80, 84, 199, 200, 217; Beijing/nultiparty talks with, 80, 82, 83; biological weapons of, 80, 84; and Bush administration, 80, 83–84, 87–88; and chemical weapons, 80, 84; and China, 5, 72, 74, 76, 79, 81, 82, 86, 122, 124, 128, 129, 131, 133, 134; and Clinton administration, 76, 77, 79; and dual-use technology, 75; fictional scenario about, 217–18; human rights in, 84, 87; and Iran, 5–6, 85, 93, 94, 100, 104–5, 108, 109, 110, 111; and Iraq, 5, 69, 85–86, 87, 129; Kelly's meeting in, 79–80; and Libya, 85, 149, 152, 157, 158, 159; and mafia, 156; missile program of, 5, 78, 82, 84–85, 86, 124, 128, 129, 131, 133, 134, 157, 158, 159, 166; as nuclear threat, 5, 7, 69, 70, 72–88, 94, 110, 140, 152, 165, 198, 199–200, 201, 217–19, 223, 224;possibility of military strike against, 84; regime survival as priority of, 87; and stopping proliferation, 221, 223, 224, 225, 229; and U.N. failures, 198, 199–200, 201; underground facilities in, 7, 76–77, 217–19; U.S. relations with, 17, 77, 87–88, 135; and U.S. security lapses, 175, 176, 178
nuclear facilities, attacks on, 211–12
Nuclear Nonproliferation Treaty (NPT), 80, 94, 130, 143, 165, 199–200, 201, 202
nuclear weapons, 5, 7, 181; acquisition of, as religous duty, 206–7; fictional scenario about, 217–19; how-to primer about, 136; and Operation Desert Storm, 45, 46; portable, 212–13; and proliferation nightmare, 204–15; and stopping proliferation, 220, 222, 224, 229–30, 231; as ultimate weapon, 229–30; U.N. failure to deal with, 198–202; and U.S. security lapses, 171–78. *See also* centrifuges; uranium enrichment; *specific nation*

oil, 18, 29–31, 63, 65–67, 68, 91, 93, 148, 162, 163, 179, 191, 199
oil-for-food program, 14, 46–48, 64, 66, 117–18, 187–98
OPEC (Organization of Petroleum Exporting Countries), 52, 53
Operation Desert Storm. *See* Persian Gulf War
Operation Iraqi Freedom: beginning of, 24; and Russia as arms supplier, 66; and Syria-Iraq deals, 164, 165; U.S. forces in, 1–4. *See also* Iraq
Osirak facility: bombing of, 19

Pacepa, Ion Mihai, 53–54, 64, 65
Pakistan, 54, 69; and China, 7, 79, 117, 124, 125, 128, 130, 131, 132, 133, 134, 135–36, 225–26; and Iran, 7, 75, 93, 97, 108–9, 128, 140; and Libya, 75, 128, 140, 145, 146, 152; missile program of, 124, 128, 130, 131, 132, 133, 134; and North Korea, 5, 7, 75, 79, 85,

86, 128, 140; nuclear program of, 7, 54, 75, 125, 128, 130, 131, 132, 135, 136, 140, 152, 175; and proliferation nightmare, 204, 206, 215; and stopping proliferation, 222, 225–26; and Taliban, 117; and U.S. security lapses, 175, 178
Palestine/Palestinians, 20, 68, 92, 148–49, 161, 191
Pan Am Flight 103. *See* Lockerbie, Scotland
passports, French, 12–13, 14–15, 25, 27
Pentagon: and proliferation nightmare, 208–9; report about Iraqi weapons by, 4–5; and stopping proliferation, 222, 223, 226, 228, 229, 230; and U.N. failures, 192, 196, 197; and U.S. support for Iraq, 181. *See also specific nation*
Perle, Richard, 51, 57
Persian Gulf War: and French-Iraqi deals, 3, 4, 19–20, 30–31; and German-Iraqi deals, 46, 54; missing U.S. pilot in, 29–30; and nuclear weapons, 44, 45, 46; and Russia, 61, 68; and Syria, 162, 163; and U.S. support for Iraq, 170, 178, 179, 180–81, 182
Pillsbury, Michael, 221, 222, 223, 224, 225
plutonium, 69, 178, 202; and Iran, 96, 97, 98, 99; and North Korea, 78, 82, 84; and proliferation nightmare, 204, 206, 211, 214
poisons, 47–48, 110–11, 125, 154, 208–12
Poland, 44, 220
Powell, Colin, 22–23, 27, 83, 84, 119–20, 225
Primakov, Yevgeni, 61, 62, 63–64, 65, 105
Project Coast, 155, 156
Proliferation Security Initiative, 88, 142, 220–21, 222, 226–27, 228
proliferation, weapons: Assad's comments about, 161, 167; efforts to stop, 142, 217–31; espionage as boosting, 171–78; fictional scenarios about, 204–5, 217–19; frightening aspects of, 135; motivations for, 8, 50; as ongoing problem, 6–7, 33, 48; serial, 69, 104–10; and threats to U.S., 6–9, 85; ultimate nightmare about, 204–15; and ultimate weapon, 229–30; U.S. negligence about, 169–84
P.T. Gulf International, 183–84
Putin, Vladimir, 57, 59, 66

Qadhafi, Moammar, 139, 143, 146, 147, 148–49, 150, 160. *See also* Libya

Rachid Hotel (Baghdad): bombardment of, 25–26
Rafsanjani, Ali Akbar Hashemi-, 91–92, 99–100
Ramadan, Taha Yassin, 42, 188
Reagan, Ronald, 83, 170, 179–80, 222
religion, 206–7
Robust Nuclear Earth Penetrator, 229–30
rogue nations. *See specific state*
Romania, 5, 53, 64, 68
Rumsfeld, Donald H.: anti-European rhetoric of, 28; and China-Iraqi deals, 118, 119; and French-Iraqi deals, 13–14, 15, 26, 27–28, 33; and German-Iraqi deals, 27–28; and Iran's nuclear program, 90, 91, 98; and North Korea, 83; "old Europe" comment by, 28; and proliferation nightmare, 205; and Russia-Iran deals, 98; and stopping proliferation, 221, 222, 229, 231; and Syria-Iraqi deals, 164; and threats to U.S., 7–8, 9; and U.S. security lapses, 171
Russia/Soviet Union, 4, 8, 54, 56–70, 170; Afghanistan war of, 221, 222; anti-Americanism in, 61, 66; biological weapons of, 212; and Bush administration, 30, 57, 58, 59, 60, 66–67; and chemical weapons, 70; and China, 69, 70, 133–34; and dual-use technology, 58, 70; fall of, 69; and France, 16, 22; and Iran, 6, 7, 68, 70, 93, 94, 97, 98, 100, 101, 104, 105, 106, 107, 109, 110, 111; and Iraq, 5, 6, 18, 21, 25, 26, 29, 30, 39, 42–43, 56–69, 121, 122, 178, 179, 180, 188, 191, 192, 193; and Libya, 70, 145, 149, 152, 157, 160; mafia in, 156, 204, 207, 212; and Milosevic, 16; missile program of, 58, 59, 67, 69, 70, 134, 157, 192, 202; and North Korea, 7, 69, 70, 86; nuclear program of, 8, 69, 70, 176, 212–13, 214; opposition to U.S. Iraq efforts by, 29, 61–62, 65–66, 186; and Pakistan, 69; and proliferation nightmare, 212–13, 214–15; and South Africa, 155, 156; and stopping proliferation, 226, 228, 229; and Syria, 59, 61, 69, 165; and U.N. failures, 186, 188, 191, 192, 193, 196; and U.S. 1998 attacks on Iraq, 63; U.S. relations with, 17, 56–58, 93, 107, 135; and U.S. security lapses, 172, 173, 175, 176, 177, 178

sanctions, U.N.: Bush's views about, 58, 121; and China, 117, 121, 132; and France, 3, 4, 20, 22, 23, 122; and Garmany, 46, 50, 54; Goods Review List for, 47, 191, 195, 196; against Iraq, 3, 4, 20, 22, 23, 25, 46, 49, 50, 54, 59, 86, 121, 122, 132, 162, 187, 188, 191–92, 193–94; against Libya, 138, 143, 146, 148, 149, 150, 151, 152, 156, 159–60; and North Korea, 86; and Russia, 57, 58, 59, 63, 68; against Serbia, 158
sanctions, U.S., 23, 117–18, 124, 125, 126–27, 135, 146, 150, 162, 225–26
Saudi Arabia, 43, 129, 130, 146, 193, 204
SCOMI Precision Engineering (SCOPE), 139, 141, 142

Senate, U.S., 22, 30, 65, 82–83, 134, 160, 226, 230
September 11, 2001, 114, 116, 166, 202, 205, 214, 227, 228
Serbia, 16–17, 115, 157, 158
Shaw, John, 19, 30–31, 59–60, 61, 122, 164, 183
Shenyang Aircraft Corporation, 72–73, 74
Siemens, 40, 45, 48
Singapore, 5, 76, 78, 142, 184
South Africa, 5, 97, 141, 155–56
South Korea, 76, 80, 82, 84, 86, 87, 177, 219
Spain, 5, 42–43, 220
Special Forces, 222–23, 224, 227, 228
Speicher, Michael Scott, 29–30
State Department, U.S.: and France, 13, 22, 26–28; and North Korea, 79–80, 83, 86–87; and proliferation nightmare, 207; and stopping proliferation, 221, 224, 225; terrorism list of, 161, 172; and U.N. failures, 193, 195, 196
State Department, U.S: *See also specific nation*
Sudan, 158, 215
suicide bombings, 208–9
superguns, 43, 48–49, 207
Sweden, 5, 42–43
Switzerland, 34, 43, 46, 157, 159, 214
Syria, 5, 17, 160–67, 229; anti-Americanism in, 161; biological weapons of, 6, 160, 166; and Bush administration, 165; and chemical weapons, 6, 160, 163–64, 165–66; and China, 122, 123, 128, 129, 131, 165, 166; and dual-use technology, 163, 165; and France, 12, 23; and Iran, 166; and Iraq, 6, 12, 23, 25, 65, 161–65, 166, 183, 194; and Kay's report, 6; missile program of, 128, 131, 160, 163–64, 166; and North Korea, 5, 85, 129, 166; nuclear program of, 5, 6, 69, 160, 165, 199; and Russia, 59, 61, 69, 165; as sponsor of terrorism, 6, 160, 161, 165, 166; and U.N. failures, 194, 198, 199

Tahir, Buhary Seyed Abu, 139–40, 141, 143
Taiwan, 33, 135, 141, 159
Taliban, 114, 115–17, 143, 205, 206, 215, 228
Tenet, George, 48, 75, 95, 146–47, 148, 149
terrorism/terrorists: motivations of, 208; and proliferation nightmare, 204–15; sponsors of, 6, 143–44, 145; and stopping proliferation, 224, 227, 228, 229; and threats to U.S., 7, 9. *See also specific nation, organization, or person*
Timmerman, Kenneth, 18, 181
Tinner family, 141
training camps, terrorist, 61, 68, 114, 116, 129, 162, 215
Treasury Department, U.S., 31, 32
Truppel, Hans-Werner, 72, 73, 74, 75–76
Turkey, 20, 42–43, 163, 166
Twetten, Thomas, 221–22

Ukraine, 4, 6, 43, 59, 93, 109, 157, 158, 160, 170, 183
ultimate weapon, 229–30
UN Monitoring, Verification, and Inspection Commission (UNMOVIC), 194–95
underground facilities, 7, 229–30. *See also specific nation*
United Arab Emirates, 20, 43, 135, 188
United Kingdom. *See* Britain
United Nations, 42, 184; appeasement by, 187–98; arms report of, 40; failures of, 186–202, 219; Iraq's declaration of arms to, 40, 120, 121; list of goods blocked for Iraq purchase, 47, 191, 195, 196; Powell's presentation before, 22–23; resolutions of, 5, 17, 59, 63; and stopping proliferation, 227–29; Zebari's comments before, 186–87. *See also* arms embargo, U.N.; oil-for-food program; sanctions, U.N.; *specific agency or nation*
United States: arms sales of, 4, 170; Chinese shipments of illegal weapons to, 124; CIA assessment of threats to, 160; exports of conventional weapons by, 170; proliferation negligence of, 169–84; security lapses in, 171–78; support for Iraq from, 5, 170, 178–84; threats to, 6–9, 219. *See also specific nation or topic*
uranium enrichment: and Germany-Iraq trade, 44, 45, 46; and Iran, 90, 92, 95, 96, 97, 98, 99, 102, 103, 105; and Libya, 140, 141, 142, 146, 151; and North Korea, 73, 74, 75, 77, 78, 79, 80, 81, 84, 94, 199, 217–19; and proliferation nightmare, 207, 211, 214, 215
Urenco, 75, 140

war on terrorism, 33, 143–44, 219
Weldon, Curt, 16–17, 22
Wolfowitz, Paul, 17, 24, 25–26, 27, 28, 221

Yakou, Regard and Sabri, 183–84
Yun Ho Jin, 72, 73, 74, 77–78